CORELDRAW 9
f/x and design

Shane Hunt

D1511778

CORIOLIS

CorelDRAW 9 f/x and design

Limits Of Liability And Disclaimer Of Warranty

Trademarks

The Coriolis Group, LLC
14455 N. Hayden Road, Suite 220
Scottsdale, Arizona 85260

480/483-0192
FAX 480/483-0193
http://www.coriolis.com

Library of Congress Cataloging-In-Publication Data
Hunt, Shane
     CorelDRAW 9 f/x and design / by Shane Hunt.
          p. cm
     Includes index.
     ISBN 1-57610-514-8
     1. Computer graphics. 2. CorelDRAW! I. Title.
T385.H852 1999
006.6'869--dc21   99-33378
                                         CIP

Printed in the United States of America
10 9 8 7 6 5 4 3 2 1

Publisher
Keith Weiskamp

Acquisitions Editor
Mariann Hansen Barsolo

Marketing Specialist
Beth Kohler

Project Editor
Michelle Stroup

Technical Reviewer
Brian Little

Production Coordinator
Meg E. Turecek

Cover Design
Jody Winkler
additional art provided by Brandon Riza

Layout Design
April Nielsen

CD-ROM Developer
Robert Clarfield

OTHER TITLES FOR THE CREATIVE PROFESSIONAL

I would like to dedicate this book to you, the reader. It takes a special kind of person to find the time and energy to broaden one's horizons and explore the unknown, especially in the fast-paced and demanding world that we live in. I applaud your tenacity and courage. We need more people like you, who are willing to take on challenges and make the extra effort to expand your horizons and creative potential.

Growing up, my teachers always rewarded me for my curiosity and creativity. I hope this book rewards yours.
—Shane Hunt

≈

ABOUT THE AUTHOR

Shane Hunt is a writer, artist, and interface design consultant with 17 years of experience in business computing, the last 10 as principal of a multi-media development company in Southern California. He has written several books on computer design techniques, including co-authoring the *CorelDRAW WOW! Book.* In addition, he is a regular contributor to CorelDRAW periodicals, including www.designer.com, Corel's Web site. When not basking in the glow of computer screens, Shane can be found in his art studio working with traditional media, or building strange and dangerous-looking contraptions.

ACKNOWLEDGMENTS

I would like to thank my friends and family for their support, and my loving and wonderful girlfriend, Dionne. I would also like to thank the brilliant people at Coriolis, who were instrumental in focusing and directing my often meandering energies and keeping me on track. In particular, I would like to thank Mariann Barsolo, acquisitions editor; Michelle Stroup, project editor; Meg Turecek, production coordinator; April Nielsen, designer of the color section, and Sharon McCarson, who lent a hand in wrapping things up in the final hour.

Finally, I would like to thank Corel Corporation, and my friends and contacts there, such as Michael Bellefeuille, Chip Maxwell, and Susan Connerty. Thanks for your help, and thanks also for putting up with my ranting and raving!

—*Shane Hunt*

FOREWORD

With computer technology advancing so quickly, the demand for exceptional computer graphics is growing, and the imaging power once reserved for an elite few is now in the hands of millions.

CorelDRAW, winner of more than 300 industry awards worldwide, offers the precision and ease of use today's artists need. Dominating the PC illustration arena, CorelDRAW is a revolutionary leader in the graphic design industry.

The first book of its kind, *CorelDRAW 9 f/x and design* will help you discover the full potential of this world-class graphics suite. Hundreds of pages filled with useful techniques, time-saving tips, and original artwork let you create professional graphics more efficiently than ever before. Learn effectively with hands-on training using the companion CD-ROM, an invaluable learning aid and art resource. Whether you're a novice or a seasoned professional, this material will allow you to design graphics that will make others sit up and take notice.

With so many powerful, easy-to-use tools and features, CorelDRAW 9 lets you unleash your creativity. Join Shane Hunt and explore the possibilities as you advance through the pages of *CorelDRAW 9 f/x and design*.

Corel Corporation

Contents At A Glance

TABLE OF CONTENTS

Chapter 12
Fifties Flashback

Chapter 13
Digital Entropy And Corporate ID

Chapter 14
Photo Collages

Chapter 15
Pulp Vision

Chapter 16
Robots, Gears, And Tentacles

Chapter 22
Beyond Two Dimensions

OVERVIEW OF
CORELDRAW 9

This chapter introduces the user to the CorelDRAW interface and universe.

CorelDRAW is the world's most popular design package. It also has the largest percentage of users who have little or no formal art background. CorelDRAW artists are computer professionals working in a variety of applications for which they need some kind of computer-generated graphics. They also need speed and flexibility. So, for simple business graphics, high-end advertising, and everything in between, CorelDRAW has become an integral part of their workday.

CorelDRAW's speed and flexibility, as well as its use by professional artists, make it stand out from the other computer art programs on the market. We aren't here just to make pretty pictures, but to put those images to work for us. You may have some art background or experience using traditional design tools, or no experience at all. I'm assuming that you're like me; that you want to get as much accomplished as you can with the smallest amount of effort and in the shortest amount of time. I have been working as a designer for over nine years and as a computer professional over half my life. I love art, I love pretty pictures, I love computers, and I even love my job. But, I'm guessing that you, like me, prefer to finish your work as quickly as possible and get the heck out of the office.

Getting To Know CorelDRAW 9

This book is about working smart. I have tried to use real-world examples and ideas you can use in your everyday work environment. My tips are from years of real-world experiences dealing with CorelDRAW on a daily basis and crunching out artwork for a living. Even if you aren't a commercial artist and creating art isn't the focus of your job (and that may be many of you), I think you'll appreciate the nature of this book. I've tried to make this a CorelDRAW book by and for Corel artisans.

In my experience, the CorelDRAW community, despite its size, has been a very close and friendly one. I hope to continue this tradition and will endeavor to make myself available for any questions or comments that may arise along the way. I will also endeavor to update the *CorelDRAW 9 f/x and design* Web site (www.slimydog.com/corelfx9) in the coming year with any news or related information. Feel free to log in now and then to check up on things, and email me with any new tips or discoveries. Hey, this is all a big adventure for me too.

Object-Oriented Package

CorelDRAW is an *object-oriented* illustration package. This means that everything breaks down into individual elements that have their own attributes (such as outline width and fill color) which the computer sees as a set of mathematical coordinates and settings. A CorelDRAW image file essentially is a set of computer instructions that the program uses to build your objects and, in turn, create your design. Object-oriented illustration with CorelDRAW objects is very efficient and, more importantly, highly versatile.

The object-oriented nature of CorelDRAW brings with it a level of flexibility unique to the medium. You can select an object and change it at any time within the life cycle of your design, something that you can't do when you're working with a bitmap program or traditional paint brush or pen and ink. This means that when a client says, "I love it, except instead of a fire theme, let's try ice...," or even makes an odd request, such as "Can we make the drop-shadows blue instead of black?" you don't have to start over; you simply change the attributes of the objects already in place. Or, before the client even asks, you can save multiple copies of the same artwork, recolor each uniquely, and present the client with a variety of options. CorelDRAW artwork is flexible, and flexibility is synonymous with *power*.

In today's competitive design climate, the advantages of working with an object-oriented application are many. Throughout this book, you'll see many effects and examples used for a specific application, but the nature of the program is such that you can use the artwork in almost any imaginable way. Artwork designed for the Web can become, with virtually no additional effort, high-end color printed material, oversized banners, coffee mugs—almost anything you can imagine. CorelDRAW images are ready to be ported to printing presses, on-screen applications, slides for presentations, even other design programs. Its flexibility is unrivaled by any other application. CorelDRAW has no hidden costs, its file sizes are not huge or unmanageable, and its output is not difficult. CorelDRAW is a commercial artist's best friend—and closest ally.

What this also means is that you never have to be satisfied with a design. You can go back and fine-tune an image and tweak a design until it is exactly what you want. Or, you can take an existing image and refine it for another application. You can customize an ad campaign to hit multiple demographics smack between the eyes. Whatever your needs, the power is yours, limited only by your imagination and your energy.

Custom Fit

In addition to creating flexible artwork, CorelDRAW itself is very flexible, with customizable tools and commands. This newest version of the software fully embraces Corel's concept of the free-flowing interactive interface, to maximize your productivity. Both the interface and tool set offer an unprecedented amount of flexibility, to make realizing your visions easier than ever. The full implementation of the interactive tool set provides access to nearly every feature from previous versions, available as an easy-to-use, powerful implement rather than a series of menus, dialog boxes, and cursor movements. Thus, you don't need to open a separate dialog box or interface to access the special effects available to you. You simply choose the appropriate interactive tool and use the on-screen features and context-sensitive options unique to that tool to accomplish what you wish.

The increased workflow is facilitated by marrying the features of the interactive tool set with the context-sensitive Property Bar. The Property Bar is an ever-present toolbar that constantly changes and allows you to access options and features of the current task. For example, if you use the Interactive Drop Shadow tool to add depth and dimension to an object, you can control the Opacity, Feathering, and even the Color options of the shadow element with the Property Bar (see Figure 1.1). With this interface paradigm, you aren't faced with a constant need to open and close specialized dialog boxes, which only clutter the workspace and hamper your workflow.

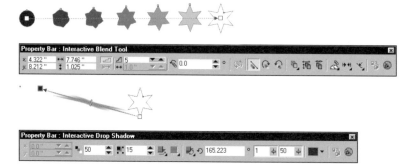

Figure 1.1

The Property Bar is a context-sensitive toolbar that offers ways to customize features and options of the currently selected tool, such as the Interactive Blend tool (top) and the Interactive Drop Shadow tool (bottom).

For features that still require the use of a specialized dialog box or options screen, CorelDRAW uses a *docker*. The docker is a dialog box that docks to the right column of your screen. This is the common docker workspace, and as you open and close dockers when you need them, they appear in this space. Other features to help you control and organize your design, such as the Object Manager, View Manager, and what have you, all dock in the docker area. This means that you can choose a handful of your most commonly used features, and dock them on the right. Tabs make switching between your favorite dockers a snap (see Figure 1.2).

Property Bar   Docker

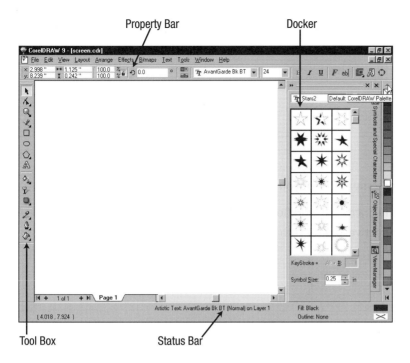

Figure 1.2
The CorelDRAW 9 workspace,
with various elements labeled.

Tool Box   Status Bar

The theme here is "customizable." If you like the docker concept, run with it and stash the boxes of your favorite features and functions on the right side of the screen. If you don't like the concept, open and close the dockers as you need them (click the small *x* in the top-right corner of the docker to close). Or, open a docker, tear it off the right column (drag on the docker with the cursor), and position and resize it anywhere you wish. This feature holds true for basically every toolbar, docker, status bar, or palette in CorelDRAW. You can tear off, reposition, resize, and even re-move, any and all of the interface components to customize the interface to your exact needs (see Figure 1.3). With the creative and quirky personalities that artists generally possess, what a great feature!

CUSTOM KEY CLICKS

Changing a keyboard shortcut in CorelDRAW 9 is easy. Simply open the Options dialog box (Ctrl+J) and click on Customize. Click on the Shortcut Keys option and find your target in the Commands hierarchy chart. For example, under the Edit folder, locate and click on Nudge. Here, you can change the SuperNudge series of commands. Click on SuperNudge Left and then click in the Press New Shortcut Key box.Now, the system is in record mode, and you can depress any keys that you want to assign to SuperNudge Left. I pressed Ctrl and the left arrow simultaneously (this was the SuperNudge Left command in CorelDRAW version 7, which I really got used to using). Now, click on the Assign button to make this the new keyboard shortcut. Easy! Reprogram any shortcuts that you wish, and then click on OK to close the Options dialog box and activate the new shortcut keys.

Figure 1.3
CorelDRAW allows you to customize your workspace to fit your needs and preferences.

In addition to being able to customize how the workspace looks, you can reprogram any of the keyboard shortcuts. This is very useful if you are upgrading to CorelDRAW 9 from a previous version and are used to certain keyboard shortcuts or have a particularly fond finger-dance that you like to do to perform special functions (see the "Custom Key Clicks" sidebar for more details).

Working In CorelDRAW

CorelDRAW is a program that allows you to follow your creative impulses. You create curves, objects, and text within your Drawing Page (the

BRING BACK THE DOCKER

If you are upgrading from version 8, and/or you don't want to be forced to use the Interactive blend (or other) tool, you can still find the hidden dockers. The quickest way to get CorelDRAW 9 to look/feel and act like V. 8 is to load the V. 8 workspace. Open the Options dialog (Ctrl+J), and click on CorelDRAW8 in the Workspaces available area. Click on the Set As Current button, then click on OK to activate. Now CorelDRAW 9 will work just like CorelDRAW 8, which you might find more appealing. The downside to this is that you lose some V.9-specific features. The better solution is to customize your CorelDRAW 9 workspace to include features that you miss from V.8, while retaining all of the new upgrades. This is easy as well. For example, to make the Ctrl+B keyboard shortcut open the now hidden Blend docker in V.9, follow these instructions.

Open the Options dialog (Ctrl+J), and then click on Customize, then Shortcut Keys in the hierarchy chart. In the Commands window, click on the Effects folder, and then Blend. Now you can create a new keyboard shortcut, or re-create the old one. Move the pointer to the Press new shortcut key area and click. Now, hold down the Ctrl key and press the letter B. This will assign Ctrl+B to open the Blend docker. Click on the Assign button, then on OK, and you're in business! You can repeat this process for any and all features in CorelDRAW 9 to restore any other now-hidden features. The *CorelDRAW 9 f/x and design* Web site (www.slimydog.com/corelfx9) will be a forum to share customized workspaces, where I will post customized workspaces from me and other artists for you to download and try out, to see how other people work. I always suggest that you customize the workspace to your taste, so you can be more efficient.

boxed area in the middle of the screen). You can work anywhere on the screen, even outside the Drawing Page, similar to how artists might have photos and cut-out elements scattered on their desks. Anything you create in your workspace will save and load to disk just fine, but anything outside of the Drawing Page will not appear in your print jobs.

You work in CorelDRAW by choosing a tool from the left-hand toolbar and then dragging on screen. For example, select the Rectangle tool and drag on screen to make a rectangle or square. No mystery here.

Some of the tools on the toolbar have a small drop-down arrow next to them. Click on this arrow to open a *flyout*, which is like opening a drawer to reveal more tools. Click on any tool in the flyout to use it.

If you have never used CorelDRAW before, I suggest that you at least work through the on-screen tutorials that ship with the program to get up to speed quickly. Start CorelDRAW and then choose Help|CorelTUTOR. This launches the CorelTUTOR program, which resides in an on-screen docker. Follow the instructions in the Introduction, and then work through the lessons to acclimate yourself quickly to the tools and features of CorelDRAW. But, to use this book, you really only need to be able to find a tool and drag it on the screen.

Vector Art Vs. Bitmaps

For the most part, CorelDRAW objects are *vector* artwork, a series of mathematical coordinates connected with a line, like an electronic dot to dot. This keeps the objects infinitely scaleable and relatively small in size. A *bitmap*, on the other hand, consists of a collection of colored pixels, the size and density of which determine the physical size and resolution of the image. A bitmap may have too much or too little image information, depending upon its size and the needs of the current project. You can

---

SUPER-SIZE, PLEASE

Bigger is better, at least when it comes to monitors. Although you can get plenty of work done at 800x600 (the screen size used in Figure 1.3), a larger monitor and screen resolution are worth their weight in gold. With technology prices falling, a 17-inch or even 21-inch monitor is not unobtainable, and the extra breathing room they afford is priceless. With so many features, functions, status bars, and toolbars on the screen, your actual image area continues to shrink. Using a big monitor and a screen resolution of 1024x768 (or higher) maximizes your CorelDRAW design potential by offering you more work room and the ability to keep more tools and dialog boxes open and at your service.

GIMME SOME HELP

If you don't know the name of a particular tool or option in CorelDRAW 9, simply hover the mouse pointer over it. Typically, a pop-up label will tell you what the tool is. So, even if you have just a beginning knowledge of the program, you should be able to follow along in the step-by-step tutorials just fine because each tool or feature is labeled for you as you go.

If you need more assistance with a tool or feature, use the online help. Press the Shift and F1 keys simultaneously to switch the on-screen cursor to the What's This? cursor (an arrow with a question mark). Now, click on the tool that you want more information about, and a larger Help balloon will offer an explanation.

For even more help, turn to the Help Topics feature under the Help menu. This opens the CorelDRAW Help window, which offers a comprehensive table of contents, an index, and search capabilities to help you locate more information on a sticky topic.

always generate a bitmap from vector artwork, but the reverse is not always true. That's why CorelDRAW is a superior starting point even for projects that will eventually become bitmaps.

Vector artwork is much more flexible than bitmaps because it is, as I said, basically a collection of coordinates. You can enlarge or reduce a CorelDRAW vector-based image without degrading the resolution or changing the file size because the computer basically needs only to reset a scale attribute for the new size. A bitmap, which is a fixed-resolution entity, does not have this flexibility.

On the left side of Figure 1.4, a happy, dancing puppy character from the CorelDRAW clip-art CD-ROM (\clipart\animals\pets) is duplicated and enlarged to create a second puppy in the foreground. If you try to do the same with a bitmap (on the right side of Figure 1.4), the resolution is fixed and becomes pixelated upon enlargement. On the other end of the spectrum, if you have a large bitmap and then duplicate it and reduce it, your image will look fine but your file size will be large. Even though you made the bitmap smaller on screen, it still contains all the image information of the original; therefore, you end up working with redundant information that just increases your file size.

Figure 1.4
Unlike a bitmap (on right), CorelDRAW vector artwork (left) can be enlarged or reduced without affecting file size or resolution.

CorelDRAW has always focused on creating and manipulating vector objects. Even from the beginning, though, you could also perform limited actions on imported bitmaps within all versions of the program. Corel has always bundled Photo-Paint, its powerful bitmap-manipulation package, along with CorelDRAW for advanced bitmap massaging. Introduced in version 7 and getting better in version 9, Photo-Paint lets you create and modify bitmaps within the CorelDRAW environment itself. In CorelDRAW 9, the integration is so seamless that you may forget the vector roots of the application.

In fact, CorelDRAW 9 blurs the line between bitmaps and vector art more than ever. Now, although some of the effects in the program act like objects, they are in fact bitmaps. The Interactive Drop Shadow tool, for example, actually is an interactive bitmap generator within CorelDRAW. The program takes user input and a set of parameters (color, size, location, opacity, edge-blur, and so on) to render a bitmap on the fly as you work. It remembers these settings for you, so that you can work with these bitmap elements just like you work with any other vector-based CorelDRAW entity (such as an Interactive Extrude element, which is vector-based but can be selected and modified at any time by changing its parameters). The Pattern and Texture fill options, available from the Fill flyout, also use pixel-based bitmap technology. So, sometimes you work with vector pieces, sometimes bitmaps, and sometimes CorelDRAW-controlled and rendered bitmaps. Other times, you'll convert your vector elements into bitmaps manually, using the Convert To Bitmaps feature.

Why would you want to convert your nice vector artwork into a less-flexible bitmap? Sometimes, you just can't get the look that you're after if your artwork is a crisp, CorelDRAW vector object. Because of the hard-edged nature of object-oriented vector artwork, you occasionally will want to convert to a bitmap to create a soft, anti-aliased edge, or to use a filter or built-in bitmap effect that simply won't work on vector artwork (which is why drop shadows, for example, must use bitmap technology, because you can't get a fuzzy-edge effect by using vector objects).

For example, our hero Albert Einstein (\clipart\carictre\historic) in Figure 1.5 (on left) is in the CorelDRAW native vector format. On the right, a shape placed in front of this artwork is given a Fish Eye lens from the Lens docker (Alt+F3). Notice how only the vector artwork in the face is distorted and not the checkerboard pattern (this checkerboard is a two-color pattern fill from the Pattern Fill dialog box, accessed from the Fill flyout). Despite being native CorelDRAW entities, drop shadows, pattern fills, and texture fills are not vector information; they are bitmaps. The Fish Eye lens effect will not distort correctly the bitmap information in a two-color pattern fill.

Now, we could redraw the checkers as individual vector box objects, and then the Fish Eye lens would work fine. However, the easier solution is to use the Bitmaps|Convert to Bitmap feature and then use a filter effect to distort the image. After you use the Convert to Bitmap dialog box to rasterize your objects (convert them to pixels), you can choose from one of many filter effects to enhance it. For example, the Bitmaps|3Deffects|Sphere command creates the rounded look in Figure 1.6 (left). The same bitmap can have a totally different look, using the

Figure 1.5

The Fish Eye lens will not distort some bitmap information, such as bitmap pattern fills or texture fills.

Bitmaps|Art Strokes|Pen & Ink command (on right). It all adds up to increased flexibility, power, and creative potential.

Figure 1.6

You can use the Convert to Bitmap dialog box to change vector art to a pixel-based image within the CorelDRAW workspace, giving you more image-manipulation power than ever before using filter effects.

The bottom line is to get the results that you want, regardless of whether the image is vector or bitmap. (I preach the philosophy of *ruthless creativity*, which is getting what you want no matter what it takes or how potentially unconventional the means.) CorelDRAW has always provided a great way to generate bitmaps, but now you can do it easier and directly within the program. This functionality blurs the line a bit between CorelDRAW and bitmap-manipulation programs such as Photo-Paint, but, as you'll see, the focus of each program is still pretty clear. Because this is a CorelDRAW book and not a Photo-Paint book, the discussion focuses on CorelDRAW's bitmap features. However, because Photo-Paint is bundled with CorelDRAW and runs circles around CorelDRAW when it comes to bitmap manipulation, I don't hesitate to turn to that program for help (as in Chapters 7 and 15, in which Photo-Paint power is critical to the techniques).

This is a book about working smart, so we don't need to be masochistic and force ourselves to work entirely in CorelDRAW when Photo-Paint may be the better solution. Along those same lines, the final chapter

BITMAPS ON PARADE

All the images in the color section in the center of this book are CMYK TIFF bitmaps printed using traditional CMYK off-set printing techniques. The bitmaps used to generate these pages were created by using the CorelDRAW Export feature (Ctrl+E). The CorelDRAW source files used for this process are the exact ones that can be found on the *CorelDRAW 9 f/x and design* companion CD-ROM. Transforming your CorelDRAW artwork into pixel-based bitmaps is often the easiest solution, especially for a cross-country, cross-application, and cross-platform project such as this book. In addition to facilitating the color section, the same bitmaps were simply down-sized and converted for use on the *CorelDRAW 9 f/x and design* Web site.

looks at working with CorelDream 3D, and other 3D modeling applications. Sometimes, even the one-two punch of CorelDRAW and Photo-Paint can't generate the images that a 3D modeling package can easily render. So, stay ruthless and smart—use the tools available to you to get the best possible results in the least amount of time using vector or bitmap technology.

The main thing to remember with bitmaps is to create images at a high enough resolution and appropriate color depth for their intended purpose. You can't use Web graphics in print, or print graphics on your Web site. But what you need to know about bitmaps can be summarized in a single paragraph (see the "Essential Bitmap Information" sidebar). Don't worry, this is just a little technical-information speed bump on our way to the graphics superhighway.

How To Use This Book

This book was written so that you can either read it straight through or just flip to a section that interests you. Some of the later chapters, however, do assume that you have learned techniques from previous chapters. Where this is the case, you will find a chapter reference so that you can just jump back and review the material as needed. For the most part though, you should be able to drop in wherever you wish and follow along step by step.

The Book

As I wrote this book, I tried to keep in mind how a person such as myself would use it. I typically buy a techniques book such as this because it has something of specific interest in the color section that makes me think, "Cool. I want to do that!" I buy the book, take it home, flip to that section, and work through the tutorial. Yippee! Instant gratification!

Then, I typically flip through the book some more, looking at the pictures and the step-by-step instructions until curiosity gets the better of me and I

PICK AND CHOOSE

To make picking and choosing a bitmaps effects filter easier, use the "best of" pages in the color section. Here you can compare a before image to an after image that has been modified with a bitmap filter effect. This way, you can just pick the result you like and choose that filter to modify your own artwork without having to spend a lot of time experimenting with each one on your own. A complete color listing of all of the CorelDRAW 9 bitmap filter effects is on the *CorelDRAW 9 f/x and design* Web site (www.slimydog.com/corelfx9), in the Art area.

ESSENTIAL BITMAP INFORMATION

Bitmaps are just collections of tiny colored dots that come together to create a picture. The problem is that you need the right number of dots with the correct number of colors in them for the application at hand. Volumes can be written on this topic alone, but it really just boils down to these essentials:

- *72 dots per inch (dpi) RGB color for on-screen applications (such as Web sites, multimedia, and PowerPoint presentations).* Use the JPEG or GIF file formats. GIF reduces your colors to 256, but is essential for Web-based animation graphics, as outlined in Chapter 21. Use JPEG when you can.

- *300 dpi CMYK color for on-paper applications (such as magazines, full-color brochures, and so forth).* Use the TIFF or PSD file formats for problem-free image transfer to other applications or to other computer users (on Macs or PCs).

Use the Export feature to convert your CorelDRAW images into bitmaps on disk, or use the Bitmaps|Convert to Bitmap dialog box to keep the transformation within your CorelDRAW workspace. Bitmaps are just too powerful to ignore, and so easy to generate.

---

find myself checking out another chapter. I then peruse the CD-ROM and check out all the goodies on it. Hey, I know the drill!

So, I have tried to tailor this book both to the jumpers and to the truly dedicated who will plow through all the material sequentially, unable to sleep until they have milked the pages dry of every secret and tip. It's up to you how you use this book. It's all here and it has no expiration date. Use and enjoy it at your own pace.

To entice you to read through the whole book and work through the tutorials, I was able to sneak in funny stories and silly life experiences here and there. Hey, I know how dull computer books can be to read (trust me, I've written enough to feel your pain). Much of the really juicy material gets the ax from the censors and the editors who just can't believe that anyone might scream and spout lengthy strings of expletives while using graphics software (you and I, of course, know better). Nonetheless, I have tried to keep the mood and tone informal and fun because I couldn't stand to write another boring technical manual. I hope you will find this book both entertaining and educational.

The Companion CD-ROM

One thing that has always bothered me about computer design books in general is that the artwork in print is not always available digitally. I hate that. Sometimes, no matter how good a set of instructions is, nothing beats loading the file and digging around in it first-hand. With an object-oriented program like CorelDRAW, this is especially true.

The reason most books don't include all the artwork on the CD-ROM is simple: Most books use a collection of artwork from other artists who, although excited to have their images in print, are not at all excited about letting people dig through their precious art files, learn all of their secrets, and steal the images for their own use. This is perfectly understandable.

However, I tossed sanity and convention to the wind and have used only my own original artwork in this book. I have drawn from over a decade of material to mix and match images to provide a variety of artwork; I've also provided each and every example on the companion CD-ROM. The files are there primarily so that you can fully understand the techniques we are discussing, but feel free to pilfer the images and use them as you like. Consider it the Crazy Uncle Shane clip-art collection, a double bonus for buying this book.

Each chapter in the book has a matching directory on the companion CD-ROM that contains the finished art and sometimes other support pieces (scans of illustrations, stock photography, and so forth). I'll point out in the text the name and location of the files in question so that you can load them and see what's going on. For the most part, each file coincides with a page in the color section as well, so you can flip there and see what we're going to work on before you load the file or read the chapter. For chapters dealing with animation or on-screen artwork (Web pages, multimedia applications, and such), I have also included the HTML code to view with your Web browser, and self-running movies or animations to demonstrate a technique. A few extra files with art are included that I thought fit a chapter or technique, and I point those out to you as we go along.

Also on the companion CD-ROM are the bonus fonts, utilities, and images that all computer books have these days. I tried to make it a CD that I would want if I were buying a computer book, so I think you'll be really happy with what you find there. In my opinion, the CD-ROM alone is worth the price of this book. So don't miss out. Load it up—I guarantee that it includes something that will bring a smile to your face or add something useful to your design day.

The Web Site

In addition to the resources in print and on the companion CD-ROM, there is the official *CorelDRAW 9 f/x and design* Web site (www.slimydog. com/corelfx9). Here, I will post any relevant information in regards to CorelDRAW 9 and this book in the coming year, such as news, reviews, patches, sample files, new techniques, and other helpful bits. With the graphics community ever-changing, it only makes sense that a live resource area be available to you to find out about news and events as they unfold. Bookmark the site and check back now and again for updates, and also to take advantage of the reference areas there (such as the bitmap filters gallery) as you need them.

Beginner To Wizard

CorelDRAW has evolved over the years from an entry-level package to a full-scale professional design suite. Along the way, with the never-ending addition of tools and functions, it has become a bit more intimidating to new users. With so much potential, the perceived learning curve seems pretty steep.

Fear not at all, because CorelDRAW 9 is as accessible to the seasoned pro as it is to the new kid on the block. The tutorials are great, the template wizards are awesome, and the documentation is very complete. You should take no time at all to get up to speed and feel comfortable working in the program.

If you are new to the program, I suggest that you go through the tutorial and work through a few projects to get used to everything before you try the examples outlined in this book. Everyone has to crawl a bit before they can walk.

Users of all levels should be able to follow along in the *CorelDRAW 9 f/x and design* tutorials. I include keyboard shortcuts throughout to make it easy to just punch up the desired command or feature. You can, of course, orient yourself with the pull-down menus and use their commands instead of the shortcuts. (I actually almost never use keyboard shortcuts. I'm definitely a mouser by nature.) In CorelDRAW, you can customize your workspace and modify your work habits to suit your exact needs, and I encourage you to do so. I have my own quirky work habits (I *refuse* to use anything but the traditional Zoom flyout, for example). If you think the way that I create something can be achieved in some other and perhaps easier way, try it. CorelDRAW is a universe full of wonder and magic, and I have yet to uncover it all. With practically yearly upgrades and constantly added features, I don't think I'll ever end this journey of discovery. So, let's get to it.

Moving On

Okay, enough of the basic introduction, bring on the f/x and design tricks! In the next chapter, we literally start with a bang as we explore fire and explosions. Like a match to gasoline, the first tutorial ignites instantly to create hot and fiery effects. So get out your protective gear, because things are going to get hot and furious right off the bat. I'm sure that you can handle it, but maybe you should have a fire extinguisher nearby....

START WITH A "BANG!"

2

This chapter works with the Interactive Blend and Interactive Fill tools to create explosion/spark effects.

Whenever I can, I peel myself away from the glow of the computers and get into my "analog" design studio. There, I work with "real" art tools (pencil, ink, watercolors, welding equipment, and so on) to satiate my desire for hands-on creativity. Although fiddling with these tools brings me great joy, my heart (and talent) lies in the comfy, less-likely-to-sever-a-finger world of computer design! My problem is that I forget what I am doing, my focus lost with the many visual distractions. For example, as I'm busy grinding away on a piece of metal, I'm so intrigued at the shower of sparks around me that I fail to notice that my hair is on fire.

The attention-getting power of fire and explosions is obvious. Such effects are bright and dynamic and have exciting visual and social connotations. Besides, it satisfies that primal urge that arises now and then just to blow something the heck up.

This chapter explores several techniques to render explosions and sparks, starting things with a "bang" by using the Interactive Blend tool to create eye-catching, dynamic explosions. With a few changes, these explosions become showers of sparks, as pinwheels or rocket-trails. This chapter also looks at using the Interactive Transparency tool to give smoke a wispy feel and to add a sense of movement to your objects.

This introductory chapter is sizzling with my philosophy of ruthless creativity. Basically, it's just a no-holds-barred approach to design, where you use your available resources to the fullest and don't hesitate to experiment or try new ways to use old tools. Just do whatever it takes to achieve the result that you want, even if it seems unconventional or even strange. Also embodied in this philosophy is the theory of *approachable* coolness—in creating these projects, I've tried to maintain a reasonable limit on the amount of effort required to do any of the tasks in this book. Personally, I hate spending too much time on one particular design; instead I prefer shortcuts and tricks that still have a high visual payoff. Take what I give you and run with it, massaging and tweaking the techniques and examples in your own twisted little ways!

Explosions

What's fun about CorelDRAW is the experience of exploring the unknown. From solving a specific design problem to conducting open-ended experiments, CorelDRAW gives you a powerful universe to explore. What thrills me is being able to get big payoffs with little creative effort! For example, I was trying to get an explosion effect without investing too much effort when I discovered the technique displayed in Figure 2.1. This section describes how you can master this technique. Here is how to blow things up:

Figure 2.1

Blending multiple sets of circles using the Acceleration feature results in a nice explosion.

1. Use the Ellipse tool to draw a circle. Duplicate this circle (use the + key on the numeric keypad) and then move the duplicate circle over and down slightly.

2. Now, drag-select both circles and repeat the duplication process until you have a blob of some 60 or so circles. To drag-select, hold down the mouse button over a blank are of the screen and drag the mouse across to select multiple objects.

3. Group them (Ctrl+G) and then fill them with solid-yellow by left-clicking on the yellow swatch (to the right of the screen). Remove any outline by right-clicking on the "no fill" color well (it looks like an *x*). Figure 2.2 shows the result.

Figure 2.2

Start with a single circle and duplicate with the + key on the numeric keypad. Keep duplicating and moving until you have a blob of circles.

4. Duplicate this group, and color the duplicate magenta. Now, ungroup the circle objects (Ctrl+U) and deselect them (click on an empty spot to deselect, or press the Esc key). One by one, click and drag each of the magenta circles away from the center, to form a scattered circle around the yellow cluster.

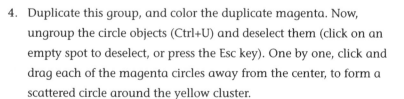

5. After you finish scattering, drag-select all the pieces or choose Select All (Ctrl+A). During this process, you also select the original yellow cluster; hold down the Shift key and click on the yellow cluster to deselect it, leaving only the desired outside circles. Now, group these objects (Ctrl+G). Figure 2.3 shows the result.

Figure 2.3

The original set of circles is duplicated, and the duplicates are scattered around, one by one.

6. Shift-select both object groups and then select the Interactive Blend tool (located on the Interactive tools toolbar). Drag from the center group to an outside circle to start the blend, which also activates the Blend Property Bar on the Property Bar, change the number of steps to 50 (see Figure 2.4). Pow! That was easy.

7. Click Object and Color Acceleration on the Property Bar to reveal the acceleration sliders. Drag the Object Acceleration slider almost all the way to the left, and drag the Color Acceleration slider just a tad to the left (you may need to disable the Link Blend Accelerations option by clicking it on the Property Bar). This Object Acceleration setting clusters the blend closer to the center, and the Color Acceleration setting results in the blend objects staying yellow longer.

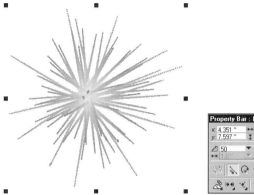

Figure 2.4

Blending the scattered objects to the inner cluster results in a convincing explosion.

8. Click on Apply to see the new blend. After applying the acceleration settings, the image looks more like fragments are being thrown violently away from the hot center (see Figure 2.5).

9. I duplicated the explosion blend group (+ key) to create vapor trails. Change the fill color of the outer control group objects to 40% black, and change the inner control group to white, either with the Uniform Fill dialog (Shift+F11) or by clicking an on-screen color well.

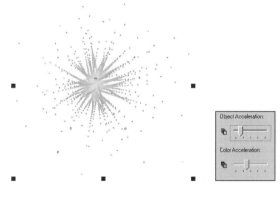

Figure 2.5

Changing the acceleration parameters clusters the blend objects more in the center, while delaying the blend from the inner to the outer color.

10. Switch back to Normal view, click on the blend group, and modify the parameters on the Property Bargain. This time, slide the acceleration sliders to the right (roughly the same distance as you slid them left) (see Figure 2.6).

11. Arrange the second vapor trails to blend behind the first (either press the Shift+PgDn shortcut for Send To Back, or right-click on the object and use the Order submenu shortcuts). Now, your exploded pieces seem to leave a trail of smoke as they blast through the cosmos! Look at Figure 2.7 to see the effect.

GET WIRED

When you work with complex blends, switching to Simple Wireframe view from the View menu is helpful, because this view shows only the control objects in a blend, thus hiding the dizzying array of in-between objects.

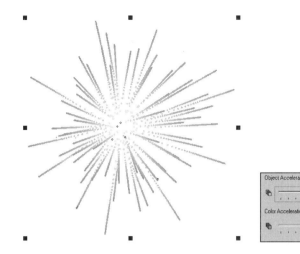

Figure 2.6
Reversing the acceleration settings creates vapor trails of the exploding objects.

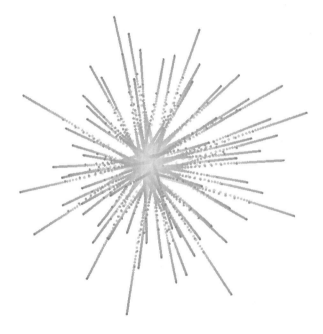

Figure 2.7
The vapor trails blend behind the scattering pieces blend enhances the explosion effect. Bang!

MOUSE TRICKS

To speed up zooming and panning in CorelDRAW, install a Microsoft Intellimouse (or compatible product). "Wheel" mice add a small dial between the left and right buttons, for easy-access control. Spinning the wheel forward and backward zooms in and out. Holding down the wheel activates a panning feature. Using a wheel mouse is, by far, the easiest way to navigate in CorelDRAW, and it's a great way to boost your productivity. The mice are not expensive (especially the Microsoft "clones") and are well worth the investment.

If you don't have a wheel mouse, you can still take advantage of many shortcuts by using the right mouse button. Right mouse-clicking reveals a pop-up menu to speed up many tasks. The task of copying and pasting, for example, is simplified with this menu. Also, changing the order (To Front, To Back, and so forth) is available from this menu, for quick rearranging.

In addition to shortcuts, you use the right mouse menu to set the Overprint value for each object on or off (see the sidebar later in this chapter for more on Overprinting).

12. To add a glowing center, place your explosion on top of a perfect circle with a white-to-dark radial fountain fill. Holding down the Ctrl key as you drag the Ellipse tool creates a perfect circle.

13. Next, drag the Interactive Fill tool across the circle to start the fountain fill process, and then click on the Radial option on the Property Bar. Drag colors off the on-screen palette to change the beginning and ending colors in the fill. Also, you can drag the two color points themselves, as well as the slider between the color chips, to change how the radial fountain fill looks and how the colors mix (see Figure 2.8).

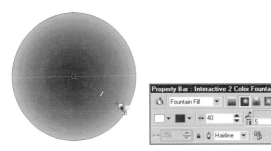

Figure 2.8

Draw circles with the Ellipse tool and then use the Interactive Fill tool to create and control fountain fills.

Duplicating the explosion is easy; simply select the control groups and recolor them, for a sky full of unique bursts. The great thing about this effect is that an explosion group will reblend itself at any size; so, like a real explosion, it is small and compact and expands as you enlarge it. The other elements in the design are explained in different parts of the book (the "chrome shading" technique is described in Chapter 5, and the "vapor trails" behind the jet are explained in Chapter 18). To manipulate the explosions—and appreciate the "live" nature of a blend—open the boom.cdr file from the \Chapt02\ subdirectory on the companion CD-ROM. Enlarge or reduce the whole blend group (or just the control groups) to see how CorelDRAW recalculates your blend each time. All the

OVERPRINTING

Overprinting is a feature that professional desktop publishers use to help control problems in the printing process, which is helpful when sending files to an image-setter to create film. For example, if you have a large body of black text over a screened-back blue photograph, enabling the Overprint Fill option prints the black text on top of the photo, without knocking out the image beneath. If you don't overprint the black text, the computer first clears away the photo underneath to create a white area for the text. The black text will fit perfectly and print in this white area, but if the printing press is slightly out of registration, you will see this white "shadow" around the text. This is bad. With overprinting, the black text is printed *over* the photo without first knocking out a white area, which eliminates print-registration problems. Use this feature to help eliminate registration problems, or to get special effects; for example, enabling Overprint Fill on a yellow object, on top of a magenta photo, creates orange where one object is printed over another.

design elements to create the image in the color section are also on the companion CD-ROM, in the file jetcover.cdr.

Pinwheels

While experimenting with explosions, I stumbled upon the spinning pinwheel variant shown in Figure 2.9; the veritable definition of serendipity—just another random, delightful discovery!

Figure 2.9

Modifying the parameters of the explosion from the Interactive Blend Property Bar instantly transforms bursts into spinning, flaming pinwheels.

Follow Steps 1 through 3 of the "Explosion" section of this chapter to create the blend control objects that you need for this pinwheel derivative (or open and select one of the blends in the boom.cdr file on the companion CD-ROM). Follow these steps to spin the wheel:

1. Start with the explosion blend group from the boom.cdr file on the companion CD-ROM. Color the inner control objects yellow and color the outer control objects red (use the Simple Wireframe view to make selecting and recoloring the blend elements easy).

2. In Normal view, click on the blend to activate the Interactive Blend Property Bar. Increase the Number of steps setting to 100, and then change the Blend direction value to 180. This puts the spin on the pinwheel.

3. Click Object and Color Acceleration and move the Object Acceleration slider to zero (or adjust the sliders to taste). Finally, click Counterclockwise Blend. This advances the pinwheel blend objects through a rainbow of colors as the blend is calculated (see Figure 2.10).

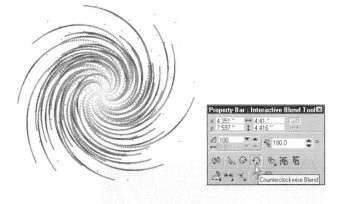

Figure 2.10

Use the Blend direction to create a pinwheel effect from the explosion blend control groups.

4. Duplicate the pinwheel blend group (using the + key on the numeric keypad) and experiment with the settings to get all kinds of different pinwheel looks.

To finish off the Fourth of July image, I imported a flag from the CorelDRAW clipart CD-ROM, found in the \clipart\flags\flying directory. (The "rocket trails" are covered in Chapter 18.) To spin the pinwheels first-hand, open the July4th.cdr file in the \Chapt02\ subdirectory of the companion CD-ROM. I feel so patriotic that I think I'll eat some apple pie.

Flaming Asteroids

Once again, my accidents become your treasures! Figure 2.11 shows another cool variant that you can use to modify the "explosion" into a rocket blast, spark-shower, comet-trail, or whatever fits your needs. Follow these steps to achieve the effect:

Figure 2.11

With a few modifications, a pinwheel can become a flaming asteroid.

1. Start with an explosion blend group (load boom.cdr and select the top explosion, deleting the other). Switch to Simple Wireframe view and drag the center blend control group to the spot from which you want the sparks to come. Switch back to Normal view, and click on the blend to activate the Interactive Blend Property Bar. Now, click Object and Color Acceleration and drag the sliders back to the center position.

2. Increase the Number of steps setting to 125 (see Figure 2.12).

Figure 2.12
Moving the control groups changes the explosion to a stream of sparks.

3. To add a random-looking spin to the spark trail, simply change the Blend Direction value in the Interactive Blend Property Bar to 360 degrees (see Figure 2.13).

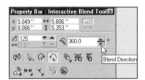

Figure 2.13
Adding a Blend Direction value makes the sparks go wild!

Beyond f/x

Fire, explosions, stars, and the like are great ways to catch a reader's eye and direct their focus toward something important. The fireworks bursts are great design elements to exploit for a "blow-out" sales brochure, or for some other design in which you need to isolate important info bits, such as prices or product names. This chapter also emphasizes "ruthless creativity." Don't be afraid to try an unconventional use of a conventional tool or design element to achieve your styling goals. The world of art and design should focus more on creativity and experimentation than on design software and tool sets.

If you are experimenting and having fun, you will have more energy and enthusiasm for your work, and your designs will reflect that, and consequently be more successful. Enjoy the ride!

Moving On

This chapter mercilessly tossed you right out of the frying pan into the fire (excuse the pun). Along the way, it hit on many cool tools and functions. You also got a taste of the "interactive" tool set (Blend, Fill, and so forth) and my philosophy of ruthless creativity. We shall maintain this frantic pace to squeeze the most out of your design day, this book, and CorelDRAW itself.

The next chapter switches from blowing things up to sculpting and carving, just to cool off a bit. The carving effects don't use the Blend feature, so you and your computer can take a breather from stepping for a spell. However, don't think your CPU won't be smokin' while it is working out the hard-core carving and beveling effects used in the next chapter—this book isn't for wimps or wimpy PCs, so keep your hands and feet inside the car at all times, and make sure the safety bar is down and locked. Off we go!

WHERE HAVE THE DOCKERS GONE?

Instead of opening dockers from the View menu, as in previous versions, this option is now under the Window menu in CorelDRAW 9. Some dockers have disappeared altogether from CorelDRAW 9, including the Blend and Contour dockers. Use the Property Bar to modify the options for these features.

SCULPTING STONE 3

This chapter works with combining objects and symbol shapes, editing/reducing nodes, using bitmap pattern fills, and creating 3D objects with the Extrude function.

People have been cutting and carving images into stone or wood since the dawn of civilization. Humans have always had the urge to make their mark and leave an indelible symbol for all to see. This tradition carries on in the world of graphic art, with everything from corporate logos to brand names incorporated in clothing design. CorelDRAW has some neat features, both simple and complex, to help you carve your own niche in the marketplace.

In this chapter, we'll create chiseled and 3D-looking objects. In the first example, we'll use the Extrude function to create stone carvings, complete with depth and shading. Then, using the Extrude Rotation option on the Interactive Extrude Property Bar we will see how to spin an object in virtual 3D space. Throw on some safety goggles, and let's get carvin'....

Shell Medallions

The technique of creating a chiseled-in-stone look is just the kind of CorelDRAW magic I love—little effort and big payoff! The results are stunning, to the point where you can stare at the finished piece and swear that you are looking at a photograph or an actual stone carving (see Figure 3.1; the same image is also shown in the color section that appears in the middle of this book). On an even cooler side of the equation, the process is highly automated, with CorelDRAW doing most of the hard work of generating shadows and highlights.

Figure 3.1
When the Bevels option (located in the Interactive Extrude Property Bar) is used in conjunction with a bitmap pattern fill, the results are very realistic.

The carved-stone illusion works because multiple extrude groups are actually working for you: an outer ring group, the actual shell shapes, and a neutral background object. In the cutout shell example, which we'll look at first, the neutral background shape shows through in the recessed, carved area. In the second example, the beveled shell object rests on the neutral background. Both techniques are very similar: the only thing that sets them apart is one small circle shape, which changes everything. By combining the circle and the shell shapes, you transform the object and, in doing so, dramatically change the way the Extrude and Bevel functions work on the object.

> **Note:** *Repeat redoes the last executed command. Using the right-click trick fools Repeat into thinking that reduce+duplicate is a single command, so you can "repeat" the process for a series of smaller circles, if you wish.*

The Cutout

Use the following process to get the cutout look:

1. With the Ellipse tool, draw a perfect circle (hold down the Ctrl key while dragging the Ellipse tool). Reduce this circle by dragging inward on the corner sizing handle while holding down the Shift key.

2. Before you release the left button, quickly right-click, which creates a duplicate, smaller circle, leaving the original circle as is.

3. Use the Repeat shortcut (Ctrl+R) to create a third circle.

4. Shift-select the smallest and largest rings and combine them (Ctrl+L). This should create a solid doughnut shape, with another circle outline on top (see Figure 3.2).

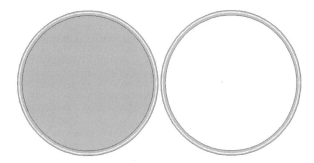

Figure 3.2
Combining two circles creates a doughnut shape.

5. Open the Symbols and Special Characters docker (Ctrl+F11, or from the Window|Dockers menu), find a shell shape in the Animals 1 gallery, and drag it onto your desktop. Enlarge and center the shell by shift-selecting both it and the circle object and then using the Align shortcuts (the letter *C* on the keyboard, then *E*).

6. Select the remaining center circle (the other two are combined into the doughnut), duplicate (+) once more, and enlarge the circle slightly. Select this ring and the shell and combine them (Ctrl+L).

This punches the shell shape through the circle, which is the last step in creating your parent shapes. Now you have three objects: a circle with the shell punched out, a simple circle background, and a doughnut ring around everything (see Figure 3.3).

Figure 3.3

Combining a circle with the shell shape, in effect, punches a shell-shaped hole through it (the Wireframe view is on the left).

GIANT SYMBOLS

The objects in the Symbols and Special Characters docker may not be to scale in relation to your design when you drag the objects onto your desktop. You can resize the objects individually after they are on your desktop, or you can change the Size value in the Symbols docker. This way, you can make the objects to scale as you drag them off the docker, which is faster than resizing them individually, especially if you are dragging many off at one time.

---

7. Select the outer ring shape and send it to the front (Shift+PgUp, or right-click and access the Order shortcuts). Drag-select all the objects and then open the Pattern Fill dialog box, shown in Figure 3.4, from the Fill tool flyout. Change the top-left set of radio buttons to the Bitmap option, which enables you to use photos of "real world" textures to colorize your objects.

8. Click on the down-pointing arrow next to the preview box to open a gallery of bitmap pattern fill options. The current process will work with any of these choices; for more options, use the Load button on the Pattern Fill dialog box. I found a bitmap pattern that I liked on the CorelDRAW CD-ROM, in the \tiles\stone\large directory (or, you can load a third-party pattern tile bitmap). The default tile size is fine, but if you prefer, you can enlarge or reduce it in the Size area of the Pattern Fill dialog box.

9. Click on OK to fill your object. At this point, all the pieces blend together in Preview mode, shown here with outlines so that you can see where each piece is located (refer to Figure 3.4).

SCREEN HOGS

The screen shots in this book often show dockers and the Property Bar as small, dialog box-type entities. When you open a docker, either with a shortcut or from the Window menu, it will be at full size on the right side of the screen. If you want to make it smaller or move it closer to what you are working on, just "tear it off" by dragging the top of the bar down and to the left. The docker reduces in size and allows you to drag it anywhere on your page. To "redock" the docker, drag it back to the right-center of the screen, against the side, and it returns to full size. The Property Bar, the on-screen palette, and even the toolbars can be similarly "torn off," resized, and repositioned. Don't be a slave to the interface; rather, customize it to your own tastes or to better serve your current task.

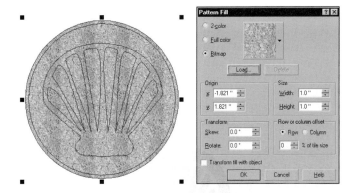

Figure 3.4
A bitmap pattern fill is the key element to creating the stone texture.

10. Now the fun begins! Work in Wireframe view (View|Wireframe) to keep things speedy. Select the outer doughnut object and then locate and select the Interactive Extrude tool (on the Interactive tool flyout). Dragging the object enables you to see that, by moving the cursor, you can control how the Interactive Extrude builds your object. In this example, you control the results by manipulating the variables on the Interactive Extrude Property Bar, so you simply need to drag to establish an active extrude group.

11. On the Interactive Extrude Property Bar, change the Depth value to 5 and double-check that the vanishing point attribute option box displays VP Locked To Object (which is the default). You can change the vanishing point by dragging the *x* on screen or by entering values in the *x* or *y* Vanishing Point Coordinate box. Drag the point to the exact center of the circle, or simply enter 0 in the Property Bar boxes.

12. Click Lighting (the light-bulb icon) and then click on the 1 light-bulb button on the pop-up dialog box that appears, to enable a single light source. Move the resulting light to the right-center position (see Figure 3.5).

13. Click Bevels and enable the Use Bevel option from the pop-up dialog box. Change the Bevel Depth option (the top spin box) to .05 inch and stick with the default, 45-degree angle. This should give your "doughnut" some depth.

Figure 3.5
The Interactive Extrude Property Bar, showing Depth and Vanishing Point settings, as well as the Lighting and Bevel pop-up dialog boxes.

DO YOU REMEMBER ROLL-UPS?

Remember when Corel introduced that spanky-fresh thing called a "roll-up"? You could open or close these dialog boxes as needed, and position them anywhere you wanted. Well, roll-ups are history in CorelDRAW 9. Because you now can move and resize dockers or access options from the Property Bar, roll-ups are redundant.

This may or may not impact the way that you work, depending on whether you are upgrading to Version 9 or are a new user. If you are a Corel veteran, you may want to use the Ctrl+E shortcut to open the Extrude roll-up, and choose extrude options from there. This shortcut now opens the Export dialog box in CorelDRAW 9, because the Extrude roll-up is gone. You have to use the Interactive Extrude tool instead, and access the options from the Property Bar. The same is true for any feature that formerly used a roll-up. You either open a similar docker or access features directly on the context-sensitive Property Bar.

SHARED VANISHING POINTS

If you have extrude groups scattered on your page and want them to share vanishing points, use the Copy VP From option on the Interactive Extrude Property Bar. By using this option, you can make all of your extrude elements appear to be in the same plane, for a convincing 3D effect.

14. Select the shell shape and then select Effects|Copy Effect|Extrude From. With the resulting arrow, click on the extrude group that you created in Step 9. With the settings "borrowed" from an existing extrude group, you can save time and ensure that both groups have the same extrude settings. Once the new extrude group is active, you can select and change any of the options on the Interactive Extrude Property Bar, enabling you to make the new group unique from the extrude group that you copied the settings from.

15. Click Bevels on the Property Bar and enable the Show Bevel Only feature for this extrude group. With a light source enabled, the surface of the extrude group becomes slightly darker than the original bitmap pattern fill, so CorelDRAW can then calculate highlight and shadow objects (see Figure 3.6). With the original bitmap pattern fill showing through, the contrast creates a nice cut-out and beveled illusion.

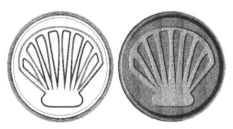

Figure 3.6
The Extrude function, with a light source and beveling options, calculates the highlights and shadows for a chiseled look (the Wireframe view is on the left).

That's it! This process yields great results, but it is mighty slow to render. You may want to work in Wireframe mode to speed things along.

Inverse

To change from the cutout look to the inverse, with the shell embossed rather than recessed, the changes are minor. First, you need to remove the circle from the shell shape and then reapply the bevel. Here is how to make the shell embossed:

1. If you are using the pieces from the previous example, be sure to save them to disk first, with a unique file name. In Simple Wireframe view, only the parent objects in blends and extrude groups (called "control curves") are displayed, making it easy to locate these objects. In a complex image such as our extrude group, even in Wireframe view there will be a lot going on.

2. So, in simple Wireframe view, select the shell shape and duplicate it (using the + key). Drag this shape off to the side. Because you selected only the control curve, your duplicate doesn't contain the extrude information.

3. With the duplicate shell selected, break it apart (Ctrl+K), delete the outer circle, and then drag-select and recombine (Ctrl+L) the pieces. This should leave you with just the original shell (see Figure 3.7).

> ### HURRY UP AND SAVE!
>
> To speed up file save times, disable the thumbnail feature. From the Save Drawing dialog box (File|Save As), change the Thumbnail option to None. A thumbnail is a nice reference graphic, but CorelDRAW must calculate every single thing in your design to create this tiny image. So, if your file has a complex extrude or series of lenses, having this feature enabled dramatically increases your save time.

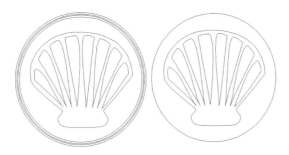

Figure 3.7
The Simple Wireframe view displays only the control curves in a blend or extrude group, which makes selecting and duplicating a control object, such as the shell shape, easy.

4. Although the Bevel function worked fine on this shape in the previous example, you need to modify it slightly in this example, because the bottoms of the scallops in the shell object are very pointy. In the previous example, because the circle shape was combined with the shell object, the bevel was inside the points, and everything rendered fine. However, removing the circle changes the cut-away area to the inside of the scallops, with the bevels now on the outside, reversing the logic of the function.

5. Creating a bevel on the outside of these really sharp points results in some unpredictable and undesirable shapes. To make things work better, you first need to round out the spikes, using the Shape tool. With the Shape tool, double-click on a point above the ending spiky node to add a node there (double-clicking on a point is the reverse short-cut, and will delete the point). Continue to add points just above both sides of the pointy scallop ends (see Figure 3.8).

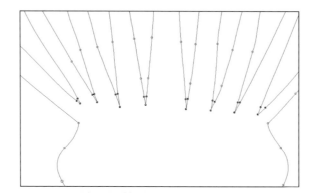

Figure 3.8

Double-click on the Shape tool on a line to add nodes above the spiky scallop ends.

6. With all the new nodes in place, drag-select the end nodes with the Shape tool and click on the Smooth button on the Property Bar. This removes the pointy ends (but with the new nodes in place), but does not dramatically change the way the object looks (see Figure 3.10). If you smooth the end points without first adding the new nodes, the scallop shapes will distort.

7. Reducing the number of nodes in the object is a good idea, too, to make the calculations simpler and smoother. With the Shape tool, drag-select all the nodes and then change the Curve Smoothness value to reduce the node count. This new slider replaces the Auto Reduce function, which did not offer any control to fine-tune your results. Use the slider to review how the node reduction impacts your object (too much reduction begins to distort your shape; too little reduction results in your object remaining overly complex).

8. Drag back and forth until you are happy with the results (see Figure 3.11).

9. Switch from Simple Wireframe view to Wireframe view. With the shell selected, choose Effects|Copy Effect|Extrude From, and then click on the extrude pieces of the original shell piece. Delete the original shell and position the new one in the center of the medallion.

With the outer circle shape around the shell removed, the extrude group rests on the original bitmap pattern background and looks embossed (see Figure 3.12).

That's the complete process for creating embossed or engraved objects. The great thing about this technique is that, at any time, you can Select All (Ctrl+A) and change the fill value, and everything automatically recalculates. In fact, I did just that, using a "wood" bitmap pattern fill, before I exported the image (Ctrl+E) as a CMYK bitmap for the color section in the middle of this book. The file is called shells.cdr and is located

No "Outside" Bevels

Unlike some bitmap plug-in filter effects (such as Alien Skin's Bevel, from the Eye Candy collection), CorelDRAW bevels only to the inside of an object. The shell in the first example appears to be beveled on the outside, because it has been combined with a larger circle, creating a solid object with the shell shape punched in it. The CorelDRAW bevel always follows along the inside edge of an object. When you remove the outer circle, the inside edge becomes the shell shape again, reversing the logic of the bevel. CorelDRAW always calculates the bevel in the same way; you just alter the logic of the object to get different results (see Figure 3.9).

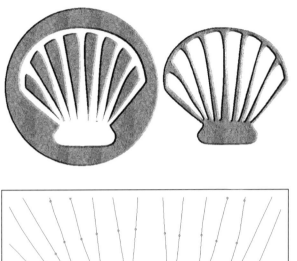

Figure 3.9

The Bevel function always creates shapes on the inside of a solid object. Combining the shell shape with a circle punches a clear area in the center, leaving the shell scallops as solids. Removing the circle makes the shell shape solid, with the scallops cut out.

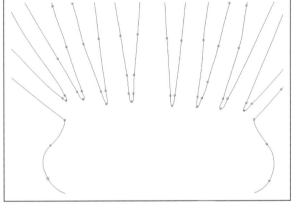

Figure 3.10

Adding points and smoothing out the scallops produce better Extrude results.

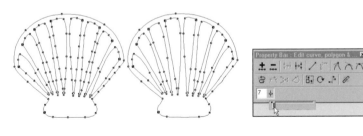

Figure 3.11

The Curve Smoothness option enables you to control how many nodes are used to create your object.

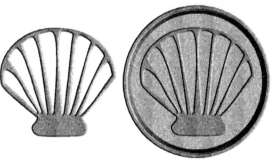

Figure 3.12

The Effects|Copy Effect option includes the option to copy an extrude from another object group. The cutout shape resting on the neutral background object creates the embossed illusion.

in the \Chap03\ folder on the companion CD-ROM, if you want to load the shell duo firsthand. The file is kind of huge, so you may want to load

shell.cdr, which is just the shell extrude group alone. Because these are
"live" extrude groups, you can modify them at any time, or you can take
the whole process one step further and spin the object in space, using the
Extrude Rotation feature. The next section is an example of just that!

Twirling Stones

An extrude group within CorelDRAW is a "live" entity, which means that
you can change the parameters for a new result at any time, or even
remove the extrude entirely. The result is an amazing amount of flexibility, because you can change the texture and orientation of your objects
whenever you want, while still maintaining the advantages of vector
artwork (as opposed to a 3D modeling package, such as CorelDream, in
which you can output images only as bitmaps, which are big and clumsy
to work with). This flexibility adds power and potential to your design
cycle and can even lend itself to animation projects.

The example in Figure 3.13 shows how you can indefinitely alter an extrude
group for the life of your design, either to add built-in flexibility (for a corporate logo that your client wants to see at different angles, for example) or
even create animated icons. (I assembled this series of twirling objects into
an animation and made the file available to you; the fxspin.avi file is in the
\Chapt03\ subdirectory on the companion CD-ROM, and on the this book's
Web site at http://www.slimydog.com/corelfx9.)

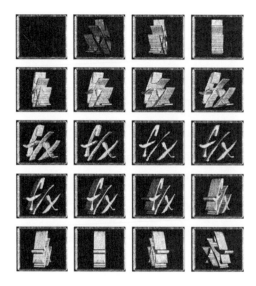

Figure 3.13
When you increment the 3D
Rotation values, the extrude
object appears to spin around.

Here is how to twirl stone objects in 3D space:

1. To make this frames-creation process for an animation as simple as
   possible, I limited the image to a single shape; this process gets too

complicated on a stack of images, like those in the medallion (but it isn't impossible, if you're a nut with lots of time on your hands!). I used a simpler text object with a static frame around it. Use the Text tool to set the f/x text on screen (the font is called Tiger Rag). In my opinion, animations benefit from solid objects that don't move and that serve as a point of reference for those that are moving. Thus, I drew two rectangles and combined them to create a frame. My Web site (where I will use this animation) has a black background, so I made the background solid black.

Rounded Corners

If you drag a node on a rectangle with the Shape tool, it changes the corners from harsh, 90-degree angles to soft rounded corners.

2. Choose Effects|Copy Effect|Extrude From to copy the extrude values from the shell medallion for the first frame. Alternatively, create your own new extrude object or, easier yet, open the fxalone.cdr file from the \Chapt03\ folder on the companion CD-ROM (see Figure 3.14).

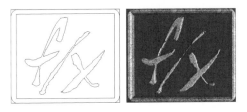

Figure 3.14
For an animation, a single extrude group is easier to manipulate, necessitating only one change per frame export.

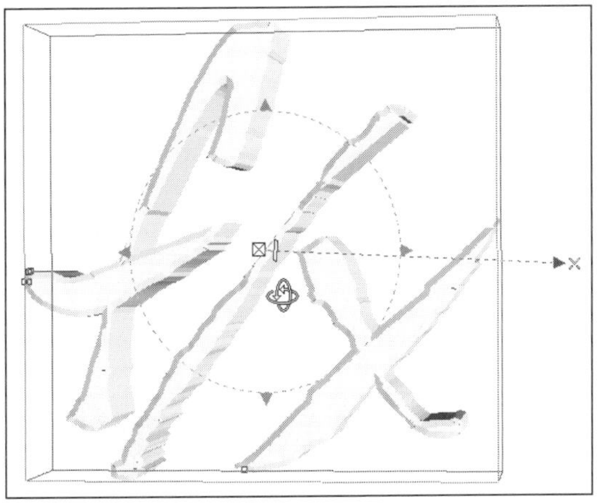

Figure 3.15
In addition to the controls in the extrude docker, you can manipulate the effect using the Interactive Extrude tool.

3. With the extrude group selected, click Extrude Rotation on the Property Bar (if you linger the pointer over a button, a ToolTip tells you the button's name). In the Rotation values dialog box, you can enter the rotation values manually.

   In this example, I increased the second value (y) by 15 for each step, to create the spinning logo illusion. I also added a second, less-intense light source on the left, so that my shading won't be solid black; that way, the shading is visible against the dark background. Enter your new values, and your object spins accordingly (see Figure 3.16).

INTERACTIVE EXTRUDE

CorelDRAW 9 adds "total control" of your extrude groups with "live" interactive object-manipulation tools (see Figure 3.15). Drag the on-screen *x* to change the vanishing point. To adjust the Depth value, drag the slider back and forth on the line pointing toward the vanishing point. Double-click on your extrude group to reveal a set of 3D rotation arrows. If you drag up or down in the center of your object with the 3D rotation arrow tool, the object spins horizontally or vertically. To rotate the object clockwise or counter-clockwise, move the cursor over the perimeter dotted-line circle and then drag. These interactive tools offer quick ways to create and modify an extrude group, but for precision and control, use the options on the Property Bar.

Figure 3.16
Incrementing the Rotation values in the Interactive Extrude Property Bar will spin your object in space.

4. Continue to create frames by incrementing the rotation value and then exporting the image (Ctrl+E) as a bitmap for assembly into an animation later (Chapter 21 covers this process in detail). You can continue to spin the object around, even until it is backward, with the *y* Rotation value at the maximum of 100 (see Figure 3.17).

Figure 3.17
The maximum *y* Rotation value of 100 spins your object completely around.

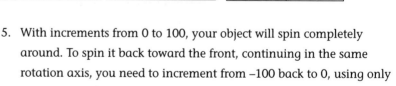

5. With increments from 0 to 100, your object will spin completely around. To spin it back toward the front, continuing in the same rotation axis, you need to increment from –100 back to 0, using only negative numbers (see Figure 3.18).

Figure 3.18
To rotate the object from back to front in the same axis of rotation, you must use the negative number range, from –100 back to 0.

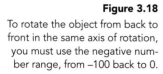

To simplify the process in Step 5, you may even want to start at –100 and work toward 0. Decide how many cells you want in your animation, and then divide by 200 (the total number of available rotation steps) to get your increment value. For example, for a 20-cell animation, you start at –100 and add 10 each time (200/20=10) to the rotation value. This generates a smoothly rotating animation.

The file fxspin.cdr in the \Chapt03\ subdirectory on the companion CD-ROM contains all the rotated objects that are used to generate the image in the color section. That subdirectory also contains the fxspin.avi file, which shows the logo moving in the assembled animation. You can also load the fxalone.cdr file from this subdirectory and practice changing the axis of rotation, to get a feel for the process before you start an animation sequence of your own. The example in this section changed only the horizontal rotation value—you could get some wild results by also incrementing the other two rotation values. Again, this is only one example of what you can do with this tool, and it isn't the most practical application. But hey, you might be as nuts as I am and want to create animations like this too!

Beyond f/x

The effects outlined in this chapter have many practical uses. Using the Extrude function is a great way to add depth and shading to any object, such as a company logo or masthead. The animation options work well to add to your Web page a logo that can sing and dance! (Scripts are available on the Web that help automate this process. Check www.i-us.com, in the "Tales from the Script" forum, for more information.) The Extrude function's power and flexibility are perfect for "carving" your niche in the Web, with graphics and buttons made of wood, stone, or any other material. Manipulating the Bevel option can also animate your stony buttons, to make them come alive as you click or roll the cursor over them (see Chapter 20 for examples). Company logos take on a new immensity when rendered in "stone" and placed predominantly in a landscape, like a giant statue. The sculpting process has endless uses. Like Bob Dylan said, "Everybody must get stoned," and with the effects in this chapter, now your images can too!

Moving On

In this chapter, we filled objects with bitmap patterns, transformed them into 3D objects, added light, shadow, and other Extrude features, and even spun them around in virtual space.

I keep babbling on about the flexibility of CorelDRAW images because I feel this is where the program is really powerful. The fact that you can constantly tweak objects is just very appealing to me! If you don't like the way something works out the first time, you can tune and massage it until it is just perfect, or you can duplicate or cut pieces to use in another project. Paint programs just don't have that kind of power, and although virtual-reality 3D universes (such as RayDream) do have that power to some extent, they don't have the output flexibility or bitmap-manipulation features that CorelDRAW has.

In the next chapter, we will explore some cool ways to take boring text elements and make them come alive in your designs. You will discover how to capture current design trends, with virtual graffiti, transparency, and glowing effects, and even make your text float freely in midair. All of this and more, none of which are available on grandpa's typewriter.

GRAFFITI,
STRESSED
TYPE, AND
BULLET HOLES

This chapter demonstrates working with the Interactive Contour, Interactive Transparency, and Interactive Drop Shadow tools, converting text to bitmaps for blurring effects, and using the PowerClip command to create a mask.

This chapter introduces popular and contemporary themes, and because this is my book, it also looks at designs from the fringe element. I find that much can be learned from artists who are far from the mainstream, even those who are from the underground design scene—regardless of what the design traditionalists think, who often scoff at these "disciplines."

We will touch upon several interesting type effects from the edge and the underground. First, we use the Interactive Contour function to achieve a flashy, graffiti look that you might find applied to a local urban surface, complete with a spray of random bullet holes. Then, we explore type effects created with the Interactive Transparency, Interactive Drop Shadow, and PowerClip tools, and also look at the blur effects from the Bitmaps menu. All of these examples will help you to get out of any humdrum art slump and add some danger to your designs!

You Write?

While promoting my own line of apparel, I met many interesting (and often frightening) characters. Hard-core, ex-con, gangbanger graffiti and tattoo artists were getting into clothing, and designs from the street were evolving into street wear. One company was promoting its apparel with a small bottle on a necklace. Inside the bottle were all kinds of different spray tips for aerosol paint cans. I thought that was pretty cool and tried to score myself a set. Don't get me wrong—I am not condoning tagging or graffiti; I hate to see anything vandalized. However, I find that the techniques are noteworthy, and I even support designated graffiti areas (such as organized murals or The Pit in Venice Beach). Personally, I love to grab a handful of spray cans and go nuts! Once I had a house with an empty, nonfunctioning swimming pool that we converted into a basketball court/skateboard park, and we covered it in graffiti. I guess I'm a *controlled* vandal.

Although I have not personally heard of anyone designing a tag or graffiti mural in CorelDRAW, anything is possible. You could easily design an entire wall at full size (Layout|Page Setup, set the Paper option to Custom, and then key in any dimensions), and then use the Tiling feature

ART ON THE STREET

Tagging is a practice in which graffiti artists mark their territory with a special icon, their nickname, or a combination of both. More often than not, a tagger is not affiliated with a gang, but just a frustrated inner-city youth seeking attention or recognition. Taggers greet one another with "You write?" to announce their status and verify that they are speaking to fellow taggers. They then compare techniques and styles as well as ambitious or dangerous *tags*. It is a subculture all of its own.

(Print|Layout|Print Tiled Pages) to output the image at actual size to create stencils, masks, or any full-size reference. Many sign companies use CorelDRAW files to generate masks, using a computer-controlled plotter that cuts out an image from giant sheets of masking material, which then can be laid down and spray painted over, to produce a crisp image. Usually, this high-end process is reserved for custom graphics on expensive cars but hey, who knows?

I imagine that re-creating the look of graffiti is more valuable to you than actually designing spray-paint graffiti projects, so I will focus on the former. In this section, we create type that has the flashy look of painted graffiti, including the texture of the wall that it is on, to achieve the result shown in Figure 4.1.

Here is how to "vandalize" a virtual wall:

1. Use the Artistic Text tool to set your headline. For my *CorelDRAW* text in Figure 4.1, I used a font called Dancin LET, but you can use this technique on any text or shape object.

2. Locate and select the Interactive Contour tool, on the Interactive Tool flyout. Drag your text from the center outward, while watching the Property Bar, which shows you how many steps are in the Contour as you go along. Stop dragging when the number of steps equals 2. You can control a contour group directly with the Interactive Contour tool, or by modifying the settings in the Property Bar. In the Property Bar, set the Offset value to .05 inch, and set the Steps value to 2. This creates the shapes needed for the multiple outline effect (see Figure 4.2).

Figure 4.1
Use the Interactive Contour tool to add multiple outlines to a shape and, with the addition of a bright color scheme, create a graffiti look. Use the piece as is, or convert the image to a bitmap and use the Wet Paint filter effect for variety.

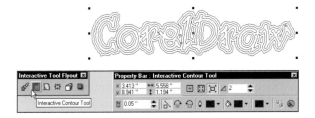

Figure 4.2
The Interactive Contour tool creates additional shapes with Offset and Steps variables, which you can control interactively or enter manually on the Property Bar or docker.

3. With the contour group selected, choose Arrange|Separate, and then choose Arrange|Ungroup. This gives you three separate curve shapes, which you can color white, black, and red (from the outside in) to create a cool look.

4. To simplify and fine-tune each contour shape, select the curve, break it apart (Ctrl+K), and then delete all the objects except the main outline. When these images are stacked, they have a bold but simple look (see Figure 4.3).

Figure 4.3

Use the shapes that result from the Contour command, or eliminate any inside shapes for a "fat" outline.

5. To add a gleam to the text, select the smallest inside curve and duplicate it. Nudge the duplicate up and to the right by using the arrow keys, and give it a white fill (Shift+F11 opens the Uniform fill dialog) and white hairline (F12 opens the Outline Pen dialog) Now, send the duplicate back one (Ctrl+PgDn) so that the original covers all but a sliver, resulting in a gleam.

6. Draw a rectangular wall behind the text and use the Texture Fill option to give it the look of a concrete wall. From the Texture Fill dialog box (open from the Fill tool flyout), change the Texture Library to Samples 7, select Concrete from the Texture list, and then click on OK (see Figure 4.4).

Figure 4.4

Offset a duplicate to create a gleam highlight. Use the Texture Fill dialog box to give a rectangle a concrete fill.

7. Use the Artistic Text tool to set more type. For the 9, I used a font called MarkerFeltWide, which has a fat, hand-drawn look to it. Give the text a fat, black .111-inch outline and enable the Behind Fill option from the Outline Pen dialog box (F12). Give this text a radial fountain fill from white to blue, using either the Fountain Fill dialog box (F11) or the Interactive Fill tool.

TEXTURE FILL IMAGE RESOLUTION

For crisper images in your high-end projects that contain texture fills, be sure to increase the Bitmap Resolution and Texture Size Limit values from the Texture Options dialog box. In the Texture Fill dialog box, click on the Options button to open the Texture Options dialog box, and then increase both options to their maximum values. This makes the texture fill usable for printed applications (the default setting of 120 dpi is just too low). Remember that these values act as multipliers when calculating the bitmap that makes up a texture fill, so your file size also increases dramatically when you increase these values. To help save disk space with this huge file, use the Advanced settings from the Save Drawing dialog box (File|Save As). Click on the Advanced button to open the Advanced Settings dialog box, and then enable the Rebuild Textures When Opening the File option. Now, CorelDRAW saves only the settings associated with texture fills, and recalculates them when you open the file, instead of saving the entire, huge bitmap to disk.

8. Use the Freehand tool to draw shapes that will become abstract reflections of the surrounding landscape, making the object look chrome-like. After you draw the abstract shapes, use the Intersection feature to trim down the blobs, so that they are within the main text shape. To do this, select one of the abstract shapes and, from the Arrange|Shaping menu, choose Intersect. In the Shaping docker, change the Leave Original options to just Target Object(s), Intersect With, and then click on the number 9 object. This creates a new object, just where the two shapes overlap, which is what we want (see Figure 4.5). Remember that this is supposed to be graffiti, so don't worry about being too detailed.

9. Move the cursor over the Polygon tool on the toolbar, right-click, and choose the Properties option. Enable the Polygon as Star option, change the Number of points/sides value to 4, and increase the Sharpness slider to 75. This makes for a nice cartoon-like sparkle. Click on OK and drag the Polygon tool to create the sparkle shape. Then, use the Pick tool to position the sparkles on the top-left edges of the chromed letter, similar to what you see in Figure 4.6.

NUDGE AND SUPERNUDGE

You can double the productivity value of the arrow keys by using the Nudge and SuperNudge options. Open the Options dialog box (Ctrl+J) and, from the Edit page, key in whatever values you want for Nudge and SuperNudge. I use a small value for Nudge (.005"), for tiny, precise movement, and a large multiplier (such as 20) for the SuperNudge value. This way, I can make tiny or big leaps as I need them, with the arrow key alone, or with the arrow+Shift keys.

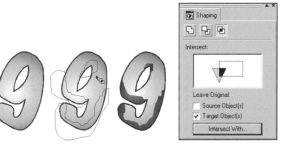

Figure 4.5

A plain text element is transformed into a "chromy" one with a radial fountain fill and objects meant to look like a reflected landscape.

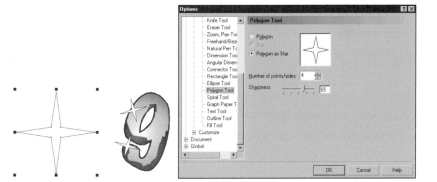

Figure 4.6

The Polygon tool creates all kinds of stars; they can have from 3 to 500 points.

10. For the *FX* text, I used the Bezier tool to hand-draw my own type. Select the Bezier tool and click on From point to point to draw a big funky *F* and then a fresh *X*. Select both objects and group them (Ctrl+G). Give the group a fat, black .222-inch outline, and from the

Note: *Dragging a node on a Star object with the Shape tool allows for unique interactive shaping, which moves all of the points in unison. Try it!*

Outline Pen dialog box (F12), enable the round option from the Corners set of radio buttons. Use the Interactive Fill tool to create a yellow-to-magenta linear fountain fill, only with a harsh transition in the center (make the start and end points close together). Finally, duplicate the group and assign no-fill and a thinner, .092-inch white outline. This thin-on-fat outline technique is an alternative to the Contour effect, with similar results (see Figure 4.7).

Figure 4.7

A fat, black outline underneath a thinner, white outline creates a multiple-outline look similar to what the Interactive Contour tool can create, but in fewer steps. A Custom color blend creates the chrome-like reflection.

11. Arrange your pieces on the rectangular wall to complete the graffiti. The next step is to riddle it with bullet holes!

12. Draw a rough circle with the Freehand tool. Switch to the Interactive Fill tool and drag from the top right to the bottom left. Click on the Conical button on the Property Bar, which creates the shading of an indentation. Use the Ellipse tool to draw a circle in the center, and then give it a medium-gray fill.

13. Duplicate the circle (+ key), offset the duplicate to the top right, give it a solid-black fill, and then send it back one (Ctrl+PgDn). This is the hole shadow (an indentation is shaded in reverse compared to how extruded objects are shaded). Select the original circle, duplicate again, and move the duplicate to the bottom left. Shade it white and send it back one, to create a gleam. Select all the bullet-hole objects and group them (Ctrl+G). Figure 4.8 shows the result.

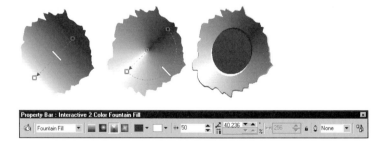

Figure 4.8

The Interactive Fill tool creates a fountain fill across the bullet-hole shape. Clicking on the Conical button changes the fill type, which provides convincing shading when teamed with a circle group.

14. Arrange your bullet-hole group on one end of the mural, duplicate it, and place the duplicate on the other end. Shift-select both groups and drag between them with the Interactive Blend tool. In the Property

Bar, reduce the Number of Steps to 5 and click on Object and Color Acceleration to open that pop-up dialog box You can change the scatter of your bullets by dragging the Object Acceleration slider to the right or left (see Figure 4.9).

 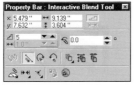

Figure 4.9
The Object Acceleration slider gives a staggered look to the bullet-hole blend.

15. That finishes the main graphic, but I added texture to make the image look more like graffiti. Select the rectangle with the texture fill and duplicate it (+ key), and then send it to the front (Shift+PgUp). On the toolbar, select the Interactive Transparency tool (looks like a wine glass) and change the transparency type from None to Texture on the Property Bar. Drag the Starting Transparency (top) and Ending Transparency (bottom) sliders to adjust the amount of texture in your letters (see Figure 4.10).

 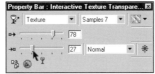

Figure 4.10
To make the art look like it is painted on a wall, use the Interactive Transparency tool and the Property Bar to adjust the opacity of the texture-filled box in front of the artwork.

16. For even more creative options, we can convert parts of the image into a bitmap, to facilitate the use of special bitmap filters (first save a copy of your file to disk before you convert anything to a bitmap, so you have a backup later).

17. Select all of your text objects, but not the wall or the bullet-hole group (the easiest way to do this is to Select All (Ctrl+A) then, holding the Shift key, click on the wall and bullet objects to de-select them). From the Bitmaps menu, choose Convert to Bitmap. Change the Color to RGB, Resolution to 300 dpi, and enable the Anti-aliasing, Transparent Background, and Use Color Profile radio buttons. Click on OK to "rasterize" (convert vector information in to pixels) your artwork.

18. With your individual objects now a single bitmap, you can make use of the many filter effects located under the Bitmaps menu. CorelDRAW 9 adds many "Creative" filters, but this example calls for Wet Paint, located on the Distort flyout. With this filter you can make your artwork look freshly painted, complete with runny drips (See Figure 4.11). You can control how "runny" the paint is with the Wetness and Percent sliders in the Wet Paint dialog box.

Figure 4.11
Converting your vector artwork into a bitmap allows you to use special Bitmap effects filters, such as Wet Paint.

Note: *A positive value for Wetness in the Wet Paint dialog will cause the light colors to "run." A negative value will control dark colors.*

You need to move the bullet-hole blend to the front (Shift+PgUp) on top of the transparent texture and keep it crisp. The results of this exercise can be seen in the color section in the middle of this book or in the bulhole.cdr file in the \Chapt04\ subdirectory on the companion CD-ROM. Load the file and fiddle with the Acceleration settings on the bullet-hole blend. Or convert the image in to a bitmap, and try other filters on it, (Palette Knife or other filters on the Art Strokes flyout look really cool!) Have fun, you cyber-vandal!

Blurry Type

In keeping with a strange trend, many artists are creating images that are actually difficult to read and purposely out of focus. As more and more design is computer-generated, a backlash seems to be taking place, with artists producing images that attempt to look anything *but* computer-generated. Artists strive for a noncomputer-generated feel with images that are purposely out of focus and designed to look out of registration, poorly photocopied, or scratchy. The irony, of course, is that computers just make these kinds of images easier to create!

Using the functions available under the Bitmap menu, we will reverse traditional logic and create objects in the foreground that are out of focus, with far-away images that are crystal clear (Figure 4.12 shows an example). This reverse-logic brings emphasis to a background image, manipulating and directing your reader's eye at your will. It is a popular design look, made easy with CorelDRAW. Here is how to "fuzz" your type:

Figure 4.12
If you convert text to bitmaps with the Transparent Background option, you can use filter effects while retaining a see-through look. You can stuff a copy of the background into a text object by using the PowerClip feature, creating a "ghost" object, as with the big number 9.

1. Use the Artistic Text tool to set your type. This technique works on any font. (I used a freaky one called MonkeyCaughtStealing from

Garage Fonts, a third-party font vendor. Check out their Web site at www.garagefonts.com.) Arrange your type on the page in the size and position that you desire. This technique involves converting the type into bitmaps, so you need to spend some time working out the layout, because after the pieces are converted, englarging them can result in low-resolution images (which are bad, bad, bad).

2. Before we proceed, import an interesting background image to help you lay out everything to your liking. I used an image from the Masters 1 CorelDRAW photo CD. Import the image and arrange the text in a way that balances the image, keeping the area of focus open for later emphasis (see Figure 4.13).

3. Draw a rectangle, with no outline or fill, around each text element (see Figure 4.14). This becomes a logical bounding box for the bitmap conversion step. If you do not provide a boundary, CorelDRAW uses the object size to calculate the bitmap size. This is fine, except that you need some breathing room beyond the edges of the text so that you can use the Blur filter.

   If you don't provide a bounding box and use the Blur filter, the effect ends abruptly at the edges and looks strange. (In CorelDRAW 8 and 9, you can use the Inflate Bitmap option from the Bitmaps menu to create this breathing room instead of drawing a bounding box.)

Figure 4.13

Import your background image and arrange your type pieces. After the type is converted into bitmaps, you can't enlarge it without losing resolution, so take some time to work out the layout.

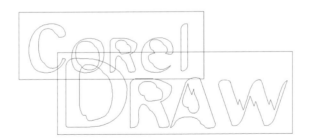

Figure 4.14

Draw a bounding box around each text element to define the limits of the bitmap. This extra area lets you use the effects filters with room to spare.

4. Select a text element and its bounding box and choose Bitmaps|Convert to Bitmap. In the Convert to Bitmap dialog box, change the Color option to Grayscale (8-bit) (or to RGB Color, if your text is in color), and enable all of the radio buttons: Anti-aliasing, Transparent Background, and Use Color Profile. Set the Resolution value to 300 and click on OK. After a few seconds, your image is transformed into a bitmap (see Figure 4.15).

5. With the bitmap selected, select Gaussian from the Bitmaps|Blur submenu. In the Gaussian Blur dialog box, drag the Radius slider to

IMAGES ON THE GO

Corel has literally hundreds of useful photo collections to choose from. You can purchase these images as whole collections on CD-ROM format, or even individually on an as-needed basis. From the Corel Web site (www.corel.com), you can gain access to its online image and clip-art library in the Corel *Studio* area. Although the CD collections are a great bargain, the real life-saver is the immediate ability to locate and download images as you need them from the Web site. This is particularly handy when you need an image to finish a project with an impending deadline. Nothing satisfies like instant gratification! The time that you save using the powerful search functions on Corel's Web site to locate images is also a value-added feature. If you budget your project wisely, you can locate, download, and exploit images as needed, and save yourself a lot of time and hassle in the long run. Remember that once you purchase and download the image, you can use it royalty-free for any and all projects you wish, now and down the road.

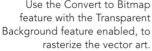
Figure 4.15
Use the Convert to Bitmap feature with the Transparent Background feature enabled, to rasterize the vector art.

the right. The further you drag, the more out of focus the type is (see Figure 4.16). Click on the Preview button so that you can see how your text looks when using different Radius settings. Click on OK when you are happy with the blur effect.

Figure 4.16
Use the Gaussian Blur dialog box to make your type seem fuzzy and out of focus. The more blur, the less in focus it seems.

Figure 4.17
Scatter the words dimensionally by using different levels of the Gaussian Blur function.

6. Repeat this process for each text element (except the 9), varying the degree of fuzziness for each word, to create the illusion of words scattered near and far. Images up close should have more blur than those far away. The concept of near and far is a bit blurry itself, however, because the background that is the farthest will also be the clearest! Experiment with the technique to get words at varied levels of focus (see Figure 4.17).

7. To give the image a darker feel, add a solid-black rectangle over everything and give it a radial fountain fill transparency. Draw the rectangle and then fill it black by clicking on the black onscreen color well. Select the Interactive Transparency tool and drag from the center out toward the edge. Change from Linear Fountain to Radial on the Property Bar and then drag the outside control node to create the mood and shading to your liking (see Figure 4.18).

8. To create the "ghost" effect in the number 9, you use the PowerClip feature. From the Options dialog box (Ctrl+J), click on Edit, disable Auto-center new PowerClip contents, and then click on OK. The default Auto-center setting automatically aligns the contents of a PowerClip to its parent container, which isn't always what you want. With this feature disabled, you can control exactly where the contents of your PowerClip will be, which is a much more powerful option, in my opinion.

9. In Normal view, select your big bitmap background by holding down the Alt key and clicking on the background bitmap. (If you don't hold down the Alt key, you select the black rectangle with the transparency. The Alt key enables you to select the objects below the front object.) Duplicate the bitmap background with the + key on the keyboard.

10. Switch to Wireframe view, choose Effects|PowerClip|Place Inside Container, and then click on the number 9. Because the duplicate bitmap is in the exact same position as the original, when you stuff it into the 9 object, you won't see anything. Use the Shift+PgUp shortcut to bring this PowerClip object to the front (see Figure 4.19).

11. To make the ghosted text stand out a little better, use the Interactive Drop Shadow tool. Drag across and down to reveal a shadow, and then fine-tune it by changing the settings on the Property Bar. I set the Opacity to 90, and the Feathering to 3 (see Figure 4.20).

12. Arrange the text elements in front of or behind the transparent black block to highlight or shade the text. I moved all the text elements in front of the transparency block, to make them pop off the page better.

The final result can be viewed in the color section in the middle of this book or in the blurry.cdr file in the \Chapt04\ subdirectory of the companion CD-ROM. The Interactive Drop Shadow shape and Transparency should still be "live," if you want to select and manipulate the settings, but the text is already converted to bitmaps. You can still select the bitmaps and add more blur, if you wish, or you can start over with your own text.

Subdued And Glowing Type

This style also falls in the category of reverse-design psychology, where text elements are de-emphasized. Instead of making text elements blurry and out of focus, they are made more subtle, using the Interactive Transparency

Figure 4.18
A solid-black rectangle becomes mood lighting when the Interactive Transparency tool transforms it into a radial fountain.

Figure 4.19
A duplicate of the background bitmap, placed into the number 9 with the PowerClip feature, creates a "ghosted" character.

Figure 4.20
The Interactive Drop Shadow creates a feathered outline effect.

Figure 4.21

Use the Interactive Transparency tool to de-emphasize text, making it more subtle. Manipulate the Interactive Drop Shadow tool to create glowing text effects.

Figure 4.22

Arrange your text elements over a background image.

tool. The secondary shapes are again created with the Interactive Contour tool, but you must take additional steps to prepare the pieces, because of their transparent nature. The Interactive Drop Shadow tool can also be used to create glowing text, such as in Figure 4.21. Here is how to make your text transparent or glowing:

1. For this effect, the text elements remain vector objects throughout the project, so you can continue to fine-tune the layout forever. Import (Ctrl+I) a background image and resize it to fit your page. I again used an image from the Corel Masters 1 photo CD. The image was too small, so I drew a black rectangle behind it at my desired page size, to create a black border into which my text could fall off. I filled this border shape with 100K and 35Y from the Uniform Fill dialog (Shift+F11).

   The yellow acts as a "kicker," which helps make large areas of black ink look darker. I chose yellow because the "transparent" text color is 20% yellow, so the areas where text and background overlap will have the same color mix (instead of, say, a cyan kicker, which would make a green tint where my text overlaps the frame).

2. Set the type with the Text tool (I used a font called Serb on the top and Modern on the bottom), fill it with a neutral color (such as pale yellow), and assign it no outline (see Figure 4.22).

3. Drag-select the top text pieces and copy (Ctrl+C) them (you need a copy later on). Select the Interactive Contour tool, and drag on one of the top text elements. Once you have an active Contour group, you can modify the parameters on the Property Bar.

4. Click on Outside, change the Contour Offset to .03 inch, and decrease Contour Steps to 1. Repeat this process with the same settings on the other two text elements (see Figure 4.23).

Figure 4.23

Use the Interactive Contour Tool to generate a set of outline shapes.

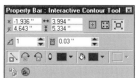

5. Drag-select all of these text elements and choose Arrange|Separate to freeze the live contour groups. Drag-select the two curves that make up each word, and combine them (Ctrl+L). This punches out the inner curve from the outer, resulting in a solid outline shape.

IS IT LIVE?

When you work within CorelDRAW, many effects stay live and recalculate often during the life of your design. Blend groups, for example, redraw themselves if you change the size, location, or any other attribute of one of the parent shapes. The same live characteristics can be observed with extrude groups, lens effects, contour groups, and even polygons, ellipses, and rectangles. If you attempt to node-edit a live rectangle with the Shape tool, you can round only the corners until you convert it to curves (Ctrl+Q). When you resize a live contour group, it recalculates the image by using the original settings, which results in a new image with effects that are out of proportion compared to the parent shapes.

6. Repeat this on the other text objects. Paste (Ctrl+V) the original text objects (still on the system "clipboard" since it was the last thing we "copied") and send them to the back (Shift+PgDn). Now you have two sets of shapes, the inside originals and the outside contour (see Figure 4.24).

Figure 4.24
Combine the contour shape with the original to get an outline object with a hollow center (shown in black). The original objects (in gray) can then shine through.

7. Give all the pieces the same pale-yellow fill (20-percent yellow) and no outline (right-click on the *x* on screen to remove any outline). Select one of the outside contours and, using the Interactive Transparency tool, drag from the top of the shape down. This creates a fade from solid yellow on top to transparent on the bottom. Repeat this process on all three outline pieces (see Figure 4.25).

Figure 4.25
Use the Interactive Transparency tool to fade the fill color in the outside pieces from solid yellow on top to transparent at the bottom.

8. Give the inside shapes the exact opposite fill. Select an inside shape and, using the Interactive Transparency tool, drag from the bottom up. Repeat for the other pieces (see Figure 4.26).

Figure 4.26

To finish the effect, use the Interactive Transparency tool again, but this time reverse the fade-out logic to fade from transparent to solid in the inside pieces.

9. To get the bottom text to glow, you basically repeat the same process that you used to get the ghosted number 9 in the previous tutorial, only with a few twists.

10. Duplicate the background bitmap (+ key) and, again, stuff it into the text by selecting Effects|PowerClip|Place Inside Container.

11. Use the Interactive Drop Shadow tool to create a shadow effect that you can modify to become a glow. Drag your text with the Interactive Drop Shadow tool, just to the edge of your text. Don't worry what kind of shadow you create with this tool, because you are going to change the options on the Property Bar in the next step.

12. Make sure that the shadow position is at X=0.0 and Y=0.0. Change Opacity to 85, and Feathering to 10. From pop-ups on the Property Bar, set the Feathering Direction to Outside, and Feathering Edges to Linear. Most importantly, click on the down arrow next to the current color chip on the Property Bar, and specify the color that you want for your glow. I clicked on the Other button and then specified 20% yellow, to match the other colors in the design (see Figure 4.27). That's it!

Figure 4.27

Modifying the Interactive Drop Shadow tool options on the Property Bar can give you a glow effect.

One Eye

The example in Figure 5.1 features another weird image that I drew, inspired by a freaky vampire tattoo that I had once seen. Using the Corel Trace program (found in the CorelDRAW 9 Graphics Utilities folder), ink artwork such as this can be converted from a bitmap image into flexible, vector-based shapes. Not only does this make colorizing the image easy, but also affords all the benefits of a CorelDRAW file (smaller files size, output flexibility, and so forth). The following steps describe how to take an ink illustration, scan and Corel Trace it, and then transform it into a color image for a tattoo-inspired record label.

Figure 5.1

Images born as tattoos can find new life as commercial artwork, as shown in this CD-ROM package design.

SMOOTH RUNNING

Before you can take advantage of the Acquire Image abilities of Corel programs to import images directly from your digital camera or scanner, you need to install these items on your computer. Scanners and cameras come with their own proprietary system drivers and scanning software, which vary by manufacturer. Generally, to install these items, you simply hook up a few cables, run an installation program supplied with the hardware, and reboot your system.

The point is that you need to perform this installation and make sure that everything is up and running before you try to use the additional hardware with CorelDRAW. If you still have some system conflicts, or the hardware isn't running correctly, then you only compound your problems by trying to work things from within CorelDRAW. For truly seamless installation, install and test your scanner or digital camera *before* you install CorelDRAW. That way, Corel identifies what you already have installed, and everything should work without a hitch.

1. In Corel Trace, scan your illustration by using the File|Acquire option (you first may have to use the Select source option if this is your first scan). The Acquire command initiates your specific hardware's scanning interface, which will vary in appearance based on the hardware's manufacturer. The software that came with my scanner has a nice interface that enables me to see what is on the scanner by clicking on Preview. It also has a dialog box that enables me to control the color depth and resolution. You can use any type of file (color, grayscale, line-art) at any resolution in Trace, but I have found that a high-resolution line-art image works best.

2. Set the options you want, drag your image around in the Preview area, and then click on Scan (see Figure 5.2).

Figure 5.2

You can open an existing bitmap file and convert it to vector artwork in Corel Trace, or you can use the Acquire feature to scan an image directly into the application.

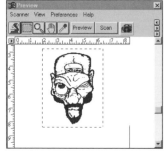

3. After you scan your image into Trace (or use File|Open to load the scan of my illustration, called buddy2.tif, from the \Chapt05\ subdirectory on the companion CD-ROM), you are ready to convert it into shapes that you can manipulate in CorelDRAW. The Trace default is Outline with an Accuracy setting of 50, which generally is fine. Click on Apply to convert your bitmap (see Figure 5.3).

4. Choose File|Save Trace Result and save the vector information as a CMX file, which you can import into CorelDRAW by selecting File|Import.

Figure 5.3

The Outline trace mode creates shapes (shown in Wireframe view on right) that you can manipulate in CorelDRAW.

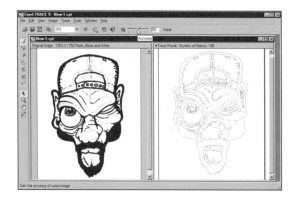

5. Back in CorelDRAW, import (Ctrl+I) the image and ungroup (Ctrl+U) the pieces. Select all the white objects and give them an appropriate color. Use a radial fountain fill from gold to sand for the skin areas to give a slight range of highlights. Remember, you can drag and drop colors right off the on-screen palette, which really speeds up the coloring process, because you don't need to select an object before you color it. Continue until all the white pieces (except the eye and the hat fastener) are colored (see Figure 5.4).

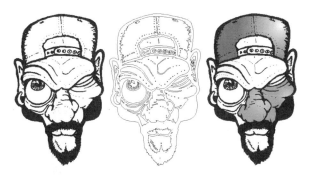

Figure 5.4

The result of converting a bitmap to vector art using Corel Trace: a collection of colored shapes on a big black pad (the wireframe is shown in the center). Select the pieces and color them to bring the image to life.

6. After you finish coloring the trace objects, you can add your own objects. Set text with the Text tool (I used a font called Bang LET on the hat), and tweak it slightly with the Interactive Envelope tool (on the Interactive tool flyout). Select the Interactive Envelope tool, change to the Envelope Single Arc mode on the Property Bar, and then drag the top-center node while holding down the Ctrl key, to create a sweeping arch distortion. Give the text a really thick .111-inch black fill and outline. Duplicate (+ key) the text and give the duplicate a less-thick .05-inch yellow outline and fill.

7. Duplicate the text again, but this time use a thin .021-inch black fill and outline to create the double outline for the text. (You can also use the Contour tool to create multiple outline effects, but the duplication process generally seems to be faster than working with a contour group.)

8. Select the thick black pad (click on the base of the beard), duplicate (+ key), send it back one (Ctrl+PgDn), and give this duplicate a thick .103-inch yellow outline. Duplicate and send it back one, with this final duplicate having a thick .222-inch black outline. Now your text and tattoo image has a freaky, thick, multiple-outline look (see Figure 5.5).

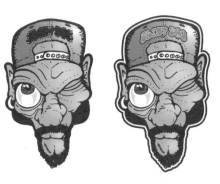

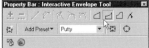

Figure 5.5

Add text and multiple-outline effects to finish off the tattoo part of your image.

9. Once again, text elements will transform the image into a functional commercial art project. Set text for the headline. I used a font called Tag LET (which seems appropriate for the graffiti look, because a "tag" is a personal graffiti icon). Convert the text to curves, so that you can break it apart. The right-hand *s* is a duplicate of the left *s*, flipped horizontally and vertically. Use the techniques outlined in Chapter 4 to get a multiple outline, using the Interactive Contour tool to finish the "grafitti-izing" of the logo.

10. Use the Rectangle tool to draw a square the size of a compact disk jewel case.

    After you draw your square, you are ready to create a brick background. Open the Pattern Fill dialog box, select the Full Color option, and then click on the Preview window to open the tile gallery. Scroll down and click on the brick wall option. Then, click on OK to fill the rectangle with the bricks.

11. Arrange your logo and face character on the CD-ROM case cover. Add any other text elements that you need, choosing fonts that stick to the street beat theme.

12. To get a more moody background than just the bright bricks afford, use a transparency effect to darken things, like you did in the last chapter. Duplicate the bricks shape (+ key) and fill it solid black. Click on the Interactive Transparency tool and change the parameters in the Property Bar, without ever actually clicking on the target object.

13. Change the type to Fountain and then click on the Radial Fountain Transparency button. The default settings should get you just what you want (see Figure 5.6).

Note: *To create objects with real-world dimensions, use the Transformation docker (open from the Arrange menu). Click on the Size button and enter measurements if you want an object at an exact size.*

This image is in the color section in the middle of this book, as well as in the cooltats.cdr file in the \Chapt05\ subdirectory on the companion CD-ROM. Open the file to see the advantages of converting illustrations into

Figure 5.6
A radial fountain transparency darkens the background bitmap pattern and makes the foreground objects stand out better.

CorelDRAW objects by using the Trace utility. Where you begin doesn't really matter; with a little effort and some CorelDRAW magic, you can mold any artwork into your desired image.

Pierce Me

A huge trend at the moment is body piercing. One of my friends has (at last count) 14 piercings. I always ask him how he gets through airports—he just smiles and waggles the bolt in his tongue at me. But I digress. Unlike tattoos or branding, very little need exists to sit down and design a piercing scheme on the computer. That would be a huge waste of time and technology. However, the implements themselves make very interesting secondary design elements (see Figure 5.7). In fact, I used some piercing hardware in the latest update of the Slimy Dog T-shirt logo. On to discuss rendering these surgical steel implements of torture....

Figure 5.7
Although using a computer to design piercing layouts is pointless, the hardware makes for interesting design elements.

Rounded Studs

Many piercing bolts have rounded ends, and after you create one bolt, you can use it in many places. Here is how to create chrome bolts with rounded chrome ends:

1. Draw a rectangle and open the Fountain Fill dialog box (F11).The key to chrome is to suggest a reflected landscape, either in color or as in this example, in shades of gray. In the Fountain Fill dialog box, set the Color Blend option to Custom, starting with white and ending with 50% black.

2. Add a black color point in the dead center (double-click on the preview ribbon to add a point, then click on a color chip to choose the color). Then, right next to this black color point, add a white one. Two color points close together like this create a harsh transition and, in this case, simulate a reflected horizon.

3. To the right of this white color point, add another white one. Change the Angle value to 90 degrees and click on OK (see Figure 5.8). This simple custom color blend is used to color virtually all the chrome elements from this point on.

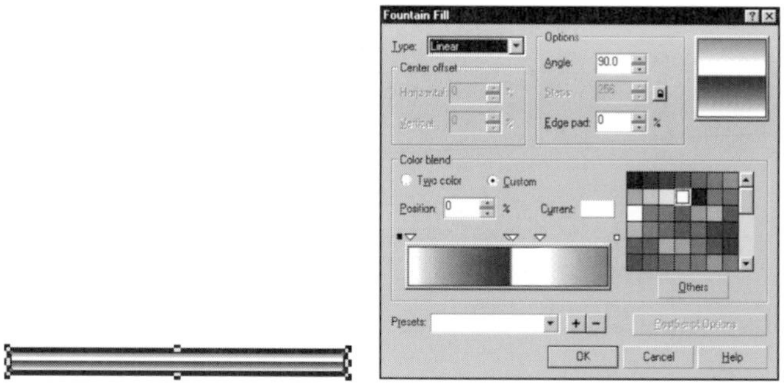

Figure 5.8

Create a metallic look with a custom color blend.

4. Use the Ellipse tool to draw a perfect circle at one end of the chrome bar. (To draw a perfect circle, hold down the Ctrl key while you drag.) Duplicate the circle (+ key) and move the duplicate to the other end. Shift-select both objects and choose Edit|Copy Properties From (Ctrl+Shift+A). Select Fill, click on OK, and then click on the bar shape, to steal the fills for the circles.

5. Open the Fountain Fill dialog box (F11), change the Type value to Radial, and change the Vertical value in the Center Offset section to 41% (or drag the center upward in the Preview window). Click on OK, and the horizon bends, making the circles look round (see Figure 5.9).

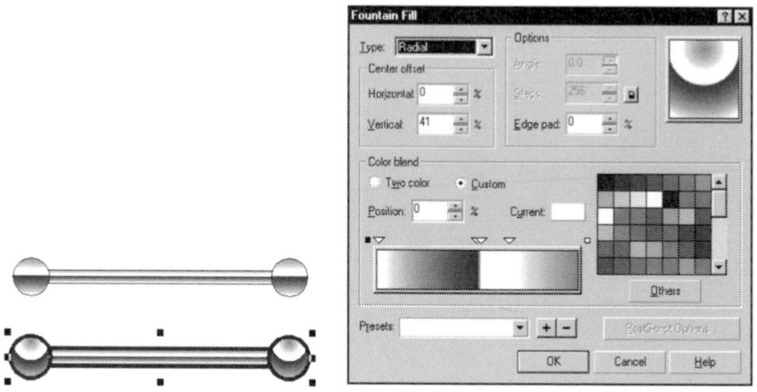

Figure 5.9

By changing the fill borrowed from the bar piece from Linear to Radial, and then offsetting the center, the circles transform into chrome balls.

To turn these round-studded objects into the "mouse dumbbells" that you see poking through the eyebrows of hardcore piercing fans, simply draw rectangles instead of circles at the ends. Use the Shape tool to round the corners of the rectangles, and use the same custom color blend to make them chrome (see Figure 5.10).

The Infamous Ring

If you haven't seen one of these rings in someone's nose or elsewhere, then you either live in a hole or don't frequent coffeehouses much. Here is how to make the curved ring with rounded ends:

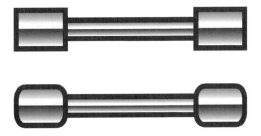

Figure 5.10
Use the Shape tool to modify the corners of a rectangle and create smooth corners.

1. Use the Ellipse tool to draw a perfect circle (remember to hold down the Ctrl key while you drag). Duplicate the circle and then downsize it by dragging a corner sizing handle inward while holding down the Shift key, to pull in all corners simultaneously. Select both circle shapes and combine them (Ctrl+L). Give this shape a radial fountain fill from 30% black to white. Use the Bezier tool to draw a shape to use to open up the end of the ring.

2. Select the new object and choose Trim from the Arrange|Shaping menu.In the Shaping docker, disable both of the Leave Original options, click on Trim, and then click on the ring shape. This cuts away the shape, leaving an open-ended ring (see Figure 5.11).

Figure 5.11
Two circles are combined to create a solid ring shape. A shape drawn with the Bezier tool serves as a cutting template to trim away an area and leave the ring open.

3. Use the Freehand tool to draw shapes to represent the reflected landscape, like you did in the last chapter. A curved metallic object like this reflects things in a very abstract way, so just take a guess at how things might look. Give these objects a radial fountain fill from black to 20% black, for a subtle shading effect. Click on Intersect on the Shaping docker to switch to that page of options.

4. Enable the Leave Original: Target Object(s) option, click on Intersect With, and then click on the ring shape (see Figure 5.12). This creates objects within the ring shape that look like reflections of the surrounding environment.

5. Position on the ring ends two of the rounded balls from the first example. Use additional circle shapes to produce round white highlights. Draw a perfect circle with the Ellipse tool and duplicate it. Offset the duplicate to the right and down, and click on Trim in the Shaping docker to switch to the Trim page.

Note: It is difficult to build custom color blends using the Interactive Fill tool on small objects, unless you zoom in close. Remember that you can also build and control a custom fill using the Fountain Fill dialog box (F11), which doesn't require you to change your current view and zoom in or out. All of the features available in the Fountain Fill dialog can be controlled with the Interactive Fill tool, and vice versa, so use which ever feature is easier for you.

Figure 5.12
Draw reflected landscape objects by hand for odd-shaped chrome pieces, such as the ring. Use the Shaping docker to trim down the shapes to create objects on the inside of the ring.

6. Disable any Leave Original options, click on Trim and then click on the other circle to cut away the areas that overlap (the opposite of Intersection). Place the highlights on the ring to make it look more dazzling.

7. To make the ring look like it's piercing the paper, draw a white rectangle at the top center of the ring, and use the Interactive Envelop tool to curve in the vertical edges. A custom color blend on this shape adds to the illusion (see Figure 5.13).

Figure 5.13
Use circle shapes to generate gleam objects, by trimming one from another. A white rectangle with an envelope makes the paper look pierced.

These pieces of piercing hardware can be worked into your current art projects, especially for those clients wanting a little hard-core edge. The Blend function gives you a great way to scatter duplicates of the objects, to create interesting patterns (see Figure 5.14).

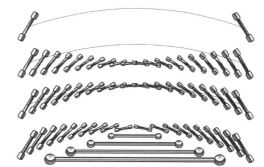

Figure 5.14
Use the Interactive Blend tool to create interesting patterns out of the piercing hardware, for use in your artwork.

The return of PowerLines to CorelDRAW 9 makes the creation of interweaving border vines, such as those I used in my logo (see Figure 5.7), a snap. PowerLines enable you to create a sweeping curve and then add the outline effect as a "live" addition, kind of like a Contour. The key features are that you can add the PowerLines to preexisting lines, and modify the shape of the "control" curve at any time. The following steps describe how to achieve a sweeping curve, and add a PowerLine effect for a tribal-pattern look:

1. Draw a straight line with the Bezier tool with two quick clicks. With the Shape tool, select both nodes, and click on the + key (or click on + on the Property Bar) to add a node, which will be perfectly centered between the selected nodes. Click on + again, and now you have five evenly spaced nodes.

2. Shift-select every other node and drag down, creating an evenly spaced zig-zag. Drag-select all the nodes and then click on Convert Line to Curve on the Property Bar. Click on Make Node Symmetrical, giving you a nice, evenly spaced curve (see Figure 5.15).

Figure 5.15
Use the Shape tool to add nodes, and then modify them from lines to symmetrical points, to create a sweeping curve.

3. On the Freehand tool flyout, click on the third-from-left option, to access the Natural Media/PowerLines tool. From the Preset gallery, choose the option that you like (in this case, the "pointy on both ends" preset). Modify the Width and Smoothing options on the Property Bar until you like what you see.

4. Since a PowerLine is "live," you can select the Shape tool and modify the original control points in the curve, to customize your "tribal" shapes into exotic designs (see Figure 5.16). I created a pattern on one side of my card, and then duplicated and flipped it for the other side.

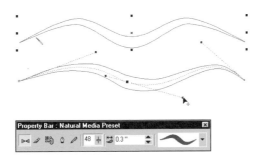

Figure 5.16
The Natural Media/PowerLines feature converts a line into a dynamic design, using a preset from the gallery. You can node-edit this line with the Shape tool.

Another idea is to stretch the hardware to pierce through artwork, either as interesting design elements or as vehicles to divert and direct attention in a design. In the color section in the middle of this book, and in the pierceme.cdr file in the \Chapt05\ subdirectory on the companion CD-ROM, you can see how I used these piercing bits to create interesting patterns, and how I worked them into a corporate logo. The pattern looks very much like the display case at a piercing parlor that I was in, with a lovely purple-haired girl trying to convince me to purchase some of the hardware. Hmm. Sorry, I'll stick to virtual augmentation for now, which leads us into the next section.

Skin Art

Yes, my job is to stick virtual tattoos on various and sundry body parts of hapless digital people. Man, my life is weird sometimes. The technique in this section has some interesting potential. You could, for example, create a "try-before-you-buy" image to see how a tattoo looks on you or a friend before you have it done (or use the art to try to talk someone out of it). Other uses are in advertising, where it seems all the rage to stick corporate logos on models and call it an ad. Save some poor model the grief and create the artwork digitally (as I did in Figure 5.17). Here is how to apply a digital tattoo:

Figure 5.17
Using transparency tricks, you can stick a tattoo on anything and anyone.

1. Find some appropriate artwork for the tattoo (a ton of great images are available in the CorelDRAW clip-art library; see the sidebar "Clip-Art Chaos"). I used a Slimy Dog logo that I had handy, and stole the wings logo from Chapter 18 (neat trick, huh, stealing from the future?).

   These two images are "spoofs" of tattoos I have seen. (The Slimy Dog head is a parody of a very popular old hot-rod-racing tattoo. Perhaps you recognize it?) Import the images into CorelDRAW along with an image of the lucky recipient. Photo-CD images are much easier to work with than real people, particularly when you're trying to tattoo them.

2. Group your images and place them where you want them. The dog head is a colorized bitmap, so find a spot that is pretty flat, because you can't distort a bitmap with an envelope. Draw a rectangle around the tattoo, with no outline or fill. Drag-select all the pieces, including the boundary rectangle, and use the Convert to Bitmap dialog box to transform the group of objects into a single, pixel-based entity.

3. Set your desired color and dithering. The critical feature is the Transparent Background option, which should be enabled, to keep the tattoo free-floating. (The bitmaps on the Corel clip-art CD, in the \objects\ folder, are already "free-floating" bitmaps.)

CLIP-ART CHAOS

My buddy showed up one day with a spanking-new wolf tattoo on his arm. It caught my eye because it was a piece of CorelDRAW clip art (see Figure 5.18). Clip art is a very handy resource, with tons of images just begging to be a part of your tattoo project. However, using this resource has a few hidden pitfalls. Clip art often won't resize correctly, especially if any heavy line weights are used, because unless the original artist chose the Scale With Image option from the Outline Pen dialog box (F12), the lines won't enlarge or reduce proportionally when you change the size of the image. This is beyond annoying, but don't despair, because your crazy Uncle Shane has yet another way to fix the artwork.

Select the offending clip art at its original size and open the Export dialog box (Ctrl+H). Change the Save As Type setting to Encapsulated PostScript (EPS), which is a vector format, similar to the native CorelDRAW format. Click on the Export button and make sure that the Include Header option is *disabled* on the EPS Export options page. Click on OK to export the image. When finished, open the Import dialog box (Ctrl+E) and change the Files of Type setting to PostScript Interpreted. Choose the Import Text as Curves option and then sit tight while CorelDRAW imports and fixes your artwork.

The lines now are set to Scale With Image, so you can enlarge and reduce to your heart's content. The downside to this technique is that if the clip art has features that translate poorly, such as fountain fills, the "fixed" file can be very complex. You need to decide whether it is worth fixing manually or just giving up and using something else.

Figure 5.18
The CorelDRAW clip-art library is filled with images and icons perfect for that tattoo look. However, resizing clip art can cause problems if line weights are not set to Scale With Image.

4. With the objects transformed into a single bitmap, creating the look of a tattoo is easy, using a transparency effect. Select the bitmap and click on the Interactive Transparency tool.

5. Change the transparency type on the Property Bar to Uniform, and drag the slider until the starting transparency is at 40%. This setting lets enough of the background color and detail show through to mute the bitmap and look darn close to a real tattoo (see Figure 5.19).

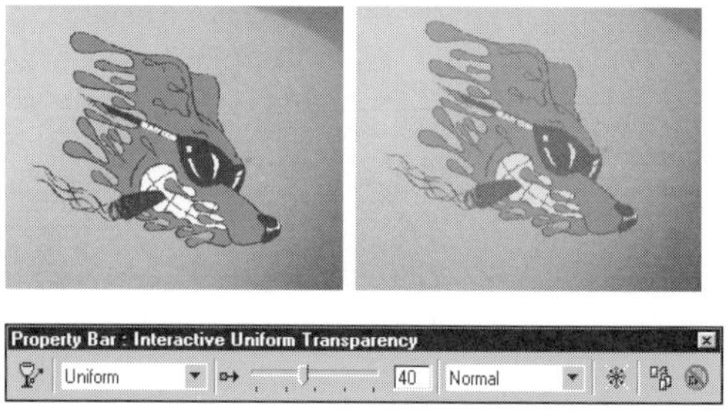

Figure 5.19
Changing the bitmap from a solid object (left) to one with a 40% Uniform transparency creates convincing skin art.

6. You can twist and distort vector-based images, such as the wings logo, to fit on top of any strange body contour. To get the logo to fit on the model's shoulder, distort the image with the Interactive Envelope tool. Remember, you can click on the Add New Envelope button on the Property Bar to "freeze" the distortion in its current state, and add a new envelope to continue to manipulate an object in multiple stages. That way, you can start with a single-arc envelope and move on to more-controlled tweaking with an unconstrained envelope (see Figure 5.20).

Figure 5.20
Use the Envelope tool to distort vector artwork so that it fits correctly on the target body part.

7. Draw a no-fill, no-outline rectangle around the wings artwork and convert it to a bitmap with the transparent background, like in step 2. While you can use the the Interactive transparency tool on a group of objects, the results won't look right with this example (you'll see through each of the objects in the group, which reveals once hidden pieces in the group, changing the look of the artwork).

8. Use the Interactive Transparency tool as before, but this time use the Linear Fountain Fill option. Drag the tool from left to right across the length of the bitmap to assign the direction of the fountain fill. This assigns the standard 100% solid to 100% transparent fill setting.

   You can control the opacity of the transparency fill with color points. White is 100% solid, and black is 100% clear, so you can drag and drop different shades of gray from the on-screen color wells onto the fill to change how the image looks. For example, drag and drop 50% black to each end point for a uniform 50% transparency.

9. Now, drag and drop 20% gray to the center, which makes the bitmap more opaque in the center (80% opaque, 20% transparent) and fade to more transparent at each edge. This makes the tattoo image seem darker as it reacts to the darker skin tone on the arm, and is more convincing than a uniform transparency (see Figure 5.21).

> **BITMAP DISTORTION**
>
> Although you can't tweak a bitmap with an envelope, some distortion options are available on the Bitmap menu. In the 3D Effects fly-out, you can try the Sphere effect to give your bitmap a touch of roundness, like a tattoo might have on a rounded body part. (See Chapter 7 for more.)

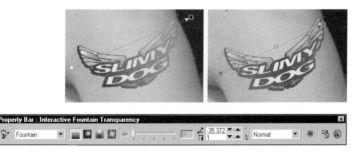

Figure 5.21
Changing and adding the opacity settings on an Interactive Fountain Transparency allows the bitmap to blend naturally with the skin tones below.

It's really a simple technique, and the results are quite convincing. See for yourself in this book's color section, or load the tatgirl.cdr file from the \Chapt05\ subdirectory on the companion CD-ROM to see firsthand what's going on.

In the file, you can see another Slimy Dog logo (like Jimmy Durante says, "I got a million of 'em!") that has been distorted with the Envelope tool to look like it's part of the hat. Modifying artwork to get it to merge into a real image is pretty easy, as you'll see in the next tutorial. The beauty of this procedure is that, unlike tattoos, it isn't permanent and is pretty painless.

Metal Makeover

Sometimes, you just have to use your powers for evil, as Figure 5.22 shows. The poor woman in this figure, an image from the Corel photo collection, will be so less-than thrilled when she sees what I have done to her beautiful portrait. This kind of image manipulation, surprisingly easy, makes you really wonder about those supermarket tabloid covers. If you see the President with green hair and piercings, you probably shouldn't panic; just chalk it up to digital manipulation. Here is how to pierce and recolor a photograph:

1. Start with a scan of the intended victim and the pieces of piercing hardware from the last section (steal them out of the pierceme.cdr file, in the \Chapt05\ subdirectory on the companion CD-ROM, to save time). Just like with Corel Trace, you can scan a photo directly into CorelDRAW by selecting File|Acquire. , making it easy to vandalize family portraits! Copy each piece of hardware into the new file and move the piercing bits in to position over the area that you want to pierce.

2. First, to add a bit more realism, duplicate the piercing piece group and use the Weld function from the Shaping docker to create a solid curve, to use as a drop shadow element. The Interactive Drop Shadow tool won't work for this, because it will just make a flat shadow that won't follow the contours of the face. Create your own curve for a shadow shape and twist and distort it into shape so that it looks correct—in this case, drooping down the bridge of the nose.

Figure 5.22

Using the PowerClip function, you can pierce your favorite model; then, using options in PhotoPaint, you can even change the color of her hair and lipstick for a total virtual makeover.

Stewart look dangerous, wild, and likely to blow smoke in your face. Tattoo art works well in logos for fringe corporations, such as those involved in alternative clothing, music, or even Web development. Speaking of the Web, imagine how freaky you could make a Web site look by using as navigation buttons metallic rings "piercing" the page? Branding also lends itself to many applications, such as taking a company logo and "branding" people, cars, or even the traditional branding victim—livestock—with the image. Like my advertisement example, branding has interesting meanings that can be worked into an advertising campaign (as does piercing, with contemporary valentines just begging for a play on the "you pierce my heart" theme).

Using a seedy nightlife theme to create a campy brochure or ad for a rather unexciting product is great fun. Just like on *Sesame Street*, "one of these things is not like the other" is an awesome concept to draw attention to a product; an element is so out of place that you can't help but react (a baby playing pool in a seedy bar, grandma and friends smoking cigars and playing poker, Hell's Angels having a tea party, and so on). The art is fun, the images are bold, and an ample supply is at hand for you to use—but don't hold me responsible if you misjudge your client and sales plummet after you put skulls and cross bones on "Grandma's Cookies"!

Moving On

In this chapter, we looked at many ways to work popular piercing/branding/tattoo artwork into your designs. We also saw how to take these elements and create "virtual makeovers," adding skin-art or metallic pieces to scanned photographs.

The next chapter moves away from this world of personal augmentation and broadens the scope to include manipulating time and space itself. Am I suffering from a "god complex"? Maybe, but I speak of using CorelDRAW tools to create the illusions of depth and perspective. Let me demonstrate....

ADDING DEPTH AND DIMENSION 6

This chapter looks at using blur and transparency effects to manipulate the field of depth; simulating dimension by skewing your artwork; and using the Blend feature to build realistically shaded objects.

Every task, whether building a house or creating a computer illustration, has a "tool of choice" for accomplishing the job. Because CorelDRAW is an object-oriented illustration package, it has a lot of built-in flexibility. This enables you to change the look of your objects almost indefinitely until you get a look that you like, making CorelDRAW the tool of choice for computer illustration.

Within CorelDRAW, you can manipulate artwork to make it appear closer to or further away from you. You can take flat-looking art and create the illusion of depth by skewing it into a perspective orientation. Or, you can use the tools to create 3D-looking artwork, either by using the Blend feature or (as you have already seen) by manipulating the Extrude tool. In any case, simulating some sort of depth and dimension is always a challenge, given the flat nature of the computer screen and the printed page. However, for all of its sophistication, fooling the ol' human eye sure doesn't take much. Let us wield the smoke and mirrors....

Distant Horizons

Although the Interactive Transparency tool continues to rank as one of my favorite CorelDRAW features, I get a bigger charge out of creating optical illusions, such as the one shown in Figure 6.1. This technique pairs the Gaussian Blur bitmap effect with the Interactive Transparency tool, to create landscapes in which you can wield god-like power over space and time. Well, not really, but you can change the field of focus, making objects appear to be either close up or far away, at your beck and call. To do so, follow these steps:

Figure 6.1

By blurring a bitmap, you take it out of focus. Stacking a blurred image on a clear original and then using the Transparency tool enables you to control what part of the image is in focus.

1. Start with a landscape photo that has some "depth" potential. The image in Figure 6.1 is from the third CorelDRAW clip-art CD-ROM, in the \photos\thebeach folder. It has a nice set of pillars that go off

This is what I call a "quick-and-dirty solution." It looks good and is convincing enough for most applications. If you want to be really technically correct, you can use the Perspective function to place the sides in a perfect 3D orientation. I'm just a big fan of idealized reality and instant gratification, as you know.

Gorilla

Although the image of an enraged primate in Figure 6.9 is one of the first things I ever drew in CorelDRAW, I still like it. New features in CorelDRAW 9 can add even more impact, to give this old beast some new life. To emphasize the wet and shiny surfaces of the eyes and mouth, I purposely made the rest of the face kind of flat and dull, compared to the original file. With the Convert to Bitmap feature available in CorelDRAW 9, we can even blur the background, making the eyes and teeth pop out even more.

This image started as a quick ink illustration of just the main features of a gorilla's face, which I scanned and traced by using the Centerline function. The hair and black outlines in the face are the results of that Centerline trace, whereas the remaining objects were created in CorelDRAW.

The use of multistage blends (as in the fangs) produces a round, realistically shaded object. Instead of blending just two objects, I blended three, to broaden the color range of the blend and add more control. The really wet look is also a basic technique of drawing tiny, solid-white circles and strategically placing them to suggest reflection and texture. I won't walk you through this whole design, because that would take too long. However, I will show you some neat tricks for the eyes and teeth, which you can work into your own monstrosities. Here is how to draw shiny eyes and fangs:

1. Use the Freehand or Bezier tool (your preference) to draw the main eye outline. The Bezier tool is great for this type of drawing, except that drawing hard edges (as in the eye corners) is difficult. If you create a curve by dragging, the node that you create is smooth.

   To create a cusped node, click—without dragging—to get a straight line. Drawing curved shapes with the Bezier tool takes some practice, and I still prefer to draw simple straight lines and then modify the curves by using the Shape tool and node-editing. This also makes for very simple, low-node-count shapes (see Figure 6.10).

Figure 6.9

Multistage blends can create the illusion of rounded objects, such as the teeth and eyes in this gorilla graphic. Converting some of the image to a bitmap and then blurring it makes the hard-edged elements pop out even more.

Figure 6.10

Often, the easiest way to create a curved shape, especially one with cusped nodes, is to draw straight lines and then use the Shape tool to edit the nodes with the Property Bar.

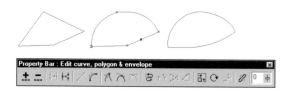

2. Draw the largest of the eye detail circles first by using the Ellipse tool and holding down the Ctrl key (to draw a perfect circle). If you habitually draw the largest objects first and the smaller ones later, you save time restacking the objects. Objects stack themselves in the order of creation, so if you draw a small circle and then a large one, the larger one will be on top of the smaller one. The same is true for duplicates.

3. Select the circle, duplicate it (+ key), and reduce it by dragging a corner sizing handle inward. This duplicate is now on top of the original. Duplicate and downsize once more for the pupil shape.

4. From the Arrange menu, choose the Shaping|Intersect option. In the docker, disable the Leave Original: Target Object(s) option. One by one, select the eye pieces (largest to smallest again, to maintain the correct order), click on Intersect With, and then click on the main eye shape. This places your iris and pupil shapes perfectly within the eye.

5. Shade the eye with a black-to-white linear fountain fill from the Fountain Fill dialog box (F11), give the two outside pieces a black fill, and give the middle piece a dark-brown fill (see Figure 6.11).

Figure 6.11

Use the Shaping docker to trim shapes to fit within a boundary object, and then color the pieces for a realistic eye.

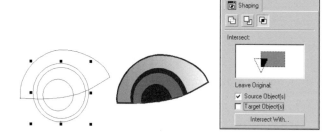

6. Select the largest black circle and Shift-select the brown one on top of it. Use the Interactive Blend tool to drag between the two shapes to create a blend. On the Property Bar, change the Number Of Steps setting to 5 (or use the default 20, for a smoother blend). Select only the top brown control curve then use the Interactive Blend tool to drag to the small black circle on top of it. The result is a compound element of three control curves and two blend groups (five total elements).

7. If you change any of the control curves, all the elements in the compound element group are affected. With this compound element selected, choose Arrange|Separate and then choose Arrange|Ungroup All. To make the retina more crisp, delete some of the resulting objects in the second blend.

8. Use the Freehand tool to draw some vein lines, following a suggested curve of the eye, and give them a red outline. Use the Freehand tool to draw objects suggesting reflected light on a wet eyeball. These shapes can be very abstract; again, just follow a suggested curve of the eye to make things look more round. Color them solid white for a stark reflection (see Figure 6.12).

Figure 6.12
Three objects blended together form a compound element. The Freehand tool draws the jagged lines of the veins, as well as the abstract reflection pieces.

9. I used this same double-blend technique on some of the teeth, to get a rounded look with a wider color range than a single blend can achieve. On some teeth, I just used a traditional blend on top of another object to accent the tooth. The trick to smooth blends is to have the same number of nodes in each control curve. To guarantee that both objects have the same number of nodes, generate the second control shape by duplicating (+) the first.

10. Use the Pick tool and sizing handles to drag, skew, and resize the duplicate. Manually sculpt the duplicate shape into its final form, using the Shape tool, rather than risk changing the node count (by using the Intersect feature, for example).

11. To shade the big fang, draw a smaller object inside the main tooth shape and give it a darker-orange fill. Duplicate this smaller object, and then shade the duplicate gray and form it with the Shape tool (to maintain a like node count). When you blend these two objects (Ctrl+B), the transition is smooth because of the like node orientation and number. Use the Freehand tool to draw shiny spots, which accent the illusion of wetness and roundness (see Figure 6.13).

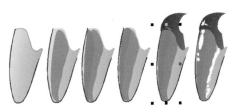

Figure 6.13
For smooth blends, both control curves need to have the same number of nodes. To ensure this, create one control node by duplicating the other. Downsize or modify the duplicate, but don't change the node count.

12. Blending original objects to smaller duplicates always produces a nice, smooth blend. Accent the round look of these blends with solid-white gleam shapes, drawn with the Freehand tool. Achieving a convincing look isn't difficult, but drawing in all the fine details takes a little time (see Figure 6.14).

Figure 6.14

Blending a large object to a smaller duplicate produces a smooth, round look. Accent with solid-white shapes to suggest wet sparkles and highlights. The Wireframe view on the left shows where the blends are located.

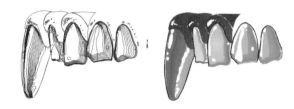

13. To take the image a step further, I needed to isolate the artwork that I wanted to keep as native CorelDRAW objects from the parts that I wanted to convert to a bitmap. The easiest way to keep track of artwork, especially a project like this in which pieces are stacked on top of others, is to build and manage different layers. CorelDRAW has the ability, like PhotoShop or other design applications, to create multiple layers for your artwork. You can move art from layer to layer, make a layer invisible, or lock a layer to prevent any changes. It's a nice feature. For this project, I created a second layer and moved the eyes and teeth objects there.

14. From the Window menu, choose Dockers|Object Manager to open the Object Manager docker, which is where you manage layers. Click the docker's small, top-right arrow to create a new layer, which creates Layer 2 on top of your existing Layer 1.

15. To move objects to a new layer, either click and drag them to the layer name in the Object Manager docker or use the Move To Layer command from the fly-out. After objects are on their own layer, you

MAKE THE NODE "COUNT"

For smooth, predictable blends, both objects need to have the same number of nodes. The status bar displays the number of nodes in the selected object; you can use the Shape tool to add or delete nodes until the numbers are the same. Then, use the Map Nodes feature (found under Miscellaneous Blend options on the Property Bar) to tell CorelDRAW from which point to start the blend on each target object.

With an active Blend group selected, click on the Map Nodes button, the arrow on the first object's starting node, and the arrow on the end object's corresponding node. This helps you to control blends that otherwise seem to give oddball results. The easiest way to get predictable results with blends is to use the same shape for all control curves. Duplicate the parent object, which ensures the same node count and orientation, and then manipulate it for the blend. You can warp, twist, downsize, and recolor the duplicate—whatever you wish—and, as long as you don't alter the node count, the blend should be smooth and predictable.

can toggle the visibility of that layer by clicking on the eye icon. I moved the eyes and teeth to their own layer and then clicked on the eye on Layer 1 to make it invisible (see Figure 6.15).

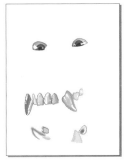

Figure 6.15

The Object Manager docker enables you to create and manage multiple layers, stack and further control the objects in your image, or make objects invisible by turning off the Display attribute for their layer.

16. With my eyes and teeth isolated on a single layer, I can lock and turn off that layer's visibility and concentrate on objects making up the rest of the face, still on Layer 1. Click the eye and pencil icon next to Layer 2 (the eye/teeth layer) to disable visibility and editing on that layer. Click Layer 1 in the Object Manager docker (to make sure that you are back on that layer) and then Select All (Ctrl+A). From the Bitmaps menu, select Convert to Bitmap. Change to CMYK, set Resolution to 300 dpi, enable Anti-aliasing, and then click OK.

    Converting such a large area into a bitmap takes a few compute cycles and produces a big file. This is unavoidable if the file is destined for print, as this one is. If you are doing on-screen artwork, such as for a Web site or presentation, you can use the RGB, 72 dpi settings, which results in a much smaller file and takes much less time to calculate (see Figure 6.16).

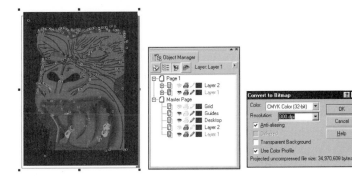

Figure 6.16

With the background objects isolated to their own layer, you can select them and use the Convert to Bitmap feature to rasterize the information.

17. After everything but the eyes and teeth are converted to a bitmap, you can use the Gaussian Blur effect, as in your first tutorial. With all but the eyes and teeth elements given the fuzz treatment, the eyes and teeth seem to jump out at you even more. To take advantage of

UNDO BLUES

Remember to save your CorelDRAW file to disk before you begin converting pieces to bitmaps. Although you can immediately Undo the command with Ctrl+Z, you can't manipulate the objects again later if you decide that you need to. So, a backup copy saved to disk with a unique file name is just cheap insurance, in case you want to go back and work with the CorelDRAW objects.

the many effects available to pixel-based art, sometimes you have no choice but to convert objects into bitmaps, an option that isn't available to vector-based objects. Because we can do both in CorelDRAW, we can have it all!

In this example, both the original and converted versions of the artwork are available in the \Chapt06\ folder. The original file, gorilla.cdr, has just the vector objects, whereas gorilla3d.cdr has all but the eye and teeth elements converted to a bitmap and given the fuzz treatment. You can also examine the blends in the teeth, for example, to see how the multi-stage, compound blend elements work to get the 3D look.

Beyond f/x

Although you may not find yourself rendering many saliva-covered teeth in your average work day, you never know what project will walk through your door. I had to create a smiling, sunglasses-and-sombrero-wearing iguana one day, and found myself drawing scales on the beast. So, even wet-fang rendering knowledge may be useful one day. The multistage blending used to create the realistic, round-looking teeth is a great way to render other tubular objects, such as coffee mugs or telephone poles.

Making flat artwork look dimensional is very common in the advertising industry, to stick corporate logos onto billboards or trucks in photos, as image comps to brain-storm promotional ideas. This chapter's field-of-focus modification techniques are very powerful ways to manipulate and direct your reader's attention subtly to different areas of your artwork, without them really realizing that you are doing so. Exaggerating depth with blur is a neat design vehicle to isolate other design elements, or to de-emphasize other aspects of your design. Sometimes, for example, you are stuck with a bad photo, such as a product shot with a busy background. By using the blur tricks, you can fuzz out the bad stuff and direct the focus towards the good areas of the photo. Remember that the Interactive Transparency tool has both Radial and Linear options, so you can create a round illusion, in which objects get sharper towards the center. Trust me, you'll find a great use for this effect some day (see Chapters 13 and 18 for more information).

Moving On

In this chapter, we tweaked the laws of nature, manipulating depth and distance with optical illusions. We twisted and slanted flat artwork into 3D-looking elements, and created rounded objects with blending techniques. Using CorelDRAW objects, or converting elements into bitmaps, you can always find a way to realize even your wildest visions. Essentially, if you can imagine it, you can create it in CorelDRAW!

In the next chapter, we examine some very interesting ways to explode your artwork into small pieces, to create a puzzle-like effect. We also examine how to manipulate the CorelDRAW tools to add the Extrude and Bevel functions to photos that we have carved and cut into any shape that we wish. It's a very "puzzling" chapter, but one that blows the lid off some unique techniques that are available only to CorelDRAW users.

PUZZLING 7 PIECES

This chapter reveals tricks that enable you to create puzzle pieces using the PowerClip feature and the Bitmap Pattern fill, and reflection illusions using the Import/ Export features.

Breaking things isn't good, unless they deserve to be broken. My cell phone, for example, has a high probability of being smashed into tiny little pieces the next time that it cuts out midconversation. In design, breaking up your image into smaller, more easily digestible chunks is also a good idea. Or, as we explore in this chapter, you may want to break apart and then piece together images, as in a puzzle or optical illusion.

In this chapter, we look at several interesting techniques, unique to CorelDRAW, that enable you to break apart and piece together images. The first example uses a PowerClip technique that automatically breaks apart a single image into many pieces. The second tutorial also takes advantage of the PowerClip, and then uses the power and ease of Photo-Paint to help create a convincing puzzle effect. The final illusion is a very strange technique, whereby multiple snapshots of the artwork-in-progress are pieced together to create the illusion of reflected surfaces. If you don't have it already, this chapter should give you that warm fuzzy happy-to-be-a-CorelDRAW-user feeling.

Picture Pieces

The PowerClip feature is a really powerful tool in CorelDRAW. It can stuff any image into any shape. You can even use the PowerClip feature on a curve that consists of multiple, unattached parts (such as a text headline). You can also put the tool to work to create puzzle pieces, such as in Figure 7.1.

Figure 7.1

If you create a complex shape by combining small paths into a single shape, you can then PowerClip an image inside of it. Then, when you break apart the PowerClip image, each little piece will have the corresponding image inside of it.

This is one of those tricks that I love, because you get a big payoff with relatively little effort. The one drawback to this technique is that the files can become big and unmanageable, because, as you'll see, when you perform the Break Apart command on a PowerClip curve with subpaths, CorelDRAW copies *all* of the image data to every resulting puzzle piece. Consequently, if you create a 10-piece puzzle from a 10MB image, when you break apart all the pieces, technically, you create a 100MB monster! Thus, to start your project, use an image that is as small as possible (fortunately, this technique is great for on-screen, low-res applications that use small bitmaps anyway). Be brave and give it a shot! With memory prices as low as they are, quit your snivelin', slap in another 32MB, and get serious! Here is how to make the puzzle pieces:

1. Import (Ctrl+I) a bitmap or any other design into a blank page (the PowerClip function works on vector and bitmap images, so you can use a CorelDRAW file instead of a photo, if you wish). Use a bitmap

that is as small as possible, and at actual size (use Bitmaps|Resample to reduce the size of the bitmap; 225 dpi is about as low as you can go for print publishing, and RGB uses less memory than CMYK).

2. Right-click on your bitmap and select Lock Object from the pop-up menu to prevent accidentally moving it during the drawing steps. Switch to Wireframe view to make seeing what you're doing easier.

3. With the Freehand and Bezier tools, map out areas of the image that would make good puzzle pieces (see Figure 7.2). Don't worry about perfection at this point; just make sure that each object is solid (click on Auto-Close Curve on the Property Bar to close any open curves automatically). After you finish drawing your puzzle pieces, draw a rectangle around the image to serve as a bounding box.

Figure 7.2

Draw shapes on top of a bitmap to create puzzle pieces. Use the image as a guide while drawing the shapes with the Bezier or Freehand tools.

4. Select one of the puzzle pieces and switch to the Shape tool (see Figure 7.3). Drag-select all the nodes and click on Make Node Smooth on the Property Bar. This removes any harsh angles.

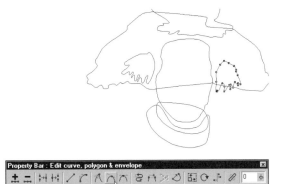

Figure 7.3

Use the Shape tool to edit the nodes and smooth out the puzzle shapes.

5. For this process, you need to create nonoverlapping pieces. This isn't too hard, but it takes a little thought and creative use of the Shaping

docker. Select the top piece, for example, and choose Arrange|
Shaping|Trim. Enable the Source Object check box, click on Trim,
and click on the piece right below your selected top piece. Predicting
the results of the Trim function takes a little practice (I still mess
things up!), as does getting the order of selection right. Keep selecting
and trimming until none of your objects overlap (see Figure 7.4).

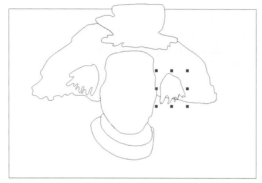

Figure 7.4
Use the Trim function to create
nonoverlapping objects.

6. After you trim away all the smaller pieces so that the objects don't
   overlap, you need to work out the problems of the bounding box,
   which also must not overlap. Drag-select all the pieces inside of the
   bounding box, click on Trim in the Shaping docker, and then click
   on the bounding box. This should punch a hole in the bounding box
   anywhere that a puzzle piece is lying on top, which is just what we
   need. I gave these pieces a fountain fill so that you could see each
   piece better (see Figure 7.5).

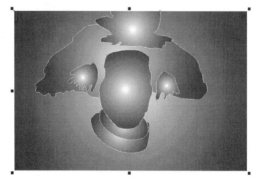

Figure 7.5
The Shaping docker's Intersect
and Trim functions help to create
each individual puzzle piece.

7. Select all the pieces, including the bounding box, and combine them
   (Ctrl+L). Select the bitmap, right-click, and select Unlock Object from
   the pop-up menu. With the bitmap selected, choose Effects|
   PowerClip|Place Inside Container and then click on the puzzle curve.
   Zing! Almost there! Figure 7.6 shows our progress thus far.

Figure 7.6
Use the PowerClip command to place the bitmap within the puzzle shapes.

8. To get puzzle pieces that you can move and rotate individually, simply select the PowerClip object and break it apart (Ctrl+K). That's it! You now have a great cyberpuzzle with which you can do whatever you want (see Figure 7.7).

Figure 7.7
When you break apart the multipart PowerClip object, each piece can be moved or rotated like a piece of a puzzle.

After your puzzle is in pieces, you can do a lot of things with it, such as animate the pieces exploding and reassembling themselves, create a cybergame, or even make an actual puzzle to cut out and assemble. You can see this file, in the exploded version, in this book's color section and in the indipuzl.cdr file in the \Chapt07\ directory on the companion CD-ROM. To see why these files are so big, load the file, select one of the small pieces, and choose Effects|PowerClip|Extract Contents. Notice how the entire original bitmap pops out of even the tiniest piece. Breaking apart a PowerClip is a great trick, but it does eat up memory.

Puzzle Parts

Puzzle analogies abound in the advertising world. I can't tell you how many times I've been asked to create images for "Bringing It All Together," or some other slogan that begs for a puzzle-like graphic. The image in Figure 7.8 was a design concept for a client that wanted to use puzzle pieces as navigation buttons in a Web site. As you move the mouse over a puzzle piece on the Web site, the piece changes from black

Figure 7.8
The PowerClip feature places images inside curved puzzle shapes. Using plug-in filters in Photo-Paint, the puzzle pieces come to life with beveling and shadow effects.

and white to color, and an identifier flashes to describe the part of the Web site to which you jump if you click on the piece.

The complexity of this image belies the simplicity with which it was created. Using CorelDRAW's PowerClip feature to stuff image shapes inside the curved puzzle pieces is a no-brainer, and getting the 3D effect is a snap using a bitmap plug-in in Photo-Paint.

Here is how to harness the power of CorelDRAW and Photo-Paint to create a complex-looking puzzle graphic quickly:

1. First, you need some puzzle pieces. Creating interlocking objects in CorelDRAW is really easy. Use the Bezier tool to create a puzzle piece. You need to draw only this single piece, so don't fret. Draw a rectangle that overlaps the puzzle piece.

2. Choose Arrange|Shaping|Trim, and enable only the Leave Original: Source Object(s) checkbox. With your drawn puzzle piece selected, click on Trim, and then on the rectangle. You now have two perfectly interlocking pieces (see Figure 7.9).

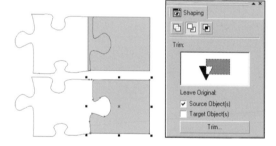

Figure 7.9
Use the Trim option in the Shaping docker to make puzzle pieces interlock.

IMPORTING MULTIPLE FILES

CorelDRAW 9 enables you to import multiple files simultaneously. Hold down the Ctrl key to select multiple files in the Import dialog box. Click on Import, and you can then size and position each individual file. This speeds up the process of populating your puzzle pieces because you can import, size, and position each bitmap in a single Import session.

3. Repeat the process until you have a collection of puzzle pieces, in whatever shapes you wish. My example has the same proportions as the computer screen (wider than tall), because it was designed for a Web page, but your puzzle can be any shape or size.

4. After your puzzle pieces are in place, give each piece a unique color, so that they stand out boldly from one another. This step just makes selecting the pieces much easier in Photo-Paint later. Select all of your pieces in their final position, and duplicate them (+ key). Position the duplicate set directly below the original set. Leave the top set of your puzzle pieces as solid-colored objects. Use the bottom set to contain your images.

5. Import a bitmap (Ctrl+I), or choose Acquire Image|Acquire to use an image from your scanner or digital camera. I used images off Corel's *Business* Photo-CD, which I purchased as part of Corel's economical

"Super Ten" *Business and Industry* Photo Packs, off its Web site (http://
www.corel.com/products/clipartandphotos/photos/superten.htm). I
don't hesitate for a moment to purchase clip-art images, because
they always come in handy, and when packaged in the "Ten Packs,"
they're obscenely cheap! I love e-business....

6. Working in Wireframe view, size and position your bitmap over your
   puzzle piece. Then, choose Effects|PowerClip|Place Inside Container
   and click on the puzzle piece. This stuffs your image inside the curve
   (see Figure 7.10). If you don't like the image's position inside the
   curve, use the Effects|PowerClip|Edit Contents command to move the
   image around inside the curve. When finished, choose Effects|
   PowerClip|Finish Editing This Level.

Figure 7.10
Use the PowerClip feature to
constrain images within a
puzzle-piece curve.

7. Repeat the process for each puzzle piece, until you have a puzzle
   filled with the images that you want. You could stop here, but I like
   to add a few steps to increase the realism. You should have two copies of your puzzle: one with colored pieces only, and one with
   image-filled pieces (see Figure 7.11).

8. Export the entire graphic (Ctrl+E), change the Files Of Type option to
   TIFF, and change the Color option to RGB. Enable the Anti-Aliasing
   and Use Color Profile checkboxes, and decide what Resolution setting is appropriate. (I always work at 300 dpi. See the tip, "Work At
   High Res," for more information.) Click on OK to create the bitmap,
   and then exit CorelDRAW.

Figure 7.11
The final steps in CorelDRAW
result in two puzzles: one with
colored pieces, and one with
picture-filled pieces.

9. Launch Photo-Paint and open the puzzle bitmap that you created in
   the preceding steps. Select the Magic Wand Mask tool, located on the
   Mask tools flyout. Click on one of the solid-colored puzzle pieces,
   which magically creates the desired selection (see Figure 7.12).

10. From the Object Picker flyout, choose the Mask Transform tool. Now,
    you can drag your puzzle-shaped selection area over the same pic-
    ture-filled puzzle piece in the duplicate set below. The solid-colored
    copy of the puzzle-piece pair makes creating this odd-shaped selec-
    tion a snap (see Figure 7.13).

Figure 7.12
Use the Magic Wand Mask tool to
select the puzzle shape quickly.

Figure 7.13

The Mask Transform tool lets you drag the selection area from the solid-colored puzzle over the bitmap-filled version.

11. With your selection now over the picture-filled puzzle piece, you are free to embellish it with a bevel. This is a snap using the Alien Skin Eye Candy filters. With this filter set installed, choose Effects|Eye Candy 3.01|Inner Bevel, which opens a dialog box that enables you to create the illusion of a 3D bevel along the contour of your selection. This is the perfect way to add depth and realism to your custom puzzle shapes. Change the Bevel Shape option to Button and then click on the green checkmark, to transform your puzzle piece (see Figure 7.14).

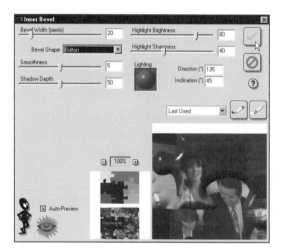

Figure 7.14

The Inner Bevel plug-in creates the illusion of a cut-out puzzle piece, adding highlights and shading along the selection contour.

12. Remove the mask (Ctrl+Shift+R) so that you can repeat the process for all the puzzle pieces.

Workaround For Masochists And Skinflints

You can achieve similar results to those in the preceding technique directly in CorelDRAW—but without the additional expense of a third-party plug-in. With some effort, you can use the Lighting and Beveling options of the Interactive Extrude tool to create the 3D-looking puzzle piece. However, the Interactive Extrude tool doesn't work on a PowerClip curve, so you lose the flexibility and ease of placing an image inside the shape by using the PowerClip feature. You can, however, create shading and beveling on a curve by using a bitmap pattern fill, as with the stone carvings in Chapter 3. Here is how to get a beveled puzzle piece directly within CorelDRAW:

POWERFUL PLUG-INS

Step 11 uses a plug-in, not included with CorelDRAW 9, called Eye Candy, from Alien Skin. Although Corel ships a lot of cool effects with its graphics suite, you may find that third-party plug-ins (from vendors such as Alien Skin, Auto f/x, and so forth) offer a quick-and-easy way to enhance your images and your productivity. Corel Photo-Paint supports any third-party plug-in that is generically labeled PhotoShop-compatible, and of course those specifically labeled Photo-Paint compatible.

When you install a plug-in, place it in the \ProgramFiles\Corel\Graphics9\Plugins folder. Or, if you already have the plug-in on your disk, just tell CorelDRAW or Photo-Paint where to find it. Open the Options dialog box (Ctrl+J), click on Plug-ins, and then click on Add. Simply select the folder in which you have plug-ins already on your system (so you don't have to install them twice on your system if, for example, you use another program, such as Adobe PhotoShop, that has plug-ins).

Most companies offer free demos of their plug-ins, so you can download and try them before you buy. For example, log in to www.alienskin.com and download the demo for Eye Candy 3.0 (or Xenofex, Alien Skin's other really cool filter set). I'm betting that you'll find the Eye Candy tool set a valuable addition to your design studio.

Another great online resource for information and links to plug-ins is www.i-us.com. This digital graphics community has several CorelDRAW/Photo-Paint-specific forums, in addition to a content area dedicated to plug-ins. This site always has an ample collection of free plug-ins to download and use immediately to enhance your design day.

1. Select your object and open the Pattern Fill dialog box from the Fill tool flyout. Enable the Bitmap radio button and then click on Load. Locate the bitmap that you want to place inside of your puzzle piece (see Figure 7.15). Click on OK to fill your object.

2. The problem with this technique is that controlling your image's position within the puzzle piece is hard, requiring you to visit the Pattern Fill dialog box several times. Open the Pattern Fill dialog box and attempt to position the graphic correctly, by modifying the Width and Height values and by toying with the x and y Origin numbers. Because this dialog box has no preview option, you have to repeat the process manually (see why I like the plug-ins solution?). With a little experimentation, you can get your picture in a satisfactory position within the puzzle piece (see Figure 7.16).

Figure 7.15

The Bitmap option in the Pattern Fill dialog box lets you select a bitmap to fill inside of your puzzle piece.

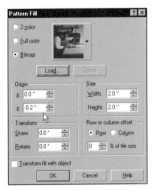

Figure 7.16

Modify the position of the image inside the curved puzzle pieces by changing the Size and Origin variables in the Pattern Fill dialog box.

3. When you finally get your image in position, you can use the Interactive Extrude tool to create the 3D-beveled look. Drag the Interactive Extrude tool up from the center of the piece to start the process. On the Property Bar, click on Lighting (the light-bulb icon) and then click on the 1 light-bulb button. Click on Bevels and enable the Use Bevel and Show Bevel Only options . This should give you results similar to the Inner Bevel bitmap plug-in (see Figure 7.17).

Figure 7.17
The Lighting and Bevel options on the Interactive Extrude Property Bar create a 3D puzzle-piece illusion.

> **Note:** You can perform other effects before you deselect your puzzle piece. For example, after you finish the Inner Bevel step, select Effects|Eye Candy 3.01|Drop Shadow to create the illusion that the puzzle piece is floating above the page. This simplicity is what makes the plug-ins a worthy investment.

The negatives outweigh the positives, in this case, which is why I always opt for the Photo-Paint/plug-in solution when building puzzle pieces. Trying to avoid the few dollars expense is hardly worth losing my sanity waiting for a page full of complex Interactive Extrude puzzle pieces to render.

You can see the results of the plug-in version of this tutorial in this book's color section. The CorelDRAW file is called puzzle.cdr, which you can find in the \Chapt07\ subdirectory of the companion CD-ROM.

Puzzling Spheres

I was showing a friend this technique in which you stuff a copy of the current file into a sphere, creating the illusion of a reflected environment. He watched the screen with wide-eyed amazement and finally said "Your job is to invent weird stuff, isn't it? Well, you're doing a good job!" Take a look at Figure 7.18 and see if you agree.

Figure 7.18
Using the Export function to "capture" the current image can result in a reflection illusion.

Yes, it is indeed my job to invent strange techniques. This image-within-an-image idea is a relatively new one for me, but already destined to be one of my favorites. It isn't really a puzzle, but the technique is reminiscent of one of those brain puzzle games, so I decided to stick it in this chapter. Here is how to create the illusion of reflecting glass or chrome-like spheres:

1. Use the Rectangle tool to draw a box the size of your target image. From the Fill tool flyout, select the Pattern Fill option. Enable the Bitmap radio button and then click on the current pattern bitmap tile or the arrow next to it to reveal the gallery of available options.

Choose a fairly geometric pattern, which helps to enhance the distortion techniques later. I chose the pattern of stones (see Figure 7.19), which will make the chrome spheres appear to be resting at the bottom of a creek bed.

 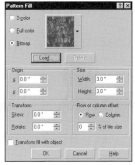

Figure 7.19

The Bitmap option from the Pattern Fill dialog box fills a rectangle with a stony-creek-bottom texture.

2. Use the Ellipse tool to draw a perfect circle, by holding down the Ctrl key as you drag. Give this circle a white fill and no outline, and then duplicate it.

3. Drag the duplicate above and away from the original, so that you can see what you're doing in Normal view. Select the top circle and choose the Interactive Transparency tool. You don't need to drag on your object to assign a transparency, because you can use the Interactive Fountain Transparency Property Bar.

4. Change the Transparency Type to Fountain and click on Radial Fountain Transparency, the second button option on the Property Bar. The logic of the default is the reverse of what we want to achieve, so drag 10% gray from the on-screen color palette and drop it on the center control point of the Interactive Transparency live control slider-line. Then, drag black off the on-screen palette and drop it on the outside color point.

5. Drag the center of the Interactive Transparency to the top and right, which creates the illusion of a reflection on a glass sphere (see Figure 7.20).

6. Select the Interactive Drop Shadow tool from the Interactive tool flyout. Click on the center of the solid-white object and drag down and to the left, to create the illusion that it's floating above the rocks and casting a shadow.

7. With the drop shadow group still selected, choose Arrange|Separate, which freezes the shadow so that you can freely manipulate the white parent circle.

WORK AT HIGH RES

You may often find yourself using the same graphic for both a Web site and a print project. However, if you design an image specifically for the Web by using low-resolution bitmaps, it will look awful in print. Instead, design everything as if it is destined for print and then simply downsize the images, as needed, for Web site use. This way, you always have the parent file on hand with the right resolution. You can always downsize the high-resolution images and create perfect graphics for the Web, but you can't work vice versa. Use the Resample dialog box in either CorelDRAW or Photo-Paint to create smaller graphics for Web sites.

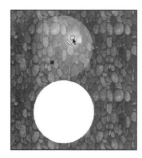

Figure 7.20

The Interactive Transparency tool transforms a solid-white circle into a glass-sphere illusion.

8. Select the white parent circle and again use the Edit|Copy Properties From command (Ctrl+Shift+A) to open the Copy Properties dialog box. Enable the Fill radio button, click on OK, and then click on the stone-filled background (see Figure 7.21). Duplicate the stone circle and set it aside, because you'll need a copy of it later.

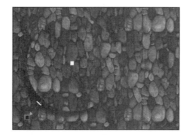

Figure 7.21

The interactive drop shadow creates the illusion of an object hovering above the creek bed.

9. Select the stone-circle object resting above the drop shadow, and choose Bitmaps|Convert to Bitmap. Change the Color option to CMYK (this project is going to print) and enable the Anti-Aliasing, Transparent Background, and Use Color Profile checkboxes. Click on OK to rasterize your object.

10. With the stone circle now a bitmap, we can distort it to look more round. Choose Bitmaps|3D Effects|Sphere to open the Sphere dialog box, in which you can control the percentage of distortion with the Percentage slider. The default setting of 25 is fine, so click on OK to transform the bitmap into a sphere (see Figure 7.22).

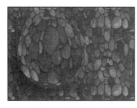
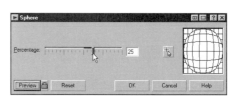

Figure 7.22

The Sphere bitmap effects filter distorts the image into a 3D-looking ball.

11. Arrange your glass-sphere circle over the stone-ball bitmap, and you have a pretty darn convincing 3D-looking image (see Figure 7.23).

Figure 7.23
Stacking the transparent circle on top of the distorted bitmap creates a convincing 3D effect.

This is good stopping point to create a nice 3D-looking sphere, and I should have left well enough alone. But, because it's physically impossible for me to leave well enough alone, I decided to take the illusion a few steps further to facilitate the illusion of reflecting a second chrome sphere. Don't panic—it's not that hard, and the results are very cool. Furthermore, you can use the effect for other applications in which you want to create the illusion of reflection. Here's how to do it:

1. Drag-select everything in your image, except the "extra" circle object that you made in Step 8, and open the Export dialog box (Ctrl+E). Create a CMYK bitmap of your scene, at 300 dpi.

2. Import the bitmap that you created in Step 1 at full size (instead of click-dragging with the special cursor that appears when you import to designate a custom import size, just click on the desktop to designate the location of the left corner of the imported image at actual size).

3. Arrange the circle duplicate that you made earlier so that it has a section of the sphere image passing through it on the bottom-left side (see Figure 7.24). Select the bitmap, choose Effects|PowerClip| Place Inside Container, and click on the circle duplicate.

Figure 7.24
Use the PowerClip feature to place the screen-capture image into another circle shape.

4. With the circle now containing a bit of a sphere reflection, repeat the Convert to Bitmap and Sphere steps (refer verbatim to Steps 9 and 10 of the previous exercise) to create a new rounded-sphere shape that

happens to also have a bit of a reflected twin. Place the new distorted bitmap under the glass-sphere shape, and you are about done (see Figure 7.25).

Figure 7.25
Using the screen-capture image in the sphere creates the illusion of reflecting another sphere.

5. Select all the elements that make up your chrome ball (including the drop shadow) and duplicate the group (+ key). Arrange the duplicate to the top right of the original, so that it looks like it's a brother to the other ball.

6. Rotate the fill bitmap on one of the balls so that the reflection is correct. This is easy. Simply hold down the Alt key and click on the ball that you want to change the reflection in, until you select the Color Bitmap (watch the status bar as you click). Then, click on the center arrows again to reveal the corner rotation arrows, which you can then drag around until your reflection illusions line up correctly (see Figure 7.26). Shazam! You are a master of illusion.

Figure 7.26
Rotating the "reflection" bitmap toward the duplicate ball group finishes the illusion.

You can find this eye-puzzle in this book's color section and on the spheres.cdr file located in the \Chapt07 subdirectory of the companion CD-ROM. It's an amazing illusion, but really simple. If you want to make the image reflect other things, such as text or other objects, you can flip-flop the image that you stuffed into the sphere.

Beyond f/x

The puzzle metaphor is a natural for advertising, and it makes for some very powerful imagery. Taking a group portrait and then pulling people out with the puzzle trick can add impact to statistics; for example, "One person in ten will be affected by violent crime...." You can create images that build themselves by using the puzzle pieces, or images that start as a whole and explode into oblivion, using the pieces to build an animation. Or, you can follow my lead and use the puzzle pieces as Web-site navigation buttons.

The optical illusion presented in the last tutorial also has some interesting potential. You could create any number of images to stuff inside the balls, to create trapped people or products, for example. Or, you could use the technique to render bubbles, to use in projects for beverages, diving equipment, or kids' toys.

A picture is worth a thousand words, as they say, and I say even more if you work in some clever CorelDRAW effects.

Moving On

In this chapter, we looked at how to make pieces, puzzles, and illusions with the PowerClip function. The PowerClip break apart trick has many uses, and they aren't limited to bitmaps. When you use CorelDRAW objects in your puzzle pieces, the files aren't nearly as large. You can also export a CorelDRAW image as a bitmap and then use a paint program to manipulate the pieces further. I like to do this because it's really easy then to use a bitmap filter effect to enhance the images further. Don't hesitate to mix and match technologies or techniques to get what you're after, or to invent your own wonderful variants. Like everything in this book, this is just a starting point. Go forth and conquer, my wicked design minions!

In the next chapter, we look at creating all kinds of "linked" artwork, using the Interactive Blend tool. From barbed wire to chain links, we will create connected strands of all kinds of wonderful design elements.

ROPE, BARBED WIRE, AND CHAINS

8

This chapter uses the Blend feature to create rope, chain, and barbed wire objects along any path that you wish.

Barbed wire, chains, and spiky shapes are popular in the tattoo community, and they also make for interesting design elements. As alternative styles become increasingly more mainstream, even the most conservative design studios may find themselves searching for appropriate art elements for a client looking for a more hardcore image. These kinds of design elements look great, and they are extremely flexible and easy to create.

In this chapter, we use the Blend function to create round wire and pointy tips, and also to create chain and rope. We work again with metallic shading (as in Chapter 5) to colorize some dangerous razor wire. All in all, we'll have a fine selection of linked and pointy things from which to choose.

The great thing about using the Blend tool for this technique is that few limitations exist to the shape of the curve that you can run the chain or rope links along, resulting in a variety of handy applications. You could easily create a signature, or any other unique shape, in chain or rope.

Rope, chain, and wire make great border elements, but they aren't limited to that purpose (see Figure 8.1, for example). The CorelDRAW clip-art CD-ROM has plenty of pieces of rope and chain in ordinary round or rectangular configurations, so your task is to come up with a solution for any strange shape that you want to create. You can accomplish this with the Blend docker and its ability to blend along a curve. The computer-accurate spacing makes such tasks as connecting chain links possible, but the same procedure could work with any shape or image (you could just as easily connect a series of plastic monkeys!). These kinds of designs are just too tedious to do by hand, but with a little computer assistance, heck, anything is possible.

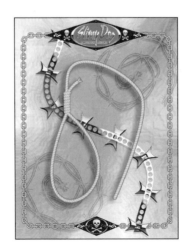

Figure 8.1
Blending objects along a path can result in chains, rope, or barbed wire in virtually any shape imaginable.

OBJECT SPRAYER

The addition of the Object Sprayer to the CorelDRAW 9 tool set promises many path-based effects, similar to the chain, rope, and wire discussed in this chapter. The Object Sprayer, available on the Curve tool flyout, references a spray list of objects, to scatter artwork along a predrawn path. Eventually, a spray list that generates a chain, rope, or wire effect may be available, but currently the spray lists consist of scattered, unlinked images (see Figure 8.2). This tool evolved from a feature in Photo-Paint 8, but it makes more sense as a CorelDRAW function, where you have infinite control over the flow path.

To use the Object Sprayer, with your path selected, choose the Artistic Media tool from the Curve tool flyout and then click on Sprayer on the Property Bar. Scroll through the spray list gallery to locate a style that you like, and then click to select that style. Easy! Now, modify the parameters (size, spacing, and so forth) on the Property Bar.

Figure 8.2

The Object Sprayer allows you to choose from a spray list gallery to assign a set of images to a path.

Danger Wire

For some reason, barbed wire just really appeals to me. It just suggests "danger" or "beware" and works in artwork for a more hardcore crowd. This market continues to grow, however, as things like cruiser bikes and gangster rap enter the mainstream. If nothing else, barbed wire makes for an interesting diversion from other, boring, border elements. Here is how to lay some barbed wire:

1. Use the Bezier tool (located on the Curve tool flyout) to draw a sweeping horizontal line with soft waves in it, by click-dragging points on the screen. On top of this line, draw another line in an opposite sweeping motion, to create the wire shape (see Figure 8.3). Try to crisscross the lines at a distance that's close to uniform, similar to how real barbed wire works. You can create barbed wire in virtually any shape or configuration, but this small piece of horizontal wire is a good place to start. Shift-select both lines and combine them (Ctrl+L).

Figure 8.3

Use the Bezier tool to create two overlapping lines in the shape of your choice.

2. Select the wire shape and give it a thick, black 8-point outline from the Outline flyout. Duplicate it and give the duplicate a thin, white hairline outline. Drag-select both stacked pieces and then locate the Interactive Blend tool from the Interactive tool flyout.

3. Carefully drag from the back thick line to the front thinner copy, to create a blend between them. This creates a round-looking wire, as the thick, black line bends to the thin, white line. Notice that the objects don't look like two separate wires at the points where they cross, because we combined the lines into one shape. If you want individual wires, don't combine them (see Figure 8.4).

Figure 8.4

Blend a thick black line into a thin white one to create a rounded wire.

4. Draw a rectangle and round out the ends by dragging a corner node with the Shape tool. Duplicate (using the + key) this shape and convert it to curves (Ctrl+Q). With the Shape tool, drag down the bottom-center node. Drag-select all the nodes in the lower half of the object and, from the Property Bar, click on Convert Curve To Line. This makes a spiky end on one of the twisted wire shapes. Duplicate the original object two more times and the spike one more time. Arrange the objects to look like the twisted, spiked, barbed-wire hub.

5. Drag-select all the objects and open the Fountain Fill dialog box (F11). Create a linear custom color blend to suggest a shaded round cylinder. Enable the Custom option and then double-click along the preview ribbon to add a color point to the blend. Change the color of this point by clicking on a color swatch in the Fountain Fill dialog box.

6. If you prefer, you can zoom in close with the Zoom tool (click on the Zoom tool and drag a box around your object to zoom in close). Now, you can use the Interactive Fill tool to create the round shading, by dragging and dropping color from the on-screen palette onto points along the Interactive Fill tool control line (see Figure 8.5).

7. Drag-select and group (Ctrl+G) the barb shapes. Duplicate the barb group and place the duplicates at each point where your wire blend crisscrosses. Double-click on the barb group to reveal the rotation arrows and drag on a corner set to spin each barb slightly to orient it to the wires below (see Figure 8.6).

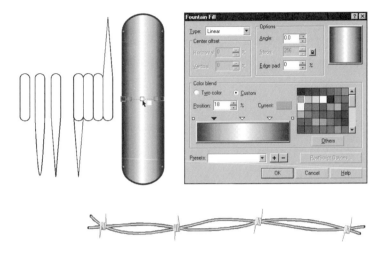

Figure 8.5

The Shape tool transforms a rectangle into a rounded wire object and then into a sharp barb. Finally, a custom color blend gives the shape a round appearance.

Figure 8.6

To finish the look, place the barb groups at the points where the wires crisscross.

You can create barbed wire in virtually any shape. Here is how to create a barbed spiral:

1. Select the Spiral tool, located on the Object flyout. Drag the Spiral tool on screen to create a spiral (use the Property Bar to control the spiral options, such as Spiral Revolutions, and so forth).

2. Place a barb group at each end of the spiral, shift-select both groups, and drag between them with the Interactive Blend tool. On the Property Bar, click on Path Properties, click on New Path, and then click on your spiral shape. This should blend the barbs along the path and space them out evenly (see Figure 8.7). On the Property Bar, you can control the number of steps and the Object Acceleration to get the even spacing that you want.

3. Use the Freehand tool to draw the wire shapes, crisscrossing at each barb point. Use the Shape tool to auto-reduce the nodes. Drag-select

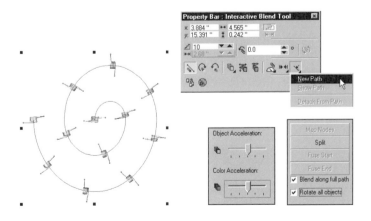

Figure 8.7

Use the Interactive Blend Tool Property Bar to space out the barb shapes along any shape (in this case, a spiral).

all the nodes in the line and then use the Curve Smoothness slider on the Property Bar to smooth out and clean up the lines (see Figure 8.8).

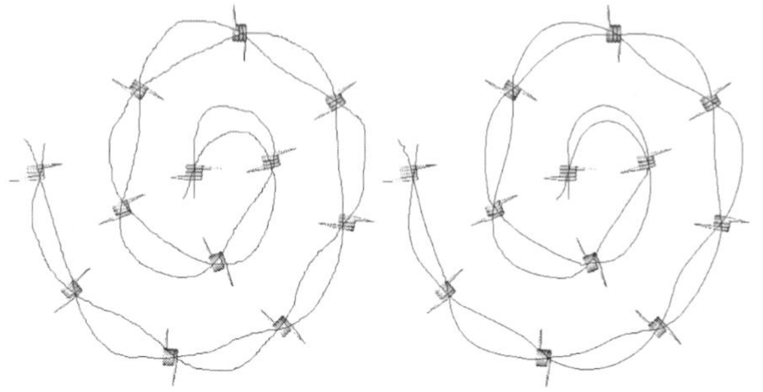

Figure 8.8

Use the Freehand tool to draw the wire shapes and then use the Shape tool to clean up the freehand-drawn lines. The blend-spaced barbs act as guidelines for drawing the wire.

4. Duplicate and blend the wire shapes as before. Send wires to the back (Shift+PgDn)—and you're done.

Razor Wire

Razor wire is usually a solid strand of metallic tape, stamped with a razor shape every few inches. This is kind of bland, so I created a more spacey-looking razor wire with more defined individual blades attached to the tape. Here is how to make my razor wire:

1. Draw a rectangle with the Rectangle tool, duplicate it (using +), and downsize the duplicate by dragging one of the corner control handles inward. From the Interactive tool flyout, select the Interactive Envelope tool.

2. Click on Envelope Straight Line Mode on the Property Bar, and then use the Shape tool to drag the top-center node of the envelope inward while holding down both the Ctrl and Shift keys. This moves all the center nodes inward simultaneously, creating a star shape (see Figure 8.9).

Figure 8.9

A rectangle becomes a razor blade with the help of a straight-line envelope.

3. Shift-select both objects and combine them (Ctrl+L). Either borrow the custom color blend from the piercing pieces in the previous chapter, create a new one with the same color scheme (with the Fountain Fill dialog box or the Interactive Fill tool), or load the blade.cdr file on the companion CD-ROM, in the \Chapt08\ folder, to copy the fill (see Figure 8.10).

links one half of the link length on each end, which makes the blending process work right (see Figure 8.17).

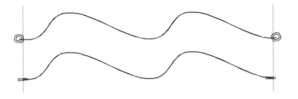

Figure 8.17
A curvy line serves as the blend path, which needs to be slightly shorter for the second set of links.

6. Shift-select the two top links and use the Interactive Blend tool to create a row of links. Click on Path Properties on the Property Bar, click on New Path, and then click on the curvy shape.

7. Click on Miscellaneous Blend Options, and enable the Rotate All Objects and Blend Along Full Path options. Repeat the process for the side links, decreasing the number of steps by two (see Figure 8.18).

Figure 8.18
Use the Interactive Blend Property Bar and the New Path option to place the duplicates along the desired path.

8. Align the two blend groups to finish the chain. If things don't align just right, increase or decrease the steps in each blend on the Property Bar until they align correctly. You may need to select the control links in each blend and move or rotate them to get things to align correctly. Typically, the smaller blend (in this case, the side links) use one less step then the larger link blend. It takes a little tweaking, but since CorelDRAW is doing all the work when you add or delete steps in the blend, you can't really complain. Figure 8.19 shows the results of this step.

Figure 8.19
Align the top and side link blends to result in a unique chain shape that follows the contour of your choice.

9. If some of the links just don't look right, you can arrange and separate the blend (choose Arrange|Separate) and then Ungroup (Ctrl+U) the objects to fine-tune them manually. This process isn't as painful as it sounds, because each line is usually in the right place, or really close, so you need to move or rotate only a few lines to make things perfect.

That's it! I used the links as a border around the page of a promotional flyer, which can be seen in the color section. To see the links in action, load the chains.cdr file in the \Chapt08\ folder on the companion CD-ROM.

Rope A Dope

I was sitting in a restaurant, having a nice dinner conversation, when I looked up and saw a guy with a nautical logo on his shirt. I turned to my girlfriend and said "Hey, I can make rope!" I then started drawing on my arm, trying to explain the process of blending a shape along any path to build the image. Although she had no idea what I was talking about and thought I was nuts, I think you might be interested. Here's how to blend an object along a path to create rope:

1. Draw a rectangle and cap it off with an oval on each end. Shift-select all three objects and open the Weld docker from the Arrange|Shaping menu. Click on Weld To and then on the selected shapes, to merge the three objects into one.

2. Squash the object vertically, and expand it horizontally by dragging the center sizing handles with the Pick tool. Double-click on the object to reveal the rotation and skew arrows. Drag the bottom-center skew arrows to the right, to create the repeating twine shape (see Figure 8.20).

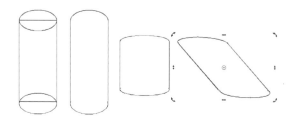

Figure 8.20
The Weld function changes simple shapes into the rope sausage, which, when squashed and skewed, is ready for the blending steps.

3. Give the twine object a radial fountain fill, from a light color to a darker one, by dragging across it with the Interactive Fill tool. Click on Radial Fountain fill in the Property Bar and then change the colors of the fill. You can click on the color chips on the Property Bar to change the colors of the fountain fill, or simply drag and drop colors directly off the on-screen color palette.

4. To test whether the shape will work for a rope blend, move it horizontally the length of the object. Before you release the mouse, right-click to create a duplicate. Use the Repeat command (Ctrl+R) to create additional, properly spaced links, to test whether your rope shape will work (see Figure 8.21).

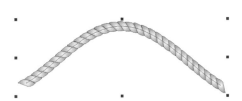

Figure 8.21
Duplicates of the rope shape link together perfectly.

5. For the rope pieces, you can use any shape as a blend path to run the rope along. The effect works well, but tends to fall flat if your blend path has sharp curves or transitions. So, keep the curves smooth and you shouldn't have any problems. Use the New Path button on the Interactive Blend Property Bar to run the rope pieces along any curve (see Figure 8.22).

Figure 8.22
Use the New Path function on the Interactive Blend Property Bar to run rope along any curve you wish.

6. The blend works great, but you need a way to cap it off, to finish the rope look. Draw a rectangle and then distort it with the Envelope function, to create a bent piece of twine. Duplicate the object, flip the duplicate, and then move the duplicate horizontally to the right, the distance of the rope piece.

7. Blend the two objects together to create other frayed ends. Choose Arrange|Separate and then choose Arrange|Ungroup All. Combine (Ctrl+L) the shapes into one curve.

8. Move a copy of the rope-twine shape beneath the frayed objects and then use the Shape tool to node-edit the object, essentially to cut it in half.

9. Take the half-twine shape and choose Arrange|Shaping|Weld, to connect it to the frayed pieces. Draw a rectangle across the point where the frays meet the twine piece, and round the edges to represent the little piece of cord that is used to keep ropes from completely unraveling. For added contrast, you can draw a black shape behind the frayed pieces, as I did, or leave them open and airy (see Figure 8.23).

10. Position the end cap group at each open end of the rope to finish it off. The same end cap will work on both ends of the rope blend (see Figure 8.24).

The next technique enables you to create sweeping rope in any size or shape, and then cap off the ends. Follow these directions to make the noose.

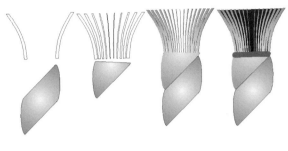

Figure 8.23

Cut a twine shape in half and weld it to a curve made from blended strands, creating an end cap for the rope blend.

Figure 8.24

Use the end caps to finish off the rope pieces.

1. Use the Bezier tool to draw a line in the shape of a hangman's noose. Place the rope pieces on each end of this curve and use the curve as the blend path to connect the rope pieces with a 200-step blend. Enable the Blend Along Full Path and Rotate All Objects options on the Interactive Blend Property Bar. You may need to add or reduce the number of steps to get the rope to build correctly (see Figure 8.25).

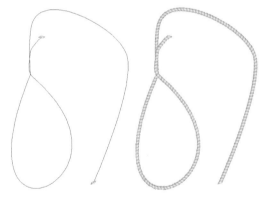

Figure 8.25

Create a blend along a "noose" path to create the hangman's rope.

2. Add the end caps to the rope to give it a finished look.

3. For the knot, you need to create a half-loop piece to cap off each end. Start with the standard shape and use the Shape tool to select and delete the top-right nodes. Fix the resulting curve so that it creates a rounded end for the rope loops. Duplicate and flip-flop this end for both sides, and group the objects. Place the noose-knot group, and then create the rest of the knots by duplicating and arranging the duplicates (see Figure 8.26).

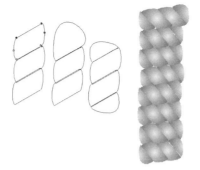

Figure 8.26
Modify a rope shape to become the end caps for the noose-knot loops. Duplicate and arrange these loops to create the signature hangman's knot.

4. To get a nice outline, drag-select all the noose pieces, group them, and then duplicate the group. Send the duplicate group behind the original and give the duplicate a thick, dark .053-inch outline and fill color. This outlines the rope as a whole, without adding an outline to every object in the front rope group.

5. With the outline group still selected, use the Interactive Drop Shadow tool from the Interactive tool flyout to add a shadow. Drag the tool across and down to create a shadow (see Figure 8.27).

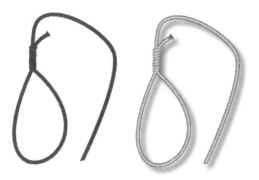

Figure 8.27
A thick-lined duplicate creates a nice outline and is also the parent shape for the drop-shadow.

Now you can entwine anything, anywhere, like some crazed rodeo rider! This technique works well with big sweeping curves, but, like the chain blends, you may need to manipulate the links manually to make all the twines look okay. Some sections in the hangman's noose in my image (which you can view in the color section) look kind of rough if you zoom in and examine the noose closely. I left these rough spots in so that you can see what kinds of problems to watch out for.

Beyond f/x

Chains, ropes, and wire are great ways to lay out a page. Because you no longer are limited to any particular size or shape for your linked graphic, your links can serpentine around and through the page as you wish. This serves not only to break up the page into smaller chunks, but also to direct the eye of the viewer to different parts of the design. Chains or rope also offer interesting associations, from Western motifs and nautical designs to creepier, darker subjects. Barbed wire can add a touch of danger to a logo, or reinforce a theme of war or persecution.

Because you can run the links along any path, you can use handwriting-style lettering to create words with a connected path, and then run the links along it. This makes for cool thematic logos or promotional graphics ("Western days," "jailhouse rock," and so forth). Blending along a path is always a great way to achieve proportionately spaced object duplicates, such as saw teeth, gears, or rivets.

Moving On

This was a fast-paced chapter, putting the Blend function to work to link wire, rope, and chain objects. Often, you'll want to create a unique chain, rope, or wire shape, and you'll need to use the Blend feature to do so. The Blend tool is a great way to space out objects evenly along a path, even if they aren't part of a linked theme (such as blending two different colored shapes along a path, for a rainbow pattern of geometric shapes around your artwork).

In the next chapter, we ignore the Blend function entirely and focus on how to circumvent a common design problem—limited resource material. Having limited resource material for a project (such as a single product shot instead of a variety to choose from) presents a situation in which you need to create more with less. We look at some simple solutions to this daunting problem, with creative duplication techniques. Rub your eyes and break out the Visine—it's time to get into double vision!

DOUBLE VISION

9

This chapter explores using multiple copies of the same image to enhance a design. It explains how to convert images into bitmap duplicates and then manipulate the bitmaps with lens effects and filters. It also demonstrates some other multiple-image design styles.

Multiple-image designs are pretty common these days; you can see them in all sorts of media, including television, print ads, and Web sites. For example, I have seen award shows where the host stands in front of a wall of TVs with a live-feed, close-up image of the host's face on the monitors, or catalogs with a close-up of a product and its full-view image as a subdued background. Web sites use this strategy a lot to produce an interesting image out of essentially one picture.

In this chapter, we look at ways to work multiple images into your artwork. This design style is a great way to add visual interest to an otherwise limited graphic. If you have ever had to try to make something from nothing, or had to stretch some customer-supplied artwork a little further than you wanted, then you will find these techniques of interest.

First, we take an illustration of a female jester and duplicate the image for both an interesting, subdued background graphic and the main focus of the design. Second, we use CorelDRAW's powerful Export features to create a bitmap background image which can be made larger and in different colors than the original foreground characters. We next create a flower-like pattern with duplicates of the same model photo and then surround the result with a chaotic pattern made from resized and recolored duplicates of the headline text. Finally, we use water as a vehicle to reflect and distort an image, to enhance a product shot. This chapter shows how even similar images and objects can be made to look very different, resulting in some very interesting design possibilities.

Jokers Wild

The jester-girl image shown in Figure 9.1 is from a T-shirt and other items commemorating the fifth anniversary of our design studio, nicknamed the Dog House because that's where Slimy Dog was whelped years before. I scanned the ink illustration to work out some other design issues, and ended up creating this double-vision layout by combining duplicates of the image in the foreground and background.

This is a great example of how you can milk a design for more than its original purpose. This image is really tall and thin, which was perfect for the T-shirt design for which it was made, but it has strange dimensions for standard print applications. By using the objects in a background image, the image was fattened up, and even though the original image is still tall and skinny the overall page is more balanced. Often, the pieces are lying right in front of you and you simply need to assemble them creatively to get what you are looking for.

Figure 9.1
Using one image in the foreground and a muted version of the same image in the background adds depth and interest without having to build entirely new pieces.

I misplaced the original illustration of the jester-girl image that I wanted to use, so I couldn't simply scan and Corel Trace the image (as in the one-eye example from Chapter 4). I could locate only a chunky 1-bit bitmap image that just didn't provide suitable results when I tried to convert it to vector by using Corel Scan (see the girlnbox.cmx file on the companion CD in the \Chapt09\ subdirectory to see my attempt at Corel Tracing the scan). However, I didn't get totally discouraged, because the bitmap still had some potential. You can set the white color of a 1-bit bitmap to nothing (by clicking on the *x* on the on-screen palette) to produce a black-ink image on a transparent background. This enables you to colorize the bitmap with shapes drawn manually with the Freehand and Bezier tools. This technique sounds difficult, but it really isn't. Here is how to combine images into a foreground/background double-vision orientation:

1. Import the bitmap (Ctrl+I) called girlnbox.tif from the companion CD in the \Chapt09\ subdirectory. Then, right-click on the bitmap to reveal the pop-up menu, and choose Lock Object. This prevents you from accidentally moving the bitmap while you're drawing shapes by hand to colorize it.

2. Switch to Wireframe view from the View menu—which enables you to see what you're doing much better—because this view displays the black bitmap as gray.

3. Use the Bezier tool to draw shapes to place behind the bitmap, to colorize it. You only need to draw shapes that fill in the clear areas (which display as white on screen), because the gray areas display in black in Normal view. You can easily create a solid shape by clicking along the contour of an area (see Figure 9.2). Don't worry about perfection because the black ink will cover anything behind it, and you can always use the Shape tool to fine-tune these curves later if necessary.

Figure 9.2
Use the Bezier tool to create shapes to color the clear areas of a 1-bit bitmap.

4. After you finish drawing your shapes, fill each shape with color to bring the black-and-white image to life. Right-click on the bitmap and select Unlock Object so that you can right-click and bring the bitmap To Front (Shift+PgUp), on top of the coloring shapes that you drew. This results in a colorized bitmap (see Figure 9.3). Save this full-color version on your hard drive so that you can work on the background duplicates.

Figure 9.3
Hand-drawn shapes (shown in Wireframe view on the left) add color to a black-and-white bitmap.

5. After you assemble your primary image group, duplicating and recoloring the objects to create the double-vision illusion is easy. (At this point, you could create a background image of jester-girl duplicates in all colors of the rainbow just by changing the hue of the coloring shapes, or use a mirror as a vehicle to exploit the double-vision trick. We'll leave these ideas for the next tutorials, and use a trick more appropriate for this jester image, which is a playing card.) A typical deck of cards uses a double-vision trick of duplicating and flipping the main image, which works great here, too. Select your jester-girl group (the bitmap and all the shapes) and choose Arrange|Transform, which opens the Transformation docker. Click on Scale and Mirror to switch to that page of options, and then enable both the Horizontal and Vertical Mirror buttons. Move the checkpoint in the grid from the center radio button to the right-center square (see Figure 9.4). When you click on Apply To Duplicate, you create a flip-flopped copy of your original in the location that you checked in the grid. If you kept on clicking on Apply To Duplicate, you could create a row of tumbling jesters!

6. With the duplicate jester-girl images in place, the playing-card motif begins to emerge. Draw a rectangle about twice as wide and about as tall as the jester girl. Curve the corners with the Shape tool to create a playing-card outline. Duplicate the card (+ key) and then

Figure 9.4
The Scale and Mirror page on the Transformation docker enables you to quickly create rotated and positioned duplicates of your original artwork.

divide the duplicate in half by adding two nodes at the center of the top and bottom lines with the Shape tool and then deleting the rest of the nodes on one side. (Or, draw another rectangle and use the Intersection tool to create the other half. Whatever works!)

7. Use the Artistic Text tool to name your playing card—in this case, "Joker". (I used a traditional-looking serif font called PalmSprings.) Change the coloring scheme so that everything that was white on the left is red on the right, and vice versa (see Figure 9.5). Select All (Ctrl+A) and then Group (Ctrl+U) your finished playing-card pieces into one easy-to-handle group.

8. Double-click on your card group and use the rotation handles to rotate the card, to break up the vertical bias that these tall figures create. To add some depth, use the Interactive Drop Shadow tool. If you drag downward-left from the center of your group, your card appears to float directly above a flat surface behind it as if you were looking down at the card (see Figure 9.6, on the left). If you drag left from the bottom of your group, your card appears to cast a shadow to its left, as if it were standing vertically on the edge of a flat surface, as viewed from the side (see Figure 9.6, on the right). Either shadow type adds a lot of depth and dimension with very little effort, and you can use the Property Bar to modify settings such as Drop Shadow Feathering and Opacity to get a look that you like.

9. This color image looks great on its own, but needs to be subdued to be appropriate for the background. With its current bright color scheme it would compete with our future foreground image. Using a lens effect is a quick and nondestructive solution to de-emphasize this artwork. I say nondestructive because a lens only changes the way that objects appear and doesn't actually modify the objects themselves. So, draw a big box over everything with the Rectangle

Figure 9.5
Transform the duplicate images into a playing card by adding a frame and reversing the color scheme for each side.

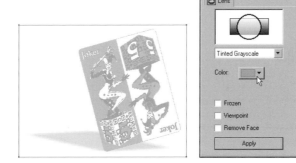

Figure 9.6

Use the Interactive Drop Shadow
tool to cast either a traditional
drop shadow or a shadow in a
horizontal perspective.

tool and select Effects|Lens (or Alt+F3). Choose the Tinted Grayscale
option to transform the colors into shades of gray. If you want to
mute the colors even more, choose black color in the Lens docker
and then choose a lighter shade of gray from the Color drop-down
menu. This creates a nice, muted tone that you can fine-tune at any
time by selecting and changing this lens value (see Figure 9.7). Remember, behind this lens object is our original, unchanged,
full-color artwork.

Figure 9.7

Use the Tinted Grayscale lens
effect to change the way the
background image appears.

10. For the main image I imported (Ctrl+I) the full-color version of the
    jester-girl image that we saved in Step 3. To make the object stand
    out even more, I gave the main outline around the object a thick
    yellow outline.

11. All that remains is to arrange the crisp color image over the back-
    ground image. Change the Color value on the lens shape that is on
    top of the background image to mute or emphasize the background.
    If you want to create the illusion that the background is out of focus,
    use the Convert to Bitmap and Gaussian Blur techniques, as out-
    lined in Chapter 6.

You can view the final image in this book's color section and in the jester-
girl playing-card file, jestrgal.cdr, in the \Chapt09\ subdirectory on the

TO EXPORT OR NOT TO EXPORT

To convert CorelDRAW objects into bitmaps you can use either the Export (Ctrl+E) dialog box or the Convert to Bitmap command from the Bitmaps menu. I have tested both methods and found that each conversion takes about the same amount of time.

The Export feature is nice because it creates a file that you can load and massage in Photo-Paint, enabling you to perform many changes or fine-tune, yet retain the original CorelDRAW objects.

The Convert to Bitmap option is super-convenient, but unless you then choose Bitmaps|Edit Bitmap to launch Photo-Paint, or Export the image, this option limits the tweaks to within CorelDRAW. In some cases, the Convert to Bitmap option is better, depending on the kind and types of changes that you want to make on the bitmap. You must remember to save the original file before you use the Convert to Bitmap option, because after you convert your objects to a bitmap you can't go back to the vector data unless you have a backup file. The choice of which option to use is a matter of personal taste, but like many things in CorelDRAW, you have more than one option from which to choose.

companion CD-ROM. Load the file to see the different effects that the unique Interactive Drop Shadow options generate.

By using a little creativity, I was able to milk this illustration one more time despite its poor resolution and odd proportions. I know that you are thinking about which of your own designs could go another round by using this technique, much to my delight.

Skull Angels

I was in the process of creating an image similar to the jester invitation with the muted-gray background when curiosity got the best of me. Instead of muting the image with the Tinted Grayscale lens, recoloring it by using other lens options is just as easy. This can dramatically change the mood of the image; in this case, it makes things more nightmarish and chaotic, which is perfect for what we want to achieve (see Figure 9.8).

Again, simply through creative duplication and manipulation we can make a single image much more unique and interesting than the original design alone. Images with seemingly limited subject matter now have almost unlimited potential variants. What could be better than getting something for nothing?

The image shown in Figure 9.8 started as a file that I created a while back, in which I colorized ink illustrations that I had drawn of an angel, skulls, and little demons. I have sort of a clip-art library of things that I have drawn, scanned, and then colorized using CorelDRAW, which I can mix and match into many twisted images (ah, the power of CorelDRAW). The angel illustration has a strange history, and if you look in the hair and folds of cloth you will find eerie faces and skulls looking back at you.

Figure 9.8
After you set up a double-vision file with Corel objects in front of a grayscale reproduction in the background, you can subdue the background (left) or get chaotic results with other lenses, such as Invert (right).

Here is how to use the double-vision technique, with dramatic, chaotic results:

1. Open the Export dialog box (Ctrl+E), change the Save As Type option to TIFF Bitmap, assign a unique file name, and click on the Export button.

2. In the Bitmap Export dialog box, change the Color option to Grayscale, the Size option to 1 to 1, and the Resolution to 300 dpi. Enable the Anti-Aliasing and Use Color Profile checkboxes, but deselect Transparent Background for this image. Click on OK to write the bitmap to disk (see Figure 9.9).

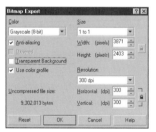

Figure 9.9
Use the Export function to create a grayscale bitmap of the angel image, to use later as a backdrop in the same file.

3. Import the image (Ctrl+I) back into your CorelDRAW drawing. CorelDRAW 9 enables you to assign the relative size of your bitmap when you Import it, so drag a very large area across and over your entire page to designate the import area, and release the mouse. This makes the image very large compared to the original artwork, creating a zoom-in effect. You can use the Shape tool to drag the nodes of the big bitmap if you want to reduce the bitmap to your page size, or stuff it into a rectangle the size of your page by using the Effects|PowerClip|Place Inside Container command.

4. Arrange the bitmap so that it is behind the original artwork, creating a powerful, double-vision image (see Figure 9.10). Downsize the original pieces and enlarge the background bitmap to create a dramatic difference in size.

Figure 9.10
To obtain an enlarged version to serve as a dramatic background image, Import the bitmap that you previously created by Exporting the original artwork.

5. As before, draw a white rectangle over the background bitmap but behind the other image pieces. Select Arrange|Order|Behind and then click on the foreground image to sandwich the rectangle behind the front objects and in front of the bitmap.

6. To achieve the muted look, open the Lens docker (Alt+F3) and choose the Transparency option. For a freaky, nightmarish look, choose Custom Color Map instead of Transparency. Select the Forward Rainbow option in the Lens docker, change the From and To colors to solid magenta, and click on Apply (see Figure 9.11).

Figure 9.11
To change the background bitmap into a strange, nightmarish backdrop, use the Custom Color Map option instead of the Transparency lens (which mutes the background).

7. For even more variety, with the lens object selected, change the fill value of the lens object from white to magenta, by clicking the on-screen magenta color chip. That is wild. Now, change the fill value to cyan. Try yellow. Wow! Fiery heat. Experiment until you find a look that you like (see Figure 9.12).

Figure 9.12
Changing the fill color value of the shape containing the Custom Color Map lens dramatically changes the look of the background.

To view a composite of images resulting from different lens settings, look in the book's color section; the original images are in the angel.cdr file in the \Chapt09\ subdirectory on the companion CD-ROM. Load the file and experiment with the lens option to produce an entirely different background look. Some of the settings that I have tried include Heat Map, Tinted Grayscale, and Color Limit. For really strange results, change the Palette rotation value with the Heat Map lens. It's such a dramatic change in the look with so little effort, I almost feel guilty about it.

World Of Weirdness

While working on the Y2K image in Chapter 14, I imagined the models standing on the planet surrounded by buzzing text elements (see Figure 9.13). Okay, so maybe I had too many double espressos that day, but that was the image that popped into my mind! When I look at the finished version of this art I can see the text buzzing around, like in a hyper ESPN 2 commercial. In fact, animating these kinds of text elements is easy, and we will in Chapter 21.

Figure 9.13
Multiple copies of text elements, enlarged and using outline-only shading, add a chaotic sense of energy to this image. The bitmap color mask lets the model bitmaps float freely on a clear background.

Note: If you enable the Show Colors radio button rather than the default Hide Colors, only the colors you select will be visible, making everything else invisible.

To free the models from their square bitmap prisons, use the magic of the Bitmap Color Mask docker, which enables you to render areas of color invisible. Again, this design technique takes a limited subject matter and makes it alive and interesting by using duplicates. Here is how to create the free-floating models and the noisy, double-vision text elements:

1. Find an image with a solid background color or use the File|Acquire command to scan a photo. You can use the Bitmap Color Mask docker to hide any color in a bitmap, which is a great way to remove the background and allow the image to float. When you use the Bitmap Color Mask docker to assign a color to be transparent, the transparency applies regardless of where the color appears; thus, if you designate a blue background as transparent, and your subject's eyes are the same color blue, they too will be transparent. So, choose your subject photo wisely.

2. To make the background transparent, select Bitmaps|Bitmap Color Mask to open the docker. In the docker, click on Color Selector (looks like an eye-dropper) and then click on the color that you want to hide, such as the white background.

   Click on Apply to make the selected color transparent and then use the Tolerance slider to fine-tune the results. A greater Tolerance value helps to eliminate a background-color halo around your subject (see Figure 9.14).

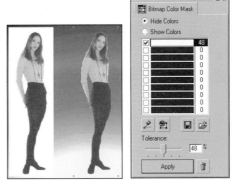

Figure 9.14
The Bitmap Color Mask tool hides selected colors in your bitmap images, so that the images appear to float free of a background.

3. With the Freehand tool, draw a horizontal line by clicking and then moving the pointer across the page while holding down the Ctrl key. Duplicate (+ key) and rotate this line 90 degrees to create a crosshair to use as a reference point to create the circle of model duplicates.

4. Select the bitmap of the model and place her at the top center of the vertical crosshair. With the model still selected, click with the Pick tool to reveal the rotation arrows and the axis of rotation. Drag the axis of rotation down until the target crosshairs match the reference crosshairs that you just drew (see Figure 9.15).

5. With the bitmap selected, open the Transformation docker (Alt+F9) and click on Scale and Mirror (it's the center button). Toggle just the Horizontal option, select the radio button in the middle of the positioning grid, and then click on Apply To Duplicate. This flip-flops and copies the bitmap in one step, without moving it.

6. Using the Pick tool, grab and drag the top-left rotation-left arrow while holding down the Ctrl key, to spin the girl around 30 degrees (see Figure 9.16).

7. Continue to duplicate and rotate the bitmap, alternating the left- and right-facing models until you complete the circle (see Figure 9.17). You have created an interesting pattern shape out of a single boring image. Not a bad trick! You can now select and delete your guidelines.

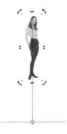

Figure 9.15
Draw two lines for reference and then change the bitmap's axis of rotation to be the point where the two lines cross.

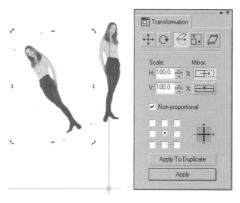

Figure 9.16
Use the Scale and Mirror options on the Transformation docker to duplicate and flip the bitmap. Then, rotate the duplicate 30 degrees by holding down the Ctrl key while dragging a rotation arrow.

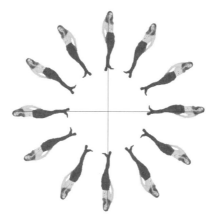

Figure 9.17
Repeat the duplicate-and-rotate process to create a ring.

8. Use the Ellipse tool to draw a circle shape and then send it To Back (Shift+PgDn).

9. Use the Interactive Fill tool to create a custom color blend.

10. Drag from the center of the circle outward and then click on Radial Fountain Fill on the Property Bar.

11. Click and drag the yellow color chip from the on-screen color palette to the center point on the interactive fill and then release it. You can drag and drop colors anywhere along the interactive fill control line to create a cascade of different colors (see Figure 9.18).

Figure 9.18
Use the Interactive Fill tool to create a brilliant custom color blend.

12. Create a fountain fill that goes from black to cyan to magenta to yellow. The redundant black points along the color blend are included to control how and where the circle fades to black. Because this object rests on a black background, without the extra points for the black the transition would be harsh and noticeable.

13. To make the models appear to be standing on the earth, Import (Ctrl+I) a bitmap of the earth from the \Objects\misc\ directory on the CorelDRAW clip-art CD-ROM. Arrange the globe behind the models, so that they seem to be standing on the earth (see Figure 9.19).

> **Note:** Use the Font List on the Property Bar to find a new typestyle (font). With your text selected, click on the current font name on the Property Bar to open the Font List. Now scroll through the list, using the pop-up sample as a visual reference to find and select a new typestyle.

Figure 9.19
Import a bitmap of the earth and arrange it behind the models to make them bigger than life.

14. Draw a black page-size rectangle and send it To Back (Shift+PgDn). Use the Text tool to set text elements around the background. (I used a font called Swis721 BlkEx BT with a gray-to-white radial fountain fill.)

15. After all the text is in place, Shift-select all the pieces, duplicate them (+ key), and use the Send Back One (Ctrl+PgDn) command. Enlarge the duplicate text shapes by dragging a corner sizing handle outward while holding down the Shift key. Give the duplicates no fill and a .023 magenta outline. One by one, arrange the word duplicates randomly around the originals (see Figure 9.20).

Figure 9.20
Set the main text elements on screen and duplicate them; then, enlarge, recolor, and scatter the duplicates.

16. Repeat the duplicate-and-scatter process two more times, each time choosing a different outline color. Scatter and enlarge these text objects even more for totally random size and placement. Don't worry if the text elements hang off the edge of the page boundary in your efforts to achieve the perfect balance of chaos (see Figure 9.21).

Figure 9.21

Duplicate, enlarge, and scatter the text objects a total of four times to create a really chaotic, energy-filled image.

17. Select All (Ctrl+A), and then hold down the Shift key and click on the black background box, which removes the box from the selection. Choose Effects|PowerClip|Place Inside Container and click on the black background box, to stuff everything inside the page limits. We'll call that controlled chaos.

You can see the results of this mayhem both in the color section and in the world.cdr file, located in the \Chapt09\ subdirectory on the companion CD-ROM. If you want to play with this image, you first need to select Effects|PowerClip|Extract. Then, you can see exactly how the Bitmap Color Mask tool works and how the custom color blend in the background circle is controlled with the multiple same-color nodes.

4X4X2

My taste in vehicles, much like my taste in art and music, has always been eclectic. I favor rugged-looking, square cars and trucks over the contemporary trend to make vehicles look like strange bulbous sea creatures! But that's just me. Figure 9.22 is an illustration that I did of a modern-day vehicle that has the classic look that I like. To broaden my design horizons I scanned and converted the illustration into CorelDRAW objects by using the Trace program. The results are crisp and detailed, and the perfect subject to illustrate several computer design tricks.

Because the vehicle now is a collection of CorelDRAW objects instead of a photograph, you can make the vehicle any color that you choose and place it in any location that you wish. You can also easily duplicate the image, flip-flop it to create the illusion of a reflection in water (as in Figure 9.22), or exploit any of the double-vision techniques.

Taking the reflection a step further, by converting the artwork into a bitmap you can add a rippling effect, and any other artistic interpretations that you wish to undertake. Here is how to get the reflecting-water effect:

1. Start with the image that you want to reflect. (It can be a collection of CorelDRAW objects, as my example is, or a scan of a photograph or any other bitmap—it doesn't matter.) Select all of your objects and open the Transformation docker (Alt+F9), then click the Scale and Mirror button. Click on the Vertical option, toggle the bottom-center checkbox in the placement grid, and click on Apply To Duplicate. This creates a flip-flopped duplicate aligned directly beneath the original (see Figure 9.23).

Figure 9.22
Using a rasterized version of your original artwork, you can get a reflection-in-water look by using bitmap filters.

 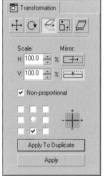

Figure 9.23
The Scale and Mirror options in the Transformation docker can duplicate and flip your artwork in a single step.

2. With your duplicates still selected, choose Bitmaps|Convert to Bitmap (unless your original object was already a bitmap, in which case your duplicate is also a bitmap, so you can skip to Step 3). Set the Color to RGB, because some filter effects (especially third-party filters, such as Kai's Power Tools, Alien Skin, and so forth) don't work on CMYK color images. Set the Resolution to what you need for your project (generally, 300 dpi for print, 72 dpi for on-screen applications), enable the Anti-Aliasing and Use Color Profile checkboxes, and then click on OK.

3. With your duplicate now a bitmap, you can take advantage of the filters under the Bitmaps menu. Select Bitmaps|Creative|Smoked Glass to modify the bitmap coloring to look more like a water reflection. In the Smoked Glass dialog box, click on Color and then select a turquoise color from the pop-up palette. Click on the Preview button to see what the image will look like, and use the Tint and

Blurring sliders to modify the results, checking the impact each time with Preview. When satisfied, click on OK to transform your bitmap (see Figure 9.24).

Figure 9.24
The Smoked Glass bitmap filter shades the duplicate to look like a reflection in water.

4. To add a ripple to the water, select Bitmaps|Distort|Ripple (imagine that!). The default Ripple settings are a bit dramatic for our purposes, so modify the parameters in the Ripple dialog box. Enable the Distort Ripple and Perpendicular Wave options. Increase the Period setting to 53, and set both Amplitude settings to 2. Click on the Preview button to test the settings. If you like what you see, click on OK; if you don't like the result, continue to modify the settings until you do (see Figure 9.25).

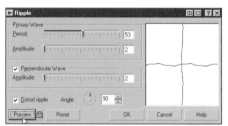

Figure 9.25
Use the Ripple bitmap distortion filter to add subtle motion to your water reflection.

5. Arrange your bitmap behind the original (Shift+PgDn), and you have your reflection effect.

You can see the finished results in this book's color section, and in the rover.cdr file in the \Chapt09\ subdirectory of the companion CD-ROM. This is a quick and easy way to double the size of an original, as in this example, where I eventually went on to place some ad copy over the reflection image. Because the parent image consists of CorelDRAW objects, and the duplication/reflection technique is so simple, you can just smile and nod happily when the client asks "Can we change the color of the car from yellow to red?"

Beyond f/x

Double-vision techniques such as those in this chapter are a great short-cut, or trick, to make a little bit of artwork go a long way. Often, you are faced with a situation in which you have painfully little original source material but plenty of space to fill. This technique enables you to get away with using the same image in the background and as the primary image in the foreground. Even if you have other options, it is a great trick and looks nice. It also doubly emphasizes the subject, but not in a harsh or even obvious way, which is a great sales and marketing tool. Product catalogs, brochures, and other support materials can benefit from the foreground/background treatment of the same subject. Another great use of the double-vision technique (if you have the resources) is to use the same subject viewed from two different angles.

Using multiple copies of the same text is also a very popular design theme. With a master set of text in place to get the message across, you are free to experiment with duplicates of the same words. Enlarging, fading, and blurring the duplicates adds visual interest and subtle emphasis without having to worry about legibility or content, because the original text is still in place. This is especially true with animation because you can have the duplicate text flying around to create a unique and atten-tion-gaining graphic. The possibilities are literally quite dizzying—you don't need bifocals to take advantage of double-vision!

Moving On

In this chapter we explored ways to expand the use of a single piece of art, from a boring solo flight to a total visual barrage. By using dupli-cates, the original artwork becomes interesting background material and other design elements are used to flesh out and augment an otherwise potentially dull or inappropriate graphic. This technique is more than practical because most designers are often called upon to make some-thing mundane look totally exciting. Our studio came by such wonderful design challenges as making bronzed turds (no joke) look interesting!

Using a lens object to change the way that things behind it look is an-other technique that has a lot of potential and is almost exclusive to CorelDRAW. From the obvious and predictable use of the Transparency lens to lighten or darken objects, to the seemingly bright and random results with the Custom Color Map, you have plenty of room for experi-mentation (the final image in this book's color section gets its wild coloring by using the Heat Map lens). These lenses also provide a great way to add color to a grayscale image that you would otherwise have to leave gray. Of course, I love lenses because they do so much with so very little actual work. How else could you take a low-quality black-and-white image brought to you by a client and actually use it in a color brochure?

From double-vision, we move on to even more bizarre tricks to play on your eyeballs. With the CorelDRAW rendering engines doing all the work, creating dizzying artwork reminiscent of the '60s psychedelic movement is easy. So throw in a Hendrix CD, plug in the lava lamp, and grab those rose-colored glasses, 'cuz we are getting into the groove, baby!

PSYCHEDELIC MIND TRIPS AND OTHER EYE CANDY

10

This chapter uses the Blend feature to create multiple copies of an object, which then are used to create bright pattern effects.

In today's chaotic climate, getting your audience's attention and pulling them into your design is harder than ever. With millions of bits of information from other sources bombarding a potential reader, your printed art, with nothing but visual tricks, must somehow stand up and scream "read me!" Creating art that is interesting enough to accomplish this isn't an easy task, but it is very possible. We have already covered many techniques that are anything but boring.

One great attention-getting device borrows from ideas that originated during the psychedelic '60s, techniques that use high-contrast coloring and dizzying patterns to create bright and, above all, interesting graphics that are impossible to ignore. The look isn't always appropriate, but when it is, it's as subtle as a car crash, with the same attention-gaining effect.

In this chapter we'll look at different ways to create attention-grabbing graphics, using a variety of dazzling techniques. The first example uses the Blend function to create multiple-outline shapes that, when combined, create dizzying patterns of light and dark colors. We look at how this technique can be custom-tailored to any shape, making it an ideal base for an advertisement. Then, we finish things off with a laser light show, again using blends, but taking advantage of the rotation options. Hope you aren't prone to motion sickness.

Figure 10.1
You can use any shape, including those custom fit to a specific application, to generate the pieces for a dazzling psychedelic effect.

Tripping Adtastic

It's the summer of love, man, with peace, happiness, joy, and the best deals in town on cellular phones. Come on down! Even something as boring as a phone suddenly looks darn interesting when it is at the center of the eye-grabbing pattern in Figure 10.1.

Using the phone object as the basis for a curve drawn by hand in CorelDRAW, you open the door to wild, eye-catching effects. Once you have the phone curve, you can create multiple copies with either the Interactive Contour tool or the Interactive Blend tool, and from there get psychedelic by using the Combine command. Here is how to create a custom shape and then create the dazzling, high-contrast checkered illusion:

1. Import the image to which you want to draw attention. You can use the Acquire command to use a photo from your digital camera or scanner, or find and Import (Ctrl+I) a piece of clip-art, as I did. I found the phone on the CorelDRAW clip-art CD-ROM, in the \objects\bus-equi (business equipment) directory. The nice thing about the images in the objects directory is that they are free-floating with transparent backgrounds so that you can stick them anywhere.

2. Use the Bezier tool to click along the edge of the phone from point to point, creating a simple, straight-line outline of the phone, starting and stopping in the same point to create a solid object (if you don't create a solid object, click on Auto-Close Curve on the Property Bar). Go back with the Shape tool and use the Property Bar options to convert lines to curves, to smooth out the edges for a smoother curve.

3. Shrink the phone outline until it is really small, duplicate it (using the + key), and enlarge the duplicate to the edge of your page. Select both outlines and drag the Interactive Blend tool between them. Use the Property Bar to set the steps to 10, resulting in the outline shown in Figure 10.2.

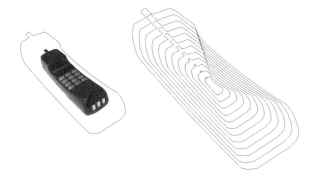

Figure 10.2
Use the Bezier tool to draw a simplified outline of the target image. A large and small duplicate of the outline are blended together.

4. Freeze the blend with the Arrange|Separate and Arrange|Ungroup All commands, and then combine (Ctrl+L) the pieces into a single curve (see Figure 10.3). Things are already getting interesting!

5. For an even more interesting effect, add a sunburst to draw the eye to the center of the graphic. Draw a perfect circle by holding down the Ctrl key as you drag the Ellipse tool. Use the Shape tool to transform the circle into just a "pizza slice" sliver, by dragging the control node to the inside of the ellipse, again while holding down the Ctrl

ON-THE-FLY TRACING

If you have a bitmap selected (such as the phone object in this example), and then choose the Freehand tool, you can perform automatic tracing functions directly within CorelDRAW. With the bitmap selected, click on the Freehand tool, move it to the left of the object, and then click. CorelDRAW now scans to the right, following along the first dark pixels that it comes across, and attempts to create a shape. You can attempt to fine-tune the results by right-clicking over the Freehand tool and modifying the Properties. Decreasing the Autotrace tracking and Corner Threshold values makes for tighter tracing. This feature really only works well with high-contrast photos, but it can usually provide a shape that, at the very least, is a good starting point, which you can then clean up with the Shape tool.

Figure 10.3

Separating the pieces in the blend and then combining them into one curve creates the fill/open pattern unique to this effect.

Figure 10.4

Dragging the control node on an ellipse with the Shape tool can transform it into a "pizza slice" object.

key (see Figure 10.4). Holding down the Ctrl key constrains the movement of the control nodes with the Shape tool to 15-degree increments, but you can obtain smaller sliver shapes by eyeballing it without using the Ctrl key.

6. Double-click on this object to reveal the rotation handles and rotation axis (the small circle in the center of your object). Drag the rotation axis point, again while holding down the Ctrl key, down to the bottom-right point of your slice. Drag a top-corner rotation handle to the right, while holding down the Ctrl handle. This snaps the rotation in 15-degree increments, so you can easily rotate the object 30 degrees. Before you release the left-mouse button, right-click to duplicate the slice. This leaves you with two copies of the slice, as shown in Figure 10.5.

Figure 10.5

Changing the axis of rotation enables you to spin around a slice in a circular fashion, and right-clicking before you release duplicates the object in one step.

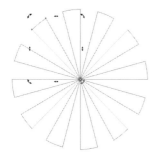

Figure 10.6

The Repeat command quickly creates a sun-burst, by duplicating/rotating the slice shape with a single keyboard shortcut (Ctrl+R).

7. With the duplicate/rotate move your last action, using the Repeat command (Ctrl+R) creates another ray of the starburst, in the desired position. Use the Repeat command a total of ten times, to spin rays into a complete circle (see Figure 10.6). The more rays that you create, the busier your design will be. For a really dizzying sunburst, use smaller slices (don't hold down the Ctrl key) and more of them. Being an extremist, I used many, smaller slices for a dizzying effect.

8. Select all the sunburst pieces and combine them (Ctrl+L). Place the sunburst so that its center is at the center of the phone, to ensure that all eyes are drawn there. Select both the sun ray and the phone curve graphic from Step 4 and combine them (see Figure 10.7). Bang! Right between the eyes. This technique could sell ice to Eskimos.

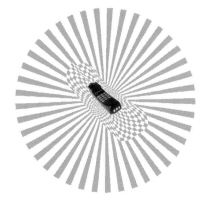

Figure 10.7
Combine the sunburst with the phone curve to create a dizzying pattern.

9. Use the Rectangle tool to draw a box the size of your page and then arrange the box around your artwork. Select all of your objects (Ctrl+A), but hold down the Shift key and deselect the page-limit rectangle that you just drew. Choose Effects|PowerClip|Place Inside Container. Click on the arrow on your page-limit rectangle to stuff all the sunburst pieces into the rectangle. With all the pieces stuffed neatly into the page limit, add some text and call it a day.

The image is exploding in this book's color section and in the phone.cdr file in the \Chapt10\ subdirectory on the companion CD-ROM. If you want to manipulate the pieces in this file, remember that you first have to extract the contents from the PowerClip (Effects|PowerClip|Extract Contents). You can select the sunburst curve, break it apart, delete the phone pieces, and steal the spokes for your own designs. Images like this that just suck your eye to the center are perfect for drawing attention to objects that fail to excite on their own.

As another bonus, the high-contrast and effective attention-getting design is perfect for low- or no-color print applications. The graphic in the color section would be just as effective if printed only in yellow and black (the phone does have some other colors in it, but they are not critical to the success of the design). You have to remember that back in the '60s when this kind of graphic was in its heyday, printing technology was low-tech, so simple one- and two-color designs were very popular—and more cost-effective. You can exploit these savings today, as well. Frugality is not an anachronistic concept.

Laser Specialties

Often associated with space scenes, laser beams also make interesting design elements by themselves. A crisp, single-colored line, blended with others, creates a dazzling light show. In the example in Figure 10.8, the

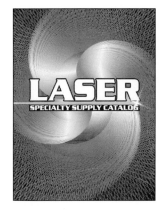

Figure 10.8
The Blend function creates not only the round laser beam, but also the background pattern and even the exploding sparkle.

busy colors of the background are a result of a blend of simple outlines, whereas the laser in the center uses the thick-to-thin-line blend technique. The center laser acts as a baseline for the text to rest on, and the blast offers a point of visual interest to draw attention to the text—no easy task in this busy sea of laser light! As they say in the laser industry, "Avoid looking into bright light with your remaining eye." Here is how to create a laser beam and sparkle effects:

1. Draw a straight line with a quick click at the starting point and the ending point with the Bezier tool. Give this line a thick .08-inch magenta outline from the Outline Pen dialog box (F12). Duplicate it (+ key) and make the duplicate a white .003-inch hairline, again from the Outline Pen dialog box. Select both and drag on them with the Interactive Blend tool, to create the round-looking laser beam (see Figure 10.9). No sweat.

Figure 10.9

Blend a thick, pink line to a thin, white one to create a rounded laser beam.

2. The sparkle in the artwork is a series of blend steps, similar to the explosions in Chapter 2. Open the Symbols and Special Characters docker, either from the Window menu or with the keyboard shortcut (Ctrl+F11). Change to the Stars1 symbol library, scroll through the gallery to locate the four-pointed star, and then drag it onto the desktop. This little shape plays a big role in this design (see Figure 10.10).

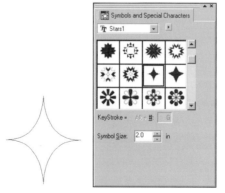

Figure 10.10

The Symbols and Special Characters docker is a valuable source of cool predrawn shapes.

3. With the Ellipse tool, draw a tiny circle. Duplicate it (+) and drag the duplicate off to the right.

4. With the Interactive Blend tool, drag between the two objects to create a blend group. Press Esc to deselect the blend, and then shift-select just

the original control circles. Align these control curves on top of one another by using the keyboard shortcuts (press C to Center horizontally and E to Center vertically). The blend pieces appear as a single object, with all the elements stacked on top of one another.

5. Press Esc to select nothing, and then drag-select the circle blend group (clicking on the stack selects only the control curve closest to you, which isn't what you want to do).

6. On the Interactive Blend Tool Property Bar, click on Path Properties and then click on New Path. Click on the star curve to run the circles along the edge of the shape. Click on Miscellaneous Blend Options and enable Blend Along Full Path. Increase the Number of steps option to 50 to create a pattern of circles along the star shape (see Figure 10.11).

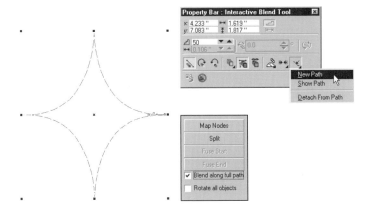

Figure 10.11
A star becomes the blend path for a series of little circles.

7. Select the blend and separate the pieces with the Arrange|Separate and Arrange|Ungroup All commands. Hold down the Shift key to deselect the star control curve, and then Group the circles (Ctrl+G).

8. Duplicate the circles (+), ungroup them (Ctrl+U), and then align them center to center (press the C and E keys). This makes them look like a small dot, which is actually a stack of 52 circles.

GIVE ME THE SYMBOLS

Not all of the symbols are installed during the Typical installation of CorelDRAW. To add more symbols or fonts, you need to call upon Win98/NT. Choose Start|Settings|Control Panel. In the Control Panel, click on the Fonts folder. Then, choose File|Install New Font. Locate the \fonts\ folder on your CorelDRAW 9 installation CD-ROM, where you'll also find the \symbols\ttf\ folder. Inside this folder you can select any of the available Symbols sets (including Stars1 and Stars2). Select the library that you want to install, and click on OK. This library now should appear in the Symbols and Special Characters docker.

9. Group these circles again (Ctrl+G) and then click on the white color chip in the on-screen color palette, to color this group of circles. Align the center stack in the center of the star shape.

10. Drag between the outside and inside circle groups with the Interactive Blend tool, to create a star burst. To give a tighter cluster of objects in the center of the blend, drag the Object Acceleration slider to the right. Pow! You have the star burst (see Figure 10.12).

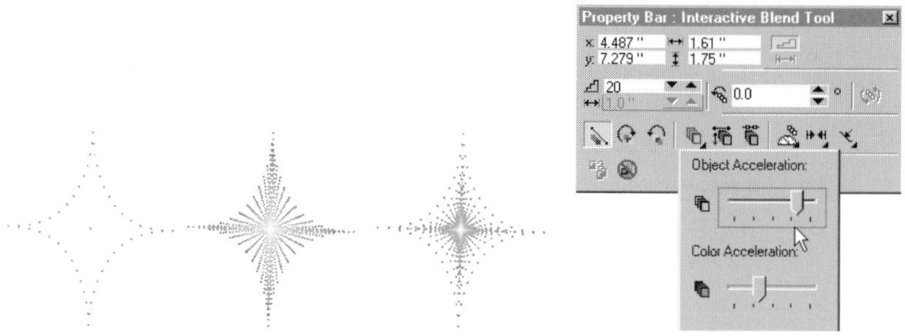

Figure 10.12

The Interactive Blend tool creates a burst by blending together the two circle groups. The Object Acceleration slider changes the blend to cluster objects closer to the center.

For the background image, you need the same star shape that you used for the burst; however, this time it will be the blend object itself rather than a blend path. Here is how to create the laser light-show background:

1. Use the star curve from the previous steps, or just grab it off the Symbols and Special Characters docker again. Double-click on the star, and drag the corner rotation handles to spin the star 45 degrees.

2. Click on the shape again to activate the sizing handles, and drag to enlarge the star way beyond the size of your page. Duplicate the star and reduce the duplicate to just a small dot in the center of the page. Shift-select both star curves and give them a .022-inch cyan outline (or as thick or thin as you wish) from the Outline Pen dialog box (F12).

3. Drag the Interactive Blend tool between the two star curves, to create a blend group. On the Property Bar, increase the Number Of Steps setting to 300.

4. To get that great spinning effect, change the Blend Direction value to 360 degrees. To get the wonderful rainbow coloring, click on Clockwise Blend on the Property Bar (see Figure 10.13). Better than a laser light show, and no parking hassles.

That's the whole process! As with the last tutorial, add a page-limit rectangle, select all (Ctrl+A), and PowerClip everything into the rectangle. Add your text, if any (I used a font called Serpentine), send your client a

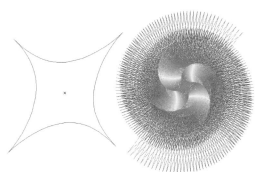

Figure 10.13

The Interactive Blend Property Bar, with 360-degrees rotation and the rainbow function enabled, creates a laser light-show blend between the two star shapes.

fat bill, and call it a day. The laser light show is starring in the color section and in the lasers.cdr file found in the \Chapt10\ subdirectory on the companion CD-ROM. Open the file and play with the laser blend for your own personal light show. For even more rotation, select either the outside or inside control curve and spin it manually.

Beyond f/x

Explosive, bright designs such as those developed in this chapter help to draw attention because of high contrast, both within the designs themselves and in a broader sense. Things naturally stand out when they are different, so for a market that is normally sedate, a bright, fun graphic might work really well. However, these images might actually look boring and ordinary in a demographic that's already suffering a glut of visual noise. Research your market so that you know whether the design is right for it, or inappropriate because of the shock value.

Almost anything can benefit from a bit of eye-blasting imagery now and then. A graphic using these techniques could draw attention to new products in an ad or to new pages in a Web site. The techniques work equally well as primary design elements or as secondary pieces such as borders or edge designs. Promotional materials, such as stickers, T-shirts, and buttons, can push design limits and benefit greatly from a violently interesting graphic that won't go unnoticed. Perhaps you could take the idea too far, though. Is a dizzying billboard that literally stops traffic a bad design? Hmmm.

Moving On

In this chapter, we looked at creating bright and bold designs using CorelDRAW. We again saw how the Blend docker can be used to create all kinds of shapes, including the simple, the mechanical, and the downright dizzying.

The examples in this chapter were extreme and used many bright colors. You can use the same kinds of techniques to get much more subtle images for more conservative designs, with muted or limited number of colors. Remember not to get carried away trying to make your artwork as loud or garish as possible, if it isn't appropriate for the task at hand. A portfolio full of loud, jarring images might appeal to record companies, but probably won't get you an account with the Fortune 500, button-down crowd.

In the next chapter, we look at how to use CorelDRAW to create comic-book heroes and heroines. We examine how to use the program to colorize ink drawings, and see that anyone can create fun and interesting cartoon characters right in CorelDRAW. Hey, I understand that not everyone is an illustrator, but I refuse to believe that you don't possess the talent necessary to create amazing artwork with CorelDRAW. You've hung in there so far—either because you have some talent or because you are some huge masochist! In either case, it's time to get into the funny pages.

COMIC BOOK HEROES

11

This chapter shows you how to create comic characters and backgrounds entirely within CorelDRAW, and how to use scanned images of hand-drawn illustrations to create bright, dynamic artwork that has a hand-drawn look and feel.

Nothing is more representative of Americana than the Sunday comic strips. These colorful and fun images have made their way out of the comic strips and into virtually every other type of media. From Roy Lichtenstein's fine art renderings of comic-style images to television commercials featuring animated cartoon characters, this style of art continues to grow in popularity.

CorelDRAW offers a flexible digital workspace that will appeal to both computer-based and pen-and-ink artists for creating stunning comic-book-style artwork. In fact, increasingly more commercially successful comic strip artists are using the computer as their medium of choice, because of the design flexibility and the thousands of nifty fonts to use for thought balloons.

For computer artists, CorelDRAW makes creating characters easy, with the ability to use common shapes augmented by flexible fill options. For traditional pen-and-ink artists, CorelDRAW offers tools for colorizing hand-drawn sketches and for creating complex scenes for their comic book characters, ranging from impressionistic to high tech. The modern virtual studio of CorelDRAW offers more flexibility than the traditional tools, enabling an artist to change and experiment with different scenes, colors, and poses quickly and easily. Art boards are out, my friend. Grab an accelerated, high-resolution video board with about 12MB of RAM instead.

This chapter shows you how to create comic-book-type characters and scenes by using CorelDRAW. We start by creating and coloring simple cartoon characters and a background for them, quickly and completely in CorelDRAW. This is a relatively simple skill that you can use to liven up all sorts of designs with minimal effort. Next, we use CorelDRAW to colorize hand-drawn and scanned artwork. You not only learn how to create a scene for hand-drawn artwork, but also learn one of my many techniques for making that scene look hand-drawn to match the artwork.

Finally, we walk through a more complex example of colorizing hand-drawn artwork and creating a dynamic high-tech scene around it. This example uses several techniques covered earlier in the book, most notably blends and repeating images. CorelDRAW really works well for cartooning and this style of artwork, so this will be a fun chapter!

Game Over

I'm amazed at how many people deny having any artistic skills. "I can only draw stick figures," people tell me when I show them some art piece that I'm working on. I don't buy this. You don't have to be dripping with talent to be a good artist; you just have to learn how to use the tools that you have available and be patient enough to work out any design problems that arise.

Take me, for example. Personally, I think I'm a lousy artist compared to my gifted associates. What my artist friends can render in one simple step takes me hours to sketch out in pencil and then ink up as line art. This is where CorelDRAW becomes the perfect creative medium for me. What I lack in talent I make up for in creativity and tenacity. I don't have to be able to draw a straight line or perfect circle—CorelDRAW does it for me. If I'm not happy with the way that a design is laid out, I can easily resize, rearrange, re-everything in CorelDRAW. It may take me a little longer, but with a little effort I can get the results that I want. I'm confident that you can too.

With very simple shapes, you can create some fun comic characters (see Figure 11.1, for example). Even the most gifted artists start with simple shapes and move on from there. The same techniques apply to creating comic characters, which can be as simple or as complex as you want. In any case, even if you stick with the simplest of shapes, you can get some pretty fun and animated characters with just a little effort. Here is how to make fun comic characters using only CorelDRAW objects:

Figure 11.1
Anyone can create comic characters in CorelDRAW using simple geometric shapes.

1. We'll start first with the girl. With the Ellipse tool, draw a circle for the head. Then, use the Ellipse tool again to draw an oval for an eye. You can freehand draw the other eye, but I like to keep things symmetrical by duplicating objects (+ key) and then moving the duplicates into place by using the Pick tool. Remember, you can always toggle between the Pick tool and the active tool by tapping the spacebar.

2. Switch to the Bezier tool and click below the character's head to create a pyramid-like object for the torso. If you don't start and stop in the same place, the object will be an open curve. Click on Auto-Close Curve on the Property Bar to convert an open path into a solid object.

3. Continue to use the Bezier tool to click around and make a skirt shape. Then, create some pointy triangles for the legs. It's easy, huh? Create the left and right arms, which require a little more attention. Finally, use the Ellipse tool to draw in other details, such as ear pieces (see Figure 11.2).

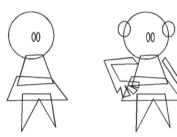

Figure 11.2
The Ellipse tool draws great circles, whereas the Bezier tool easily draws straight-lined objects with single clicks from point to point.

4. Draw more circles to fill in details, such as the shoulders and big poofy hair. To speed things up and keep everything symmetrical, duplicate like object shapes (such as ears, hair, and so on) and flip-flop the duplicate horizontally by dragging a left-center sizing handle to the right while holding down the Ctrl key. You should start to see the girl figure emerge from the simple shapes (see Figure 11.3).

Figure 11.3
Duplicate and flip-flop objects to speed things along, and keep the like object pairs symmetrical.

5. Our figure looks very much like a stick person, or robot, which is fine, but I like my cartoons more gooey. With the Shape tool, select an object, such as an arm or leg, drag-select all the nodes, and use the node-edit features on the Property Bar. Click on Convert Line To Curve and then click on Make Node Smooth. This converts the straight and pointy objects into mushy sausages (see Figure 11.4).

6. Fine-tune the objects with the Shape tool. Some pieces, such as the feet, need to have the nodes changed back to cusps, so that you can make them pointy again. You can get carried away, as I do, massaging the pieces until you get them just right. Start to fill the pieces with colors and arrange them in front and behind each other, to make the girl come to life (see Figure 11.5).

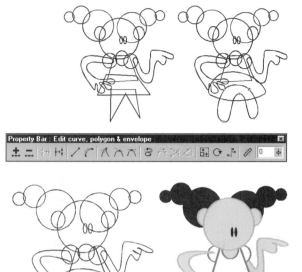

Figure 11.4
Use the node-edit features on the Property Bar to convert the lines to curves and smooth out the nodes.

Figure 11.5
The Shape tool makes fine-tuning the objects easy, so that you can get the exact lines and curves that you want. Assign outline and fill colors to change the wireframe objects into solid objects.

7. To add pieces such as the hair and the socks, don't try to draw objects that fit together, because that takes too long. Draw a simple object with the Freehand tool and then use the Arrange|Shaping|Intersect command to create a new object where the two overlap. This way, you can quickly create custom-fit pieces for many details (see Figure 11.6).

Figure 11.6
Use the Shaping|Intersection feature to create new shapes where objects overlap, for such things as socks and hair.

8. Add small details, such as circles for gleam shapes and fingernails, to finish up the girl character.

9. For the boy, first I used the Freehand tool to draw the pieces, and then I cleaned things up by using the Shape tool and node-edit options on the Property Bar. Which tool you are more comfortable working with will depend on how adept you are at using the mouse. My Freehand mouse shapes looked darned pathetic until I cleaned

them up with the Shape tool. Once again, by using the Intersection tool, big, simple shapes, such as the circles, trim down nicely to become hair and other objects (see Figure 11.7).

10. Color and stack the pieces like you did with the girl. For the pants, open the Pattern Fill dialog box from the Fill flyout. Click the down arrow next to the current pattern to open the gallery of patterns, and select the 2-Color checker pattern. Click on the Front color chip and change it to red, and then click on OK to fill (see Figure 11.8).

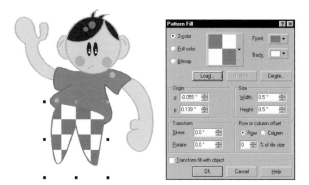

Characters alone aren't very interesting; they need to be in a scene. For these simple characters, I thought a video-game-type scenario would work well. Here is how to create an abstract, high-tech scene for simple comic characters:

1. Use the Rectangle tool to draw a horizontal rectangle, and then use the Shape tool to round the corners.

2. Duplicate this object many times and arrange the duplicates randomly, varying the height and width of each copy. Fill some of the objects, and leave others with no fill and a heavy .40-inch outline. For an interesting look, I used three shades of blue for all the outline and fill attributes. When you use the same color for a fill in one object and the outline in another, the point where they overlap disappears.

9. For the target shapes in the background, first draw a circle and use the downsize/duplicate right-mouse trick to create a series of four circles. Draw lines for crosshairs, and add text to designate values for the rings. Drag-select the entire bunch and combine them (Ctrl+L). Use the skew arrows to distort the target (see Figure 11.26).

Figure 11.26
Circles become a target object with the addition of crosshairs and text.

10. Select the target curve and give it a magenta outline with no fill. Duplicate it (+ key), move the duplicate down, and give it a unique outline color. Repeat the process to build a tower of targets, like some high-tech 3D map (see Figure 11.27).

11. The little crosshair grid is simply an *x* blended to a duplicate across the page. When you freeze this blend (Arrange|Separate), you can blend it again to a duplicate on the other side of the page. I also used this method to create the grid of squares. You can also use the Graph Paper tool, located in the Polygon tool flyout, to make grids on the page (see Chapter 17 for more information).

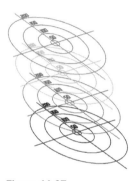

Figure 11.27
Duplicates of the target shape stack to suggest 3D space.

12. Right-click to open the Properties dialog box for the Graph Paper tool, and type the number of cells for the grid's width and height. Then, click-drag to create a graph-paper object (see Figure 11.28).

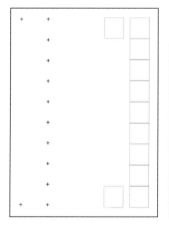
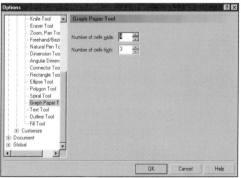

Figure 11.28
Blending objects creates even-spaced patterns for the x and square grid elements. You can also use the Graph Paper tool to create grids.

13. While working on this project, I really wanted some sort of Japanese writing on it. I called my friend in San Francisco, and she faxed me the characters, which I digitized directly by using a fax-modem. I used the Corel Trace utility to trace the objects (which spell out

"Sword of Beauty"), but I was unhappy with how thin they were. By using a thick .055-inch outline, I got the width that I wanted (see Figure 11.29).

Figure 11.29

Corel Trace can convert bitmaps from any source, including fax/modems, into vector artwork. The thin characters were beefed up with a heavy line weight.

14. Arrange the characters and other design elements to create a busy image that creates a mood of urgency and excitement. To add more depth, layer objects, such as pieces of the grid, in front of and behind the main character shape. Draw a rectangle for the page limit and send it to the back.

15. Open the Texture Fill dialog box from the Fill tool flyout. In the Samples 9 Texture Library, locate Wood Grain in the Texture List. Change the mineral colors from the default greens to dark blue and pink, again. This creates interesting visual noise in the background (See Figure 11.30).

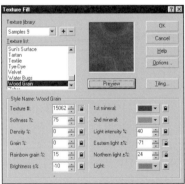

Figure 11.30

Use the Texture Fill dialog box to create a customized pattern by changing the color chips.

16. Depending on the amount of chaos you want in your scene, you can add more elements. I added straight dotted lines. You can make any outline a dotted line by changing the Style option in the Outline Pen dialog box (F12).

You can view the finished poster in this book's color section or in the companion CD-ROM's sword.cdr file in the \Chapt11\ subdirectory. This image includes so much action that would be too tedious to draw by hand, yet it still retains the look of a real cartoon because the main character started as an ink illustration.

More and more, I mix and match media to create the images that I dream up. The computer affords so many design opportunities that would be far too tedious to do by hand. For example, choose Bitmaps|Plug-Ins|Fancy|Terrazzo to open a dialog box in which you can convert a bitmap into a dizzying pattern design, which serves as a cool background variant (see Figure 11.31).

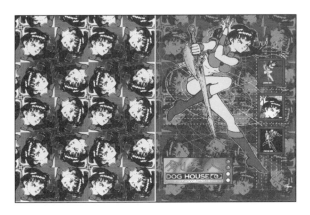

Figure 11.31

The Terrazzo bitmap filter creates patterns from your images.

Beyond f/x

The potential is endless for a computer-based comic strip. A black-and-white strip could be colorized (or vice versa) and the text converted into different typestyles, or even other languages. The same images for print can migrate into animations and Web sites, or pop up on merchandise—you name it. Beyond comic strips, the techniques for colorizing hand-drawn illustrations lend themselves to many applications. You could use a hand-drawn illustration as the basis for an advertisement, using the same kind of coloring techniques from this chapter, to avoid a cookie-cutter, computer-generated look. Using screen-captures to create additional artwork for a design is also a great way to milk more out of your design day without adding much effort (such as the double-vision techniques in Chapter 9). A background pattern based upon a screen capture (or a piece of a screen capture) adds a unique look to your design without adding much effort.

Moving On

In this chapter, we looked at mixing traditional ink illustrations with CorelDRAW objects. For all you nonillustrators, we looked at creating creatures and characters entirely within CorelDRAW, using simple shapes and geometric objects.

The great thing about assembling comic scenes in CorelDRAW is that you can then go beyond the static printed page right into action-media.

Because you can move and manipulate the characters within the scenes, you are only a heartbeat away from animating them. If you take the time to create multiple poses for the same character, you can then go right into animation mode. In fact, this new kind of computer animation is gaining in popularity, with a series already airing on cable.

In the next chapter, we continue to explore animated options and uses for CorelDRAW. In keeping with the low-tech/high-tech theme, we'll endeavor to create designs and images reminiscent of the middle-half of this century. Contemporary design tools such as CorelDRAW make creating crisp and visually engaging designs a snap, even for anachronistic images. So, crawl into your bomb shelter, grab a TV dinner, and get ready for a '50s flashback!

CORELDRAW 9
STUDIO

This color studio includes final images from all step-by-step projects in this book and a visual gallery to the best of the new bitmap effect filters found in CorelDRAW 9. All images are also available on this book's CD-ROM in CorelDRAW format, so you can "load and learn." Use this section for reference, inspiration, or as a quick guide to cool techniques outlined in this book. When you see something you like, point finger, exclaim "Cool!" then flip to the chapter that explains the process. Enjoy!

Using the Interactive Blend tool on two sets of circle shapes can result in dynamic explosion effects (Chapter 2).

Modifying the parameters of the "explosion" blend on the Interactive Blend Property Bar can transform the group into colorful spinning pinwheels (Chapter 2).

Changing the positions of control objects in an active blend group can give you comet tails or rocket trails (Chapter 2). High-step blends consisting of specially shaded circle objects can result in solid-looking tubes and tentacles (Chapter 16).

The Lighting, Shading, and Beveling options on the Interactive Extrude Property Bar transform flat shapes into cut- and carved-looking objects (Chapter 3).

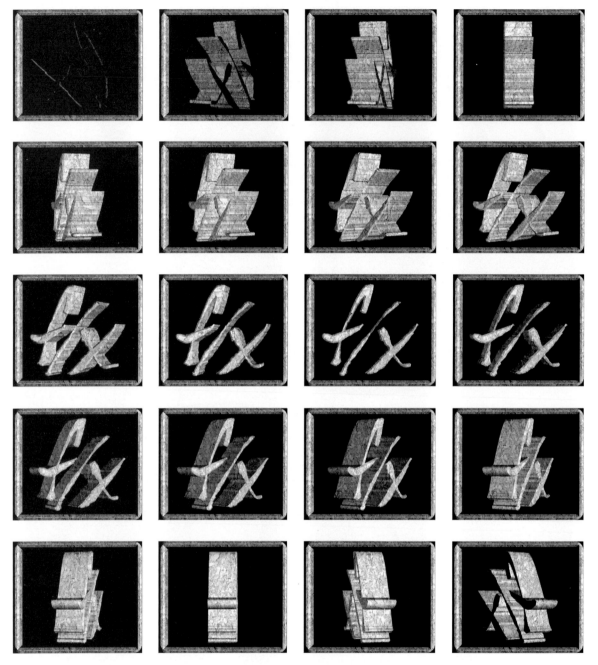

Modifying the Rotation parameters on the Interactive Extrude Property Bar can make objects appear to spin in space, an effect that lends itself well to animations for Web sites (Chapter 3).

Shading techniques, coupled with multiple outlines generated with the Interactive Contour tool, can give your text a flashy and bold look (Chapter 4). Converting the image to a bitmap allows for artistic manipulation through filter effects. The bottom image has the Wet Paint filter applied for a wet and drippy appearance without the hard edges of the original.

By converting vector objects into bitmaps directly within CorelDRAW, you can then exploit a new range of effects. The type was blurred to change the field of depth, while the PowerClip and Interactive Drop Shadow features create the "ghosted" look (Chapter 4).

The Interactive Transparency tool enables you to control the opacity of objects, while manipulation of the Interactive Drop Shadow feature can create a "glow" effect (Chapter 4).

Tattoo-inspired artwork is right at home in some designs, such as this music CD cover and logo for a surf-apparel company (Chapter 5).

Computer-aided design techniques enable you to add tattoo and piercing elements to your favorite digital victims, and even recolor hair and lips for a complete digital makeover (Chapter 5).

The addition of a "brand" transforms this clip-art image into an eye-catching advertisement (Chapter 5).

By modifying the focus of an image, you can redirect the reader's attention to any part of your design (Chapter 6).

Using skew and rotation techniques, you can place flat artwork into a 3D-looking orientation (Chapter 6).

Multistage blend techniques create round and shiny-looking objects, while selective blurring makes some details appear to leap off the page (Chapter 6).

Special PowerClip tricks automate the task of breaking an image into puzzle-like pieces (Chapter 7).

While the PowerClip feature makes stuffing images into puzzle-shapes easy, a few easy tricks in Photo-Paint add the finishing touch of a rounded bevel to these puzzle pieces (Chapter 7).

By creating snapshots of artwork in progress, you can easily create complex-looking optical illusions (Chapter 7).

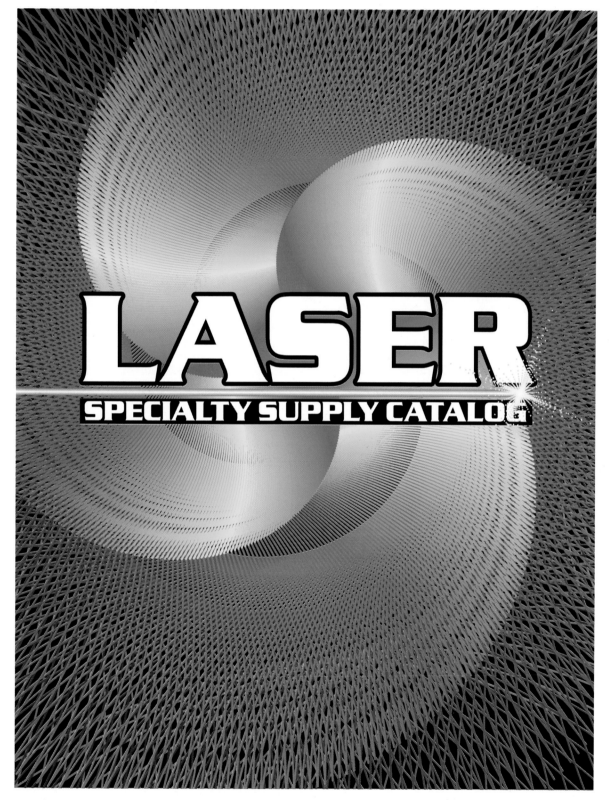

Modifying the parameters on the Interactive Blend Property Bar can create instant wins with colorful, dynamic images that are a snap to produce (Chapter 10).

Even the "artistically challenged" can create fresh and fun comic-book characters out of simple shapes. Lens and distortion effects "stick" images to cyber Silly Putty (Chapter 11).

Using simple techniques, you can easily combine hand-drawn characters in a computer scene that has been modified with bitmap filters, giving everything a "hand-drawn" feel (Chapter 11).

By converting hand-drawn images into CorelDRAW objects, you can easily colorize them and place the finished character in any computer-generated scenario (Chapter 11).

Taking design cues from the past, modern-day designers—armed with the speed and precision that technology offers—can quickly create clean and efficient designs (Chapter 12).

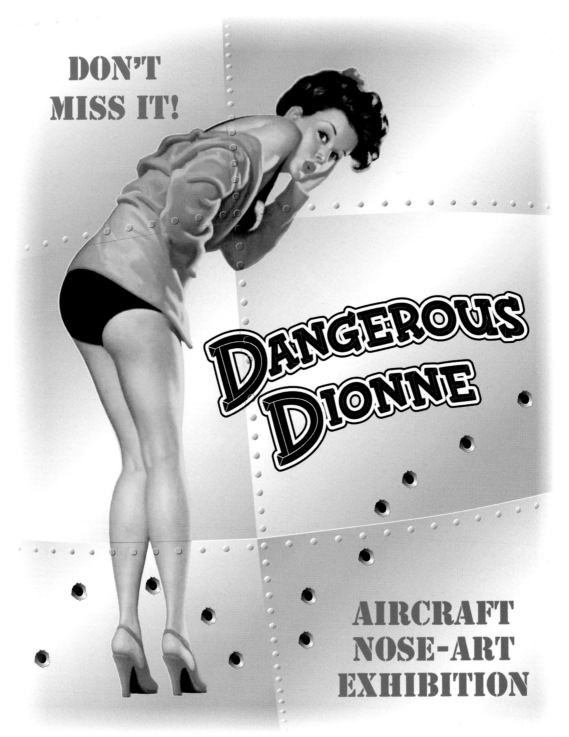

DON'T MISS IT!

DANGEROUS DIONNE

AIRCRAFT NOSE-ART EXHIBITION

Computerized tricks, such as bitmap color masks, "frozen" lens effects, and the Interactive Transparency tool features, come together to create an image reminiscent of the late '40s (Chapter 12).

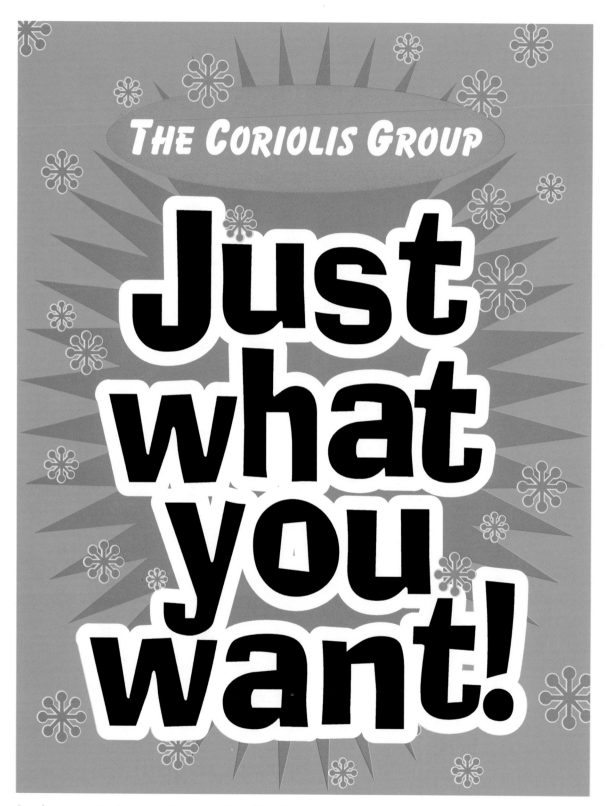

Simple, geometric shapes, bold text, and a quirky color scheme create a "retro" design, perfect for clients wanting a "flashback" feel (Chapter 12).

PowerClip tricks coupled with period-looking geometric shapes create another image perfect for the TV generation (Chapter 12).

Using a motif made popular by '70s-style household products, the Interactive Fill tool creates the bright fill effects with just a few mouse clicks (Chapter 13).

Combining contemporary design elements, including 3D-rendered images and strong geometric shapes, results in a contemporary image that is appealing to the video-game set (Chapter 13).

Combining hand-drawn cartoon characters with a computer-generated background and then "twisting" the combination with the Interactive Distortion tool creates a chaotic art nightmare (Chapter 13).

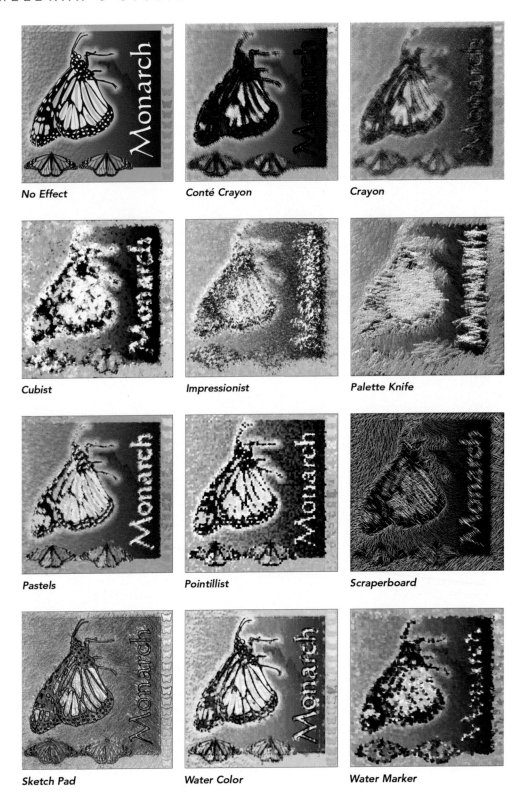

No Effect

Conté Crayon

Crayon

Cubist

Impressionist

Palette Knife

Pastels

Pointillist

Scraperboard

Sketch Pad

Water Color

Water Marker

This visual listing includes some of the more useful bitmap effects available within CorelDRAW and Photo-Paint, so that you can see what they do beforehand to make picking bitmaps more streamlined (Chapter 13).

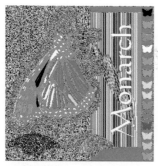

Bit Planes

Halftone

Psychedelic

Solarize

Find Edges

Crafts-Puzzle

Crystalize

Fabric-Needlepoint

Frame

Glass Block

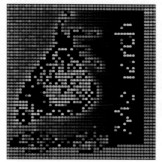

Kid's Play-Light Pegs

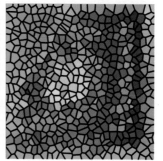

Stained Glass

Importing bitmaps into CorelDRAW has always been a snap, but with the addition of many artistic filter effects, you can follow any artistic impulse. New tools in CorelDRAW 9, such as the Object Sprayer and Interactive Mesh Fill tool, provide more creative control (Chapter 13).

The Interactive Blend tool can create gear shapes, which are then brought to life by using the Interactive Extrude tool (Chapter 16).

Gear shapes make interesting design elements, with their multiple spokes and mechanical appearance (Chapter 16).

CorelDRAW automates the tasks used to create repeated images, such as "tesselations" and other patterns using like shapes (Chapter 19).

Seamless tile designs, perfect for background tiles on Web pages, are easy to render once you understand the principle of "hiding the repeat" (Chapter 19).

The flexibility of the CorelDRAW workspace is perfect for designing and building a Web site, such as this home-page mockup. You can then export the images individually or perform a quick screen capture to get only the pieces that you need (Chapter 20).

You can design the graphical elements for a Web site in CorelDRAW and then assemble the pages by using traditional HTML programming, as in the top example. Or, you can use the Publish To Internet features to generate a Web page directly from your CorelDRAW file, as in the bottom example (Chapter 20).

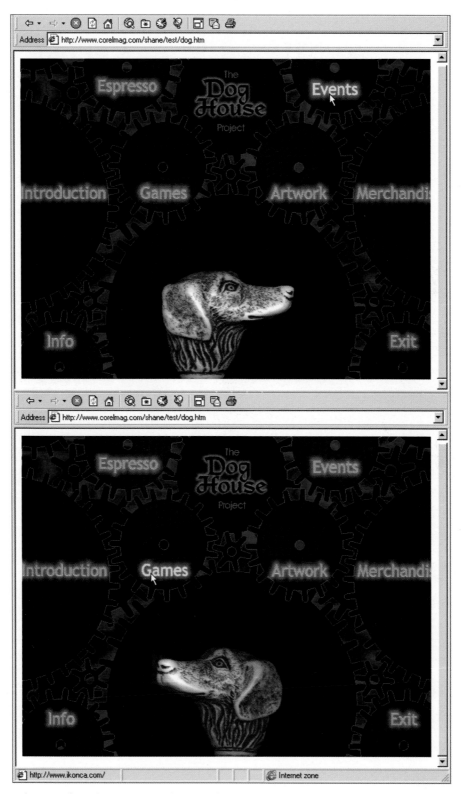

CorelDRAW makes interface design easy with cut-and-paste compatibility between applications. You can build your artwork in CorelDRAW and then port it effortlessly to another application builder, such as Macromedia Director, which was used to bring to life this information kiosk design (Chapter 20).

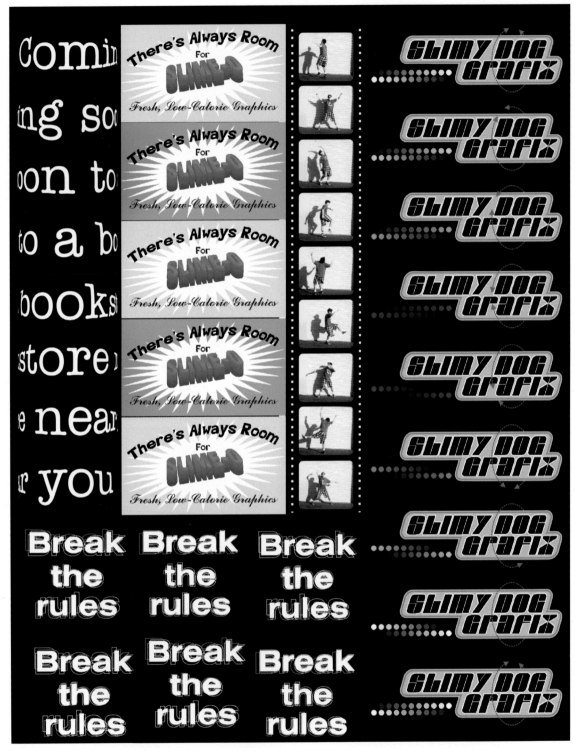

You can generate multiple cells for an animation in CorelDRAW and then build and give the animation life in Photo-Paint (Chapter 21).

Importing special shapes generated in CorelDRAW into a 3D spline-modeling package (such as Raydream, 3D Studio, or TrueSpace) makes rendering complex objects a snap (Chapter 22).

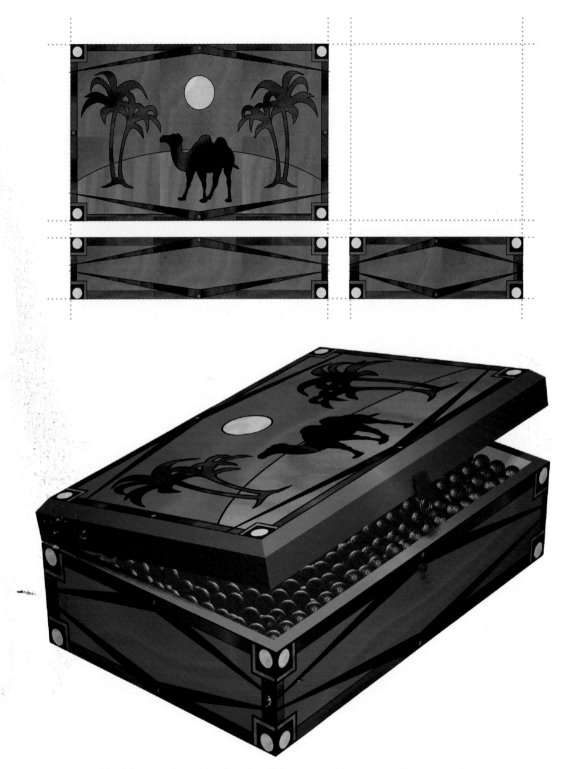

You can design and build a complex "label" in CorelDRAW, to add a unique design or color scheme to your objects built in Raydream or other 3D applications (Chapter 22).

Using both special shapes and a "blueprint" bitmap generated in CorelDRAW, a 3D scene comes alive (Chapter 22).

This image, along with all the others in this color section, is available as a CorelDRAW file on the companion CD-ROM. Load the files and see firsthand how the techniques work, or simply modify the images for your own use. (The original photo of Mona Lisa is from the Corel digital-stock photo collection, which allows you to select and purchase images online.)

FIFTIES FLASHBACK

In this chapter, we exploit simplistic but sound design principles and images from the past, and use modern, computerized techniques to take them into the future.

Back when life was simpler, before computers, before nine versions of CorelDRAW, designs also were simpler. Because every aspect of the design process was more difficult to do, often requiring physical cutting and pasting, art had a clean-cut look to it. Designs were thought out way in advance, and many more interim steps were involved to make sure the end result was perfect. The less-is-more lesson here is worth looking into, though, because in our digital age of visual noise and information overload, simplicity seems darn appealing.

Too much art these days is created with the goal of satisfying an artist's "see what I can do" ego rather than simply trying to solve the design problems for the project at hand. Often, the appropriateness of the outcome is questionable; not every piece of art needs to be dripping with technical complexity. Use your technical ability to create good designs faster, and use the extra time doing something else, like, uh..., well, I can't remember, but something other than working on the computer.

In this chapter, we create simple but visually engaging pieces that have a retro look to them (and not limited to the '50s, I just liked how that title sounded). In the first example, we see how a simple, two-color design using classic and clean page layout can produce an interesting and professional-looking design that's right at home in the modern world. Then, continuing with the theme, a simple layout is brought to life and given a retro look with select shape, font, and color choices. After that, we switch on the "idiot box" to work the American pastime into another flashback image; we'll use the PowerClip function and other tricks to put an image on TV. Finally, we capture the spirit of a '40s pinup, launching scans of images from the past into the present in the form of digital stock photography. The technology of the present works well to create images from the past.

Contact

I am a huge fan of the history of art and graphic design. So much can be learned from the past, and if nothing else, books on the subject serve as great sources of inspiration. Many times, I have been stumped trying to come up with some new look or design twist, only to find the art history archives were the catalyst necessary to ignite my creativity. If you haven't already taken some time to peruse through books on the topics of art and graphic design history, I recommend you do so.

The image in Figure 12.1 has a simple and clean layout that takes advantage of a commodity many people lose sight of: white space. An adage in design states: "It's not always what's there, but what isn't there that's important."

Figure 12.1
Modern artists can learn from the past, to create simple, cost-efficient designs that are interesting and professional.

WHAT ISN'T THERE

My favorite example of the importance of what *isn't* there is a story that, like Figure 12.1, involves airplane silhou-ettes. During World War II, the British were searching for ways to reduce their losses, and they got mighty creative in the process. After each mission, an artist would come out and inspect a returning airplane for bullet holes and flak damage. They marked the damaged areas of the plane on a sheet of cellophane that had a diagram of the plane on it. Then, they stacked up sheets from many different damaged planes until a pattern began to emerge for that model of aircraft. Distinct areas of light and dark created a pattern of damage that was common to the returning aircraft. They took this graphic to the aircraft factories and had them add armor and reinforcement to the planes on the areas in the diagrams where the hit markings *weren't,* because these blank areas on the diagrams represented where the planes that *didn't* make it back were hit. Pretty clever, eh? What's *not* there can be mighty important.

To keep down costs on a project, you're often limited to one or two ink colors. Use the white color of the paper as a third color option, creating interesting patterns and making use of the negative space in a positive way. The white creates nice areas of contrast and rest where the eye can linger away from visual noise. Trying to cram as much as possible into a design is such a natural tendency, but you'll find that less is more, and it's also very effective.

Here's how to use contemporary tools to create a clean, two-color design:

1. Use the Rectangle tool to draw a box the size of your paper and then open the Transformation docker. Click on Scale and Mirror (the middle button in the row of five buttons at the top of the docker) to open that page of options. Set the H (Horizontal) Scale value to 50% and click on Apply to Duplicate. This creates a rectangle that is half the width of the original. Click on Apply to Duplicate again to create a shape one quarter as wide as the page.

2. Shift-select all of these shapes and choose Arrange|Align and Distrib-ute to open the dialog box to align the elements to the right (or simply use the single keyboard shortcut *R*).

3. Select just the full-size rectangle and, on the Transformation docker/ Scale and Mirror page, change the Vertical value to 50%, set the Horizontal value back to 100%, and click on Apply To Duplicate. With the new duplicate selected, change the Vertical value to 80% and again click on Apply To Duplicate. Shift-select these objects and align them to the top (the keyboard shortcut is *T*). This divides the page into neat and orderly sections (see Figure 12.2).

4. Select the quarter-page vertical block and fill it black. Now, flip-flop it by dragging the right-center control handle left while holding down the Ctrl key.

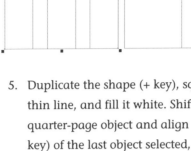

Figure 12.2

The Scale and Mirror page of the Transformation docker divides the page object horizontally and vertically to create an orderly page layout design.

Note: *If your Interactive Blend doesn't result in even-spaced objects, check the settings on the Property Bar. Click on Object and Color Acceleration and move the sliders to the middle, neutral position. This should result in even blend spacing.*

5. Duplicate the shape (+ key), squeeze it horizontally until it is just a thin line, and fill it white. Shift-select both the thin box and the quarter-page object and align them to the vertical center (press the C key) of the last object selected, in this case, the quarter page object.

6. Duplicate the thin white line, Shift-select both it and the quarter-page object, and align it to the Left (press the L key).

7. Select both thin rectangles and use the Interactive Blend tool to create a blend that produces a perfectly spaced pattern on half of the quarter-page black object (see Figure 12.3). Use the Property Bar to modify the number of steps in the active blend group, if you wish.

Figure 12.3

Use the new single-key shortcuts or the Align and Distribute dialog box to place white lines in the center and on the left of the black shape; then, blend them together.

8. Open the Symbols and Special Characters docker (Ctrl+F11), select the Transportation symbols library, scroll down until you find a plane that you like, and drag it onto the desktop. Flip the plane vertically, fill it white with no outline, and move the plane to the bottom of the page.

9. Shift-select the quarter-page shape and align the plane to its vertical center. Duplicate the plane and drag the duplicate up the page while holding down the Ctrl key, to keep it aligned with the original. Use the Interactive Blend tool to create an active blend between them, reducing the steps to 5 on the Property Bar (see Figure 12.4).

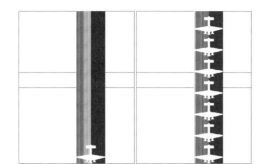

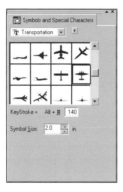

Figure 12.4

Use a plane from the Symbols and Special Characters docker as a white silhouette and then create an evenly spaced row of them by using the Interactive Blend tool.

10. Select and color the sections of the design in white and green. Green is a nice, neutral color that has universal appeal. (For a cooler look, you could substitute light blue; for a hotter look, substitute orange or red.) If this job were destined to go to press at your local print shop, you would want to use a spot color for the green. Thus, choose Windows|Color Palettes|Pantone Matching System to switch to a spot color theme. Each spot color outputs as a single plate when you create color-separated film to give to your printer.

COLOR LANDMINES

CorelDRAW 9 will display multiple palettes simultaneously on your screen. Be careful not to mix and match colors from different palette types accidentally, or you may end up with more color plates than you want or need. For example, if you use both the Pantone Black and the default CMYK Black, you'll end up with two separate color plates, both requiring black ink. You can use this mix and match technology to get some cool printing effects (like using a spot-color to designate an area to add a shiny varnish to parts of your design).

If you do accidentally build a project using Pantone Spot colors instead of the usual CMYK palette, don't panic. CorelDRAW can convert Spot colors automatically to CMYK during the printing process. From the Print options dialog (Ctrl+P), click on the Separations tab to open that page of options. Enable the Print Separations option, and below that, also Convert spot colors to CMYK. Now you will only produce the standard four-color plates (Cyan, Magenta, Yellow and Black) necessary to reproduce your artwork in traditional off-set printing (such as the color section in the middle of this book).

Duplicate the guideline shapes and reduce them with the Scale and Mirror page to produce proportional copies of the guideline shapes. You may need to change the order in which the objects are stacked. The Arrange|Order|In Front Of and Arrange|Order|Behind commands make stacking easy. Use the Align and Distribute dialog box or the keyboard shortcuts to keep all objects perfectly aligned.

11. Draw a perfect circle in the top-left box of the page and align it to the top-left area in the box. Duplicate the circle and then downsize it by dragging a corner handle inward while holding down the Ctrl key. Shift-select the original circle and combine (Ctrl+L) the two. To trim away the right side, draw a rectangle over the trim area and use the Arrange|Shaping|Trim command to create a big letter *C*. Set the rest of the letters by using the Text tool. I used a classic-looking font called Futura Bk (see Figure 12.5).

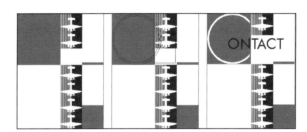

Figure 12.5

Divide the page with color and shapes and then create a big letter *C* from a perfect circle, to stay with the clean, geometric look of the design.

12. To make *ON* white, simply Shift-select the two control nodes for those two letters by using the Shape tool, and then click on the white on-screen color well. You can use the Shape tool to modify each letter in a text object, if you wish. The question mark in the lower-right corner consists of the same shape as the big *C*, but downsized and rotated with two white bars to create a *?* object.

COLOR TRICKS

Understand the parameters of a job before you begin to build the artwork. For a two-color job, such as the project in this tutorial, using a CMYK color for a traditional offset printing project is illogical. CMYK colors result in additional film and higher printing charges. Use a spot color from the Pantone Matching System instead, which creates only one color plate on output. Because this book doesn't use spot color (it uses CMYK), I chose Grass Green, which is a CMYK color choice from the on-screen palette. In the real world, I would have chosen Pantone 3288 CV as the fill color and produced exactly the artwork that my printer needs, which is a separate color plate for each color (black and green).

Alternatively, you can use CMYK colors to produce the color plates for spot-color jobs, such as this one. If I chose Green from Corel's on-screen palette, which is 100Y and 100C, I could still produce just two color plates by printing only the black and yellow. I wouldn't print the cyan plate, because I don't need it for printing. I just need to label the "yellow" film as "Pantone 3288 CV," so that my printer uses that ink instead of yellow. The color separations are the same. Why do this? Well, if your artwork is already set up as CMYK, but you really don't need all the color plates for printing, you can use this trick to save time and money.

13. Okay, I admit to modernizing the look a bit with the addition of a drop shadow, but it's just so easy. Select the original full-size rectangle and drag the Interactive Drop Shadow tool down and to the right to create a traditional drop shadow. You can change the parameters, such as Feathering and Opacity values, on the Property Bar (see Figure 12.6).

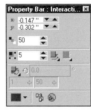

Figure 12.6

Use like shapes when possible to save time; the *C* can become a *?*. The Interactive Drop Shadow tool gives you a quick and easy way to add convincing depth to an object.

Well, perhaps this image isn't as exciting as some that we have created so far, but I think it's important to address simple design strategies, too. You can view the finished piece in this book's color section and in the contact.cdr file in the \Chapt12\ subdirectory on the companion CD-ROM. I like this graphic because you start with the layout, dividing the page into neat quadrants, and then add pieces to enhance visual interest. By nature, humans like to divide and conquer, and subconsciously that's still how we digest visual information. Neat and tidy sections are appealing, which is why you'll find that most good design has pages that are divided into easy-to-digest chunks. Take a clue from the past and don't over-design a project.

Avocados, Plums, And Carrots

The '90s has this strange mix of the previous four decades, especially in areas such as art and fashion. Today's trends borrow heavily from the past, but simultaneously mix in pieces of the present. Nothing beats seeing a kid in bell-bottoms playing with a Game Boy to mess with your head! Or, how about oldies music on CD-ROM?

Getting a retro look means sticking to the formula of the times. Older graphics use lower-tech printing and design methods, which help to define the look. Simple geometric shapes, natural colors (avocado green, carrot orange, plum purple, banana yellow, and so on), and fonts from

Figure 12.7

In addition to kitschy design and funky fonts, the right choice of colors really screams retro-funky (see color section in the middle of this book to get the full effect).

the same era all add up to a blast-from-the-past look (see Figure 12.7 and the finished image in the color section in the middle of the book to see what colors I am talking about).

These designs are all the rage again, as people appreciate not only the look but also the simplicity at all levels of production. Here is how to capture that groovelicious look:

1. Draw a rectangle and fill it with a lovely avocado green. To create colors that aren't on the on-screen palette, open the Uniform Fill dialog box (Shift+F11). Click on a green color in the Rainbow slider to get started, and then drag the selector in the mixing window to change the CMYK values. I use a color reference swatch book, which tells me the CMYK values that I need to use to get certain colors in printing.

   This is a handy item, especially when trying to convert spot colors into CMYK (CorelDRAW now does this automatically and fairly accurately, but I like to double-check). For the green, the values are C-47, M-0, Y-88, and K-0, which you can type directly into the Uniform Fill dialog box, when using the CMYK color model. Now, draw an oval with the Ellipse tool and fill it with a what's-up-doc orange (C-0, M-60, Y-100, K-0).

2. With the Text tool, set your ad copy on the page. (I used a font called Balloon for the top text, and AdLib for the lower text.) Use the Shape tool to Shift-select the nodes of the first letters of the top text. Double-click on one of the nodes to open the Format Text dialog box, and add 10 to the value in the Size box. Click on OK to enlarge just these selected letters.

3. Using the Shape tool, select the second text element and drag the bottom-left arrow up to change the line spacing. This reduces the vertical space between the words.

4. Using the Shape tool again, select and drag the letters one at a time so that they aren't all aligned along the baseline, to make them seem more excited. Give these words a thick, white .333-inch outline and enable the Behind Fill option from the Outline Pen dialog box (F12) (see Figure 12.8).

5. Open the Symbols and Special Characters docker (Ctrl+F11) and locate the Stars1 Library. Scroll down until you find the star that looks like the jacks child's toy (a little metal star with rounded ends on the points that your mom always was stepping on) and drag it

COLOR CONSISTENCY

Matching on-screen colors to their printed counterparts has always been a problem. In CorelDRAW 9, a color-corrected display is the default, with the on-screen images very closely representing their printed values. The Corel Color Manager utility will help you to fine-tune your equipment to provide the best on-screen color representation possible. I work with color correction enabled, so that I see an image on my screen that is close to the CMYK printed equivalent. If you are working on Web graphics, however, you may be surprised if you work with CMYK color correction while creating RGB graphics. So, set your screen for the task at hand. In CorelDRAW 9, open the Options menu (Ctrl+J), and on the Global|Color Management options page, you can turn on or off the Calibrate Colors for Display (the default is on).

If you are really serious about calibrating color, forget the gadgets, gizmos, and companion software; just do the math. So many variables (including heat, color of your clothing, time of day, and so on) change the way that on-screen colors look that the chances of ever calibrating your monitor are nil. However, you can monitor the color mixes in your artwork and compare the mathematical values to a trustworthy printed reference. Use a printed swatch book to pick a color, and then key in the CMYK values for that color as your fill value in the Uniform Fill dialog box (Shift+F11). How it looks on screen doesn't really matter; the printed result should look like the color that you keyed in, or close.

Make sure that your printed reference is new, not faded, and from a reputable source. Compare the final printed version to the reference and take notes on how the color varies so that you can adjust the colors the next time. Differences in output machines, film developing chemistry, printing presses, and so on all alter the outcome, so you have to track what happens, so you'll know how to fix things. If jobs that you send to your local print shop always look blue, you need to adjust the levels of cyan in your artwork. If things look green, you may need to increase the magenta level. (Green is yellow and cyan, so what's left? Magenta.) Unfortunately, no plug-in replacement or upgrade is available for good ol' real-world experience.

Figure 12.8
You can change the letter and line spacing, in addition to manipulating each letter individually, using the Shape tool.

onto the desktop. Give it a plum/pink fill (C-5, M-75, Y-0, K-0) with a .029-inch yellow outline, and enable the Behind Fill outline option from the Outline Pen dialog box (F12). Duplicate and arrange a whole bunch of these jacks, enlarging or reducing the duplicates as you go, to create a random-looking barrage of those non-slip shower flowers (see Figure 12.9).

6. For the final element, I wanted a starburst-looking shape. You can either use the Interactive Deformation tool's Zipper mode to distort an oval into this object, or use the Polygon tool, as I did. Right-click on the Polygon tool and click on Properties to open the tool's Options dialog box.

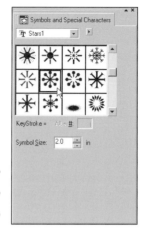

Figure 12.9
Use the Symbols and Special Characters docker to find the perfect star icon to duplicate and scatter around your page.

7. Enable the Polygon as Star option, change the Number of Points/ Sides value to 44, and drag the Sharpness slider until you get the look that you're after. Click on OK and drag the Polygon tool onto the desktop, to draw the object. (Remember, the Shape tool is useful for fine-tuning a polygon object, if necessary.) Fill this funky polygon with cyan and call it a day (see Figure 12.10).

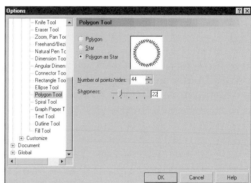

Figure 12.10
Use the Polygon tool to create a circular burst behind the text.

You can view this image in the book's color section and in the 50sad.cdr file in the \Chapt12\ subdirectory on the companion CD-ROM. The burst in the file is a curve, so the Shape tool won't perform the same way as it would if the burst was still an active polygon. Open the Polygon tool settings, draw a star, and see then how the Shape tool changes things. Remember, with the Shape tool you can drag the outside points or the inside points to modify an active Polygon or Polygon as Star object.

Classic TV

Part of putting together any contemporary project is working out the peripheral details. Corresponding Web sites, brochures, mailers, post-cards—you name it—all start to pop up on your job board. The fun thing is combining the past with the present. For example, a Web site design could benefit from the clean, quirky styling of a retro look incorporated with modern twists such as animation or interactive buttons.

This design is just such a project, in which a printed image works into an on-screen Web experience (see Figure 12.11). I decided that a television is a good way to swap images for an animation, in a campy, classic-TV kind of spoof, to add motion and interest to a Web page. You can create a series of images for the screen and swap them to create animation cells, to make your television change channels. For the Web, you would want to slice the image into three separate GIFs, so that just the center is animated, to cut down the load time and file size (see my example in Chapter 20).

This exercise walks through the process of putting the first image into a screen shape and making that image look like it's appearing on an old 1950s vintage TV. We also create a background that combines retro coloring and modern objects, and even throw in some modernistic text effects.

Figure 12.11

Even a simple-looking design can benefit from high-end tricks. The TV image is a bitmap and static lines stuffed into a screen shape with the PowerClip feature; the design elements are Symbols; and the FX logo was created with the Combine function.

1. Draw a TV screen by creating a rectangle and curving the corners with the Shape tool. Import an image for your screen (I used a photo from \photos\entertain directory on the CorelDRAW clip-art CD-ROM). Select the photo and align it to your screen.

2. Choose Effects|PowerClip|Place Inside Container and then click on the screen. Because you'll be stuffing this image into a different screen object later, again using the PowerClip function, this step is just to help you visualize the screen and aid in the layout of the TV graphic (see Figure 12.12).

Figure 12.12

Put an image into the TV screen with the PowerClip function.

3. To create scan lines or static, use the Interactive Blend tool to create a row of straight lines across the screen. "For snow" instead of static, increase the number of blend steps and, in the Outline Pen dialog box (F12), change the line style to dotted. Add any text or other tidbits to your screen, to create the program that you want to display.

4. Drag-select everything and select Bitmaps|Convert to Bitmap. I used the Grayscale Color setting for a "golden age of television" look, but you could set it to RGB, to get an old-fashioned-color-TV look. (If you use RGB, choose Effects|Color Adjustment|Color Balance to reveal

sliders with which you can add yellow to your image, making the picture look like my uncle's old TV set.) Convert the bitmap to either Grayscale or RGB, and click on OK (see Figure 12.13).

Figure 12.13

Use the Convert to Bitmap command to transform your pieces into a pixel-based image. Then use the Bitmap filters to add noise or change the colors of your image.

5. Now we need a TV. I did a file search on the CorelDRAW clip-art CD for "tv*.*" to see what was out there. I find this is faster than thumbing through the reference book, although I always have the book close at hand. The search gave me 11 choices, and I picked one from the \clipart\home\electron directory on the CorelDRAW clip-art CD-ROM. Import (Ctrl+I) the TV clip-art and use the Ungroup (Ctrl+U) function to make selecting the individual objects possible.

6. Click on your image object that you want to showcase in the television screen to reveal the Rotation and Skew arrows, and drag the left skew arrow up to tilt your image into position.

7. Switch to Wireframe view, choose Effects|PowerClip|Place Inside Container, and then click on the clip-art TV screen shape. Hey, look, your art is on TV!

8. For a final touch, add a white rectangle with curved corners to the top of the screen and use the Interactive Transparency tool to turn the solid box into a subtle gleam (see Figure 12.14).

Figure 12.14

Your custom image is placed in the picture tube with the PowerClip feature. The TV screen is given a highlight by applying an Interactive Transparency lens to a solid-white box.

9. Position your TV in the center of the page. Draw two kidney-shaped blobs, oh-so-typical of '50s design, either by using the Bezier tool or by starting with a curved-corner rectangle and converting it to curves (Ctrl+Q) and then editing the nodes. Use the Shape tool to delete all but two of the nodes, for a relaxed, sweeping blob (see Figure 12.15).

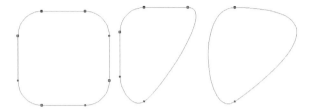

Figure 12.15
Node-edit a rectangle into a kidney shape.

10. Duplicate and flip-flop the blob, and arrange the original and the duplicate behind the TV shape. Fill one with a light, chalky yellow (Y-60) and the other with a pale green (C-47, Y-88).

11. To create a pattern of abstract objects, use shapes from the Symbols and Special Characters docker. Open the docker (Ctrl+F11) and drag shapes from the Electronics symbols library for a high-tech but interesting abstract pattern (see Figure 12.16). Drag off the symbols and color them ice blue (C-40).

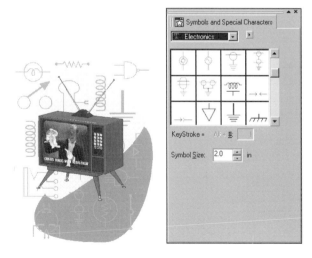

Figure 12.16
Use the Symbols and Special Characters docker to decorate the page with interesting objects.

12. The FX Channel logo, with its reversed-out areas, is actually easy to create using the CorelDRAW Combine command. Draw a perfect square and then use the Text tool to set the text *F* and *X* as separate text elements. Align the letters to the upper-left and lower-right corners inside the box.

13. Select the box and duplicate it twice. Move one duplicate up and to the left and use the Arrange|Shaping|Trim command to create a flopped-over *L* shape.

14. Select the other box duplicate and drag the top-left corner inward to downsize it, so that the area of the box that passes through the *F* is about as thick as the flopped-over *L* shape passing through the *X*. Convert this box to curves (Ctrl+Q) and double-click on the bottom-right node with the Shape tool to delete it, resulting in a triangle.

15. Drag-select all three objects and combine them (Ctrl+L), creating an inverse color scheme where the objects overlap. Keep in mind that these white areas are open, and that anything below this image will show through the holes. To prevent this, draw a white box behind the *FX* curve that is large enough to accommodate the rotated CHANNEL text (see Figure 12.17).

Figure 12.17
Create three objects that, when combined, create an interesting logo with an alternating black/white pattern.

You can view this image in this book's color section and in the classictv.cdr file in the \Chapt12\ subdirectory on the companion CD-ROM. I usually disable the Auto-Center PowerClip Contents option from the Edit page in the Options dialog box (Ctrl+J), but to make a series of animation cells using the television, leave it enabled. Then you can select a bitmap and stuff it into the TV screen frame by using the PowerClip function, and it automatically centers in the same step. You can then select the TV objects and export them as a single GIF for use in an animation that automatically changes the channels on a Web site graphic. Chapter 21 discusses animation more thoroughly.

Pinup Posters

I love the image in Figure 12.18. It has such a classic look, and thanks to modern imaging tricks, with a few clicks, it can even be yellowed and weathered to look old. Sometimes, I mix so many modern tricks with classic art that I feel like I could stop time.

This image uses a derivative of the retro formula to achieve the desired look. Instead of symbol shapes, a pinup illustration from the era provides the first piece of the puzzle. The pinup girl alone provides a date reference for the image, with a classic '40s-era pose, hairstyle, clothing, illustration style, and even coloring scheme. The font is from a new collection of old-style fonts from House Industries (which, for licensing reasons, aren't on the companion CD-ROM); it looks like the hand-lettered style used to personalize aircraft bombers during World War II. Here is how to create an old-style pinup graphic:

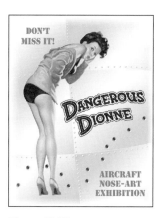

Figure 12.18
Adding rivets and other details changes a classic pinup image from a third-party clip-art collection into a convincing piece of aircraft nose-art.

1. Locate an appropriate pinup girl graphic. Time Tunnel (www.timetunnel.com), a unique supplier of digital images, was gracious enough to provide us with a sample collection of its images, including its brand-new Pinups collection. Start Photo-Paint and load the file called pinup1.jpg, located in the \timetunl\ directory on the companion CD-ROM. This is a great-looking image with the signature style of '40s pinups. You first need to prepare the bitmap in Photo-Paint for use in CorelDRAW. Before you import your images into CorelDRAW, you should always take control of them, making sure that they are the correct size and color depth in Photo-Paint. This saves you some headaches later.

2. With the image loaded in Photo-Paint, make sure that the size and resolution are correct, which you can monitor from the Resample dialog box. From the Image menu, open the Resample dialog box and make sure that the resolution is 300 dpi and that the dimensions are what you want. Click on OK to close the dialog box. Select Image|Mode|CMYK Color to convert the image to CMYK for printing.

3. Next, we need to remove the busy background, to use the Bitmap Color Mask in CorelDRAW. You could paint away the background by using a neutral color, such as white, but I thought of a different approach for this graphic. The background is cyan, but we don't really need cyan anywhere in this graphic (the orange tones in the model consist of yellow and magenta, with her hair and bathing suit in shades of black). Removing cyan from the image also cleans up the background and solves our background problem.

   Choose Image|Adjust|Level Equalization. Change to the Cyan channel in the Equalize section and drag the right Output Range arrow all the way to the left. Click on OK to modify the image. This removes the cyan from the background, leaving only a faint-yellow tint, which you can get rid of by increasing the Brightness and Contrast from the Brightness-Contrast-Intensity dialog box (Ctrl+B). Save the bitmap and exit Photo-Paint (see Figure 12.19).

4. Start CorelDRAW and begin a new drawing—the pinup girl needs an airplane to be stuck on, reminiscent of World War II nose-art. To simulate a plane, create the look of riveted metal sheets. To start, draw a

Figure 12.19
Use the Level Equalization dialog box in Photo-Paint to remove the cyan background pattern. Use other Photo-paint features, check the physical size and resolution, and also increase the brightness and contrast of the pinup girl image, before you import it into CorelDRAW.

rectangle. From the Fountain Fill (F11) dialog box, use a Preset to add a cool, custom coloring scheme. Click on the down-arrow next to the Presets box on the Fountain Fill dialog box, and scroll down until you find the Cylinder-Grey 02 option (see Figure 12.20). This has a nice, metallic look to it. Change the Angle value to –45 degrees and click on OK.

Figure 12.20
Use the Presets option in the Fountain Fill dialog box to assign a preprogrammed custom color blend to your object.

5. Draw a circle in each corner of the rectangle and fill the circles with the same metallic custom color blend as the rectangle to make them look like rivets.

6. Drag the Interactive Blend tool between the two top circles and change the number of steps on the Property Bar to 15 to create an even-spaced row of rivets. Repeat the same blend for all the corner rivets to create a blend group of rivets all around the edge of the object (see Figure 12.21).

7. Duplicate and arrange the riveted panel to create a large wall of metal sheeting. To get away from the cloned look, select every alternate sheet and reverse the angle of the fountain fill from –45 to 135

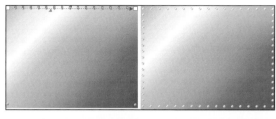

Figure 12.21

A rectangle with a preset fountain fill becomes a riveted metal sheet when four circles create rivet rows with the help of the Interactive Blend tool.

degrees, by adjusting the Angle value in the Fountain Fill dialog box (F11). This creates a more flowing color scheme. Select all the shapes and rotate them 5 degrees to avoid a grid-like feel.

8. Draw a rectangle the size of your page over the sheets. Open the Lens docker (Alt+F3) and apply a Fish Eye lens to distort the sheets so that they look like an aircraft fuselage. Change the Rate to 50% to give a slight distortion that is perfect for this application. Enable the Frozen option and click on Apply. You end up with a collection of pieces that are distorted and trimmed down to the desired page size (see Figure 12.22). You can then delete or save the original panels to disk. At this stage, things were looking busy, so I deleted a bunch of the rivets.

Figure 12.22

Modify the fountain fills to create areas of light and dark. Use the Fish Eye lens to distort the objects slightly for the look of a rounded plane fuselage.

QUICKLY COPY OUTLINES AND FILLS

A quick way to copy outline and fill attributes from one object to another is to use the right-mouse button. Select the object *from* which you want to borrow an outline or fill, click and hold down the right mouse button over this object, and then drag over the object *to* which you want to copy (the cursor changes to target crosshairs). When you release the right-mouse button, a pop-up menu enables you to Copy Fill Here, Copy Outline Here, or even Copy All Properties.

9. Use the Import (Ctrl+I) feature to bring your color-corrected pinup image into this design. Size and position the bitmap on top of the metal-looking objects. Choose Bitmaps|Bitmap Color Mask, and use the Eyedropper tool to select and hide the white background in the pinup bitmap. Bump up the Tolerance value to 24% and click on Apply. This should leave just the image of the pinup on the side of the airplane.

10. To get the look of raised rivets (a bit of an artistic leap, because airplane rivets really are flush and flat), add a highlight and gleam to each rivet. It isn't hard. First, select all the rivets in Wireframe view and combine them into one curve. Then, duplicate the curve, offset it down and to the right, and use the Arrange|Shaping|Trim function to get the shadow shapes. Repeat the process, moving the duplicate to the top and left, to get the highlight shapes. The shadow shapes are filled black, the highlights are filled white, and all are given a 50% Transparency lens (see Figure 12.23).

11. Set your text to name the plane. Pilots were very superstitious and sentimental, and would name their planes after sweethearts back home. Modify the text with the Interactive Envelope tool to give it a curved look. (I used a font called Fink from House Industries.) Using the Behind Fill option from the Outline Pen dialog box (F12), give the text a really thick .133-inch black outline, duplicate it, and give the duplicate a thinner .083-inch white outline. This gives the text the double-outline look (see Figure 12.24).

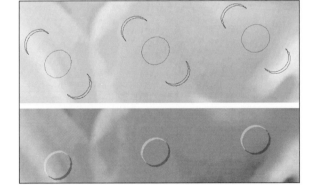

Figure 12.23

Use the Trim function to create highlight and shadow shapes from a duplicate of the rivets (top, in Wireframe view). When given a 50% Transparency lens, the rivets look round and shiny (bottom).

Figure 12.24

To name the plane, use a retro-looking font distorted with an envelope and given the double-outline effect.

12. Swipe the bullet holes from Chapter 4 to add a sense of danger to the graphic. To get the image to fade away to white, use the Interactive Transparency tool on white rectangles. Draw white rectangles over each edge and use the Interactive Transparency tool to drag from the outside inward to get the fade-away look (see Figure 12.25).

You can see the final image in this book's color section and in the pinup.cdr file in the \Chapt12\ subdirectory on the companion CD-ROM.

Beyond f/x

In what I'll call a reaction *against* the computer design revolution, more and more designs are embracing a retro or low-tech look. This is great news for everyone, because old-school images are easy on the eyes, simple to build, and usually a breeze to output and print.

Everything from annual reports to advertising campaigns can benefit from the simple but eye-catching look of the past. Using existing stock images, such as the pinup girl, adds a sense of nostalgia to artwork, with little effort on your part. In fact, you can "stand on the shoulders of giants," as the saying goes, and use amazing artwork from the ever-growing copyright-free archives, and use them as your own. What a cool deal, especially with trends the way they are. Why not use those images and start your own line of nostalgic silk ties, or promotional posters, or whatever you can dream up.

I'm a huge fan of the retro look and will be working it into every design opportunity that I can. The beauty of using this kind of artwork is that it's really hard for things to go wrong—very few color-correction hassles are involved, and if the colors end up looking kind of funky, you just call it an effect and pretend that you did it on purpose.

Moving On

In this chapter, we looked at ways to exploit the modern conveniences of CorelDRAW to create designs that look like they are from past decades. We also looked at how to achieve the modern retro look by combining old design ideas with more modern ones. And, we proved that you can create artwork that is really fun and engaging without losing its simplicity.

In the next chapter, we blast from the past into the present...and then beyond. We'll see how the simplicity of computer-aided design is resulting in a new type of techno imagery. Using the automation features in CorelDRAW and borrowing images from 3D rendering software, this new style is seemingly haphazard and busy, but in the end becomes a balanced, workable design. Lose those poodle skirts, watch a copy of *Blade Runner*, and get ready for some digital entropy!

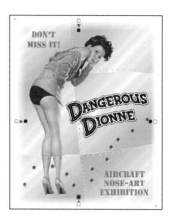

Figure 12.25
The Interactive Transparency tool transforms solid-white rectangles into effects-shades that create a soft-edged look.

4. In addition to the position and size of the 3D object, you can control light and shadow effects if the default Ambient lighting doesn't appeal to you. Click on the Distant/Ambient button on the Property Bar, with the ducky selected. Change the type to Spot and then click on the + button to add a spotlight. You can enable shading and even change the color of the light. Illuminate the figure to your tastes and click on OK when finished. You can then manipulate the spotlight within the mini-3D scene by using the movement and rotation tools in the 3D Toolbox window. Figure 13.5 shows how the ducky ended up after my manipulation of the 3D interface within CorelDRAW.

Figure 13.5
Use the Property Bar's many 3D features, including lighting, shading, and rendering options, to get the highlights and shadows just the way that you want them on your 3DMF object.

5. When you are finished manipulating your object, click on a blank area of the desktop with the Pick tool to exit the 3D editing mode. 3D objects such as this are similar to bitmaps with clear backgrounds (such as the objects mentioned in the sidebar), so you can add CorelDRAW objects on top of or underneath them with no sweat.

6. With your duck in place, draw a perfect circle around it. Duplicate (+ key) and enlarge the circle with the sizing handles, and move the duplicate down, off-center horizontally.

7. Use the Interactive Blend tool to drag between the two circles to create an active blend. Use the Property Bar to modify the blend. Change the number of steps to 20 and then click on the Object and Color Acceleration button. Adjust the Object Acceleration slider to make the circles closer together at the center (see Figure 13.6).

8. Select the ring-blend group, choose Arrange|Separate, and then choose Arrange|Ungroup All. Combine the objects (Ctrl+L) to create solid ring shapes. Use the Rectangle tool to draw a rectangle for the page limit.

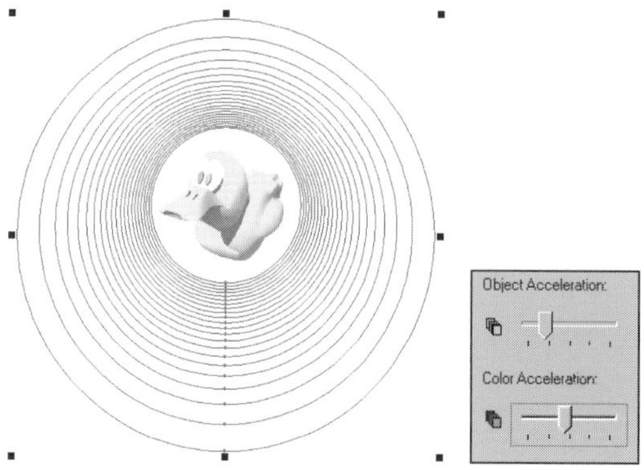

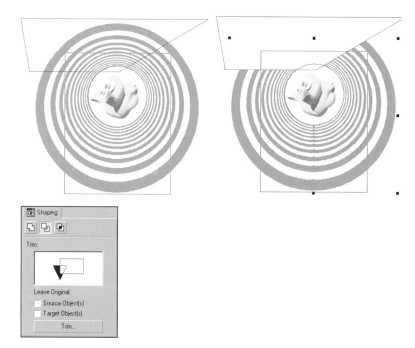

Figure 13.6

Use the Interactive Blend tool and the Property Bar to create a set of rings that get closer together in the center.

9. Hack off the top-left sections of the rings by drawing a shape using the Bezier tool. With your newly drawn trim-shape selected, choose Arrange|Shaping|Trim. In the Shaping docker, disable the Leave Original options, click on the bottom Trim button, and then click on the rings (see Figure 13.7).

Figure 13.7

Freezing the blend enables you to combine the circles into a multi-ring shape. The odd shape across the top (on left) is used to cut away a section of the rings, using the Trim option of the Shaping docker (on right).

10. Give the ring objects an orange fill and no outline. With the Interactive Extrude tool, drag on the ring shape, but not too far. Use the Property Bar to fine-tune your extrude group. Change both the x and y Vanishing Point coordinates to 0, so that the extrude shapes point toward the center of the page. Click on Color (looks like a color wheel), and then click on Use Solid Color (the center-top button in

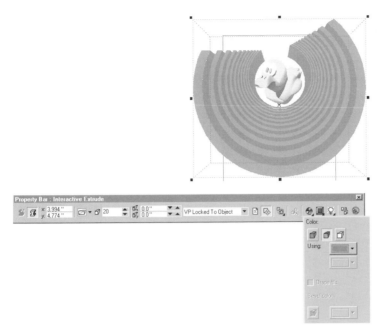

Figure 13.8
The Interactive Extrude tool adds shapes, with a solid fill color assigned by using the Color option on the Property Bar.

the pop up menu). Click on the drop-down arrow next to the active color chip and select a burnt-orange color (see Figure 13.8).

11. Choose Arrange|Separate to obtain independent control over your extrude shapes. Give the front rings a pink .023-inch outline (part of this look is created by using many colors from a very similar palette; in this case, light and dark tones of orange).

12. Fill the page rectangle with black and bring the duck to the front (Shift+PgUp). Draw some more circles behind the duck, and you have the basic page layout finished (see Figure 13.9).

13. The shapes around the duck began as pizza-slice shapes. A white circle then was placed on top of a large portion of the inner pizza, thus hiding that area and making the remaining, outer objects

Figure 13.9
Arrange the elements on the page and separate the extrude elements, so that you can give only the front objects an outline.

look like arced rectangles. Draw a circle and then use the Shape tool to drag the node to the right, on the *inside* of the circle, to create a pizza-slice shape. Duplicate and color the pizza-slice shapes in the same orange tones, throwing in a black one here and there for contrast. To create the solid and dotted arcs, use the Shape tool to drag a circle node on the *outside*, which creates an arc line (see Figure 13.10).

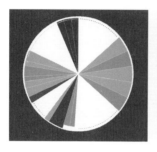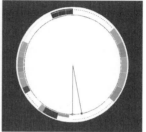

Figure 13.10

Create circle slices and arcs by dragging the control node on an ellipse with the Shape tool.

14. Placing some text in the circle area creates an interesting look. Draw a circle and then switch to the Text tool. Drag the pointer over the circle so that the pointer changes from crosshairs into a bracket shape, and then click. When you type, the letters are centered on the top of the circle. Or, you can type the text, Shift-select both the text and the circle, and choose Text|Fit Text to Path. Then you can change the placement of the text with the options on the Property Bar, so that you can place the text on the bottom, inside, outside, or even choose a different letter orientation (see Figure 13.11).

Figure 13.11

After you choose Fit Text to Path, the Property Bar gives you many options for arranging text along a curve or, in this case, a circle.

15. To add the busy array of images, open the Symbols docker (Ctrl+F11). Drag and arrange a mixed jumble of pieces to create that international-communication look. Use characters from Japanese, Korean, and Arabic alphabets to get a real global-village feel.

The rest of the design is pretty straightforward. I arranged all kinds of symbols and text around the page to create a busy but interesting ad design. The evenly-spaced cutouts along the edge and top of the card are just two white shapes blended together. The big logo in the center is a scanned image of a marker-drawn word, converted to vector artwork by using CorelTrace, and then skewed with the Perspective tool. When finished, all the pieces were constrained into the page rectangle using the PowerClip function.

You can view this image in this book's color section and in the ducky.cdr file nestled in the \Chapt13\ subdirectory on the companion CD-ROM. Due to technical and legal reasons (I can't redistribute unaltered Corel clip art, which is what a 3DMF file essentially is), the ducky image in this file is just a bitmap. You can either open your own copy of CorelDream and create a new 3DMF file to experiment on in CorelDRAW, using the 3D functions, or use any other real-world photo to get the effect. To check out the CorelDRAW file pieces, remember that you have to use the PowerClip|Extract Contents function to see anything.

Fourth Dimension

I can safely say that Norman Rockwell isn't exactly a big influence on my artistic style. If you guessed Salvador Dali, Robert Williams, Hans Rudi Giger, Edvard Munch, Albrecht Deurer, or Hieronymus Bosch, you would be much more on the mark. I draw inspiration from all kinds of artwork, sometimes as a spoof, often just as a starting point.

The nightmarish vision in Figure 13.12 is another example of mixing classic gargoyle-type images with computer-generated effects. It is also a mixture of low-tech, hand-drawn images brought to life within CorelDRAWS's high-tech, automated, digital canvas.

The background is the result of mixing the Twister effect and a texture fill, while a lens effect alters the image within the chain portal. This is the kind of art that would be too tedious to render by hand, but by mixing in scanned ink images it maintains a traditional cartoonish feel while still exploiting high-tech computer effects (see Chapter 11 for more details).

The centerpiece is a mixture of techniques that we have already covered and artwork from my archives (which, with your purchase of this book, essentially are now *your* archives as well). The chain portal can be created with the techniques outlined in Chapter 8, blending link objects around a circle. The gargoyle guards are the same ones found in the skull angel image, only now they are gray. They are a group of objects consisting of a black-and-white bitmap colorized with shapes. For this design, only the main

Figure 13.12
Mixing hand-drawn ink images with a plethora of CorelDRAW effects, including texture fills, a lens, and the new Interactive Distortion tool with the Twister option, creates a nightmarish vortex into the unknown.

gargoyle body was recolored (you have to love CorelDRAW for this kind of simplicity). Here is how to mix technologies to create whirling vortex scenes:

1. To manipulate an object within a group, you first need to select it. Press the Ctrl key, click on the main fill object within the group, and select only that object. Open the Fountain Fill dialog box (F11) and assign a new body-color scheme to the gargoyle (see Figure 13.13).

Figure 13.13
The Ctrl key enables you to select a single object within a group so that you can manipulate it without first ungrouping or otherwise affecting the other objects.

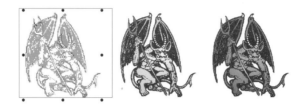

2. Press the Esc key to deselect the subgroup object, and then select the gargoyle group. Duplicate it (+ key) and flip-flop the gargoyle by dragging the left-center control node rightward while holding down the Ctrl key. Arrange the gargoyles on either side of the chain gate. I'm the king of image swiping: I grabbed the f/x logo from Chapter 2 and plunked it into the center of the chains. Use the technique from the Piercing Bits example (Chapter 5) to recolor the *CorelDRAW* and *9,* using a red-and-yellow color scheme to match the future background (see Figure 13.14).

Figure 13.14
Bits and pieces come together to create a new image.

3. With the CorelDRAW clip-art book (the handy printed reference to the clip-art CD-ROM that ships with CorelDRAW) open to the Crests section, I spotted a file with some nifty design nuggets waiting to be mined (see Figure 3.15). Import a file with cool knife objects from the \clipart\crests\misc directory on the CorelDRAW clip-art CD-ROM. Ungroup the objects and delete all but the pointy pieces.

4. Arrange these objects around the chain circle like rays of the sun, duplicating any objects that you need to finish the pattern. Use a white-to-cyan fountain fill (F11) to create a random reflection in the pieces. Create one side and then duplicate and flip for the other (see Figure 13.15).

5. The bat is an illustration that I created just for this image, so it isn't all borrowed. This image was scanned and colorized just like every other black-and-white bitmap in this book, but with one notable difference. Because the wings need to be behind the chains, and the head needs to be in front, two bitmaps are actually in the image. For the second bitmap I used a white brush in Photo-Paint to paint over the areas behind the chains. (To keep the task within CorelDRAW, you could create a shape for the head, PowerClip the bat pieces into it, and then place the PowerClip in front of the chain.) The bat consists of a coloring object, and the original, whole bitmap is behind the chain. On top of the chain are the pieces to colorize the face, and the bitmap with the areas painted away, resulting in the back/front illusion (see Figure 13.16).

> **BEHIND THE LIMITS**
>
> If you are having trouble selecting CorelDRAW objects behind a bitmap (even in Wireframe view), you need to disable the Pick tool's Treat Objects as Filled option, which is the default. Disabling this option gives you more functionality in Wireframe view. Right-click on the Pick tool and choose Properties. From the Options dialog box on the Pick Tool page, disable the Treat All Objects as Filled option.

Figure 13.15
Pieces from a clip-art crest are recolored and arranged to use in the new image.

Figure 13.16
A duplicate of the bat bitmap, with areas painted away is in front of the chain objects, while the original bitmap is behind the chain objects.

6. To create the spinning vortex shape, first draw a perfect circle with the Ellipse tool. With the Shape tool, create a thin, pizza-slice shape by dragging the nodes on the circle toward the inside of the circle.

7. With the Pick tool, convert the object to curves (Ctrl+Q) and then change the axis of rotation to the top-center of the object. Use the rotate/right-mouse duplicate trick (as outlined in Chapter 10, when you created a similar shape) to create the wheel spoke design (see Figure 13.17).

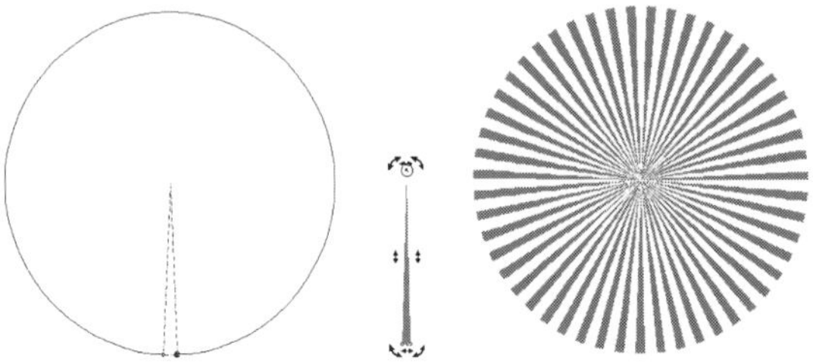

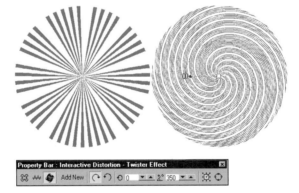

Figure 13.17

Create a spinning wheel by duplicating and spinning ellipse slivers made by dragging on a circle with the Shape tool.

8. Randomly delete every fourth spoke or so to create open areas in the vortex. Drag-select all the remaining spinning wheel objects and combine them (Ctrl+L).

9. Select the Interactive Distortion tool from the Interactive Blend tool flyout. On the Property Bar, click on the Twister Distortion button, adjust the Additional Degrees to 350, and press Enter (see Figure 13.18). Convert the vortex to curves (Ctrl+Q).

Figure 13.18

The Twister option on the Interactive Distortion tool Property Bar spins the object into a vortex illusion.

10. Fill the vortex shape with a custom color blend by using the Interactive Fill tool; use an alternating yellow-red pattern. With the vortex shape selected, choose Arrange|Shaping|Intersect. Enable only the Target Objects Leave Original option, click on Intersect With, and then click on your rectangular page-border object. This limits the vortex shape to within the desired page size (see Figure 13.19).

11. Arrange the new vortex shape and page frame behind the ghoul gate. Use a yellow outline on the vortex object (to make it stand out more).

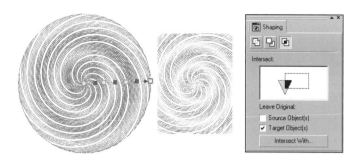

Figure 13.19
Color and trim down the vortex shape to fit within the page.

12. Select the page frame, and from the Fill Tool flyout, open the Texture Fill dialog box and change the Texture Library to Styles. Browse the list until you find Mineral, Cloudy 2 Colors. Select it, change the mineral colors from brown and cream to purple and yellow, and click on OK. (For abstract backgrounds, you can leave the default Texture Fill values; but to avoid chunky images, increase the values in the Texture Options dialog box, opened by clicking on the Options button.)

13. To change the mood in the area inside the chain, draw a circle behind the gate and in front of the background and then open the Lens docker (Alt+F3) to change things. I used a Transparency lens filled purple and given a 50-percent transparency rate. You could make things even crazier with another lens choice, such as Invert or Heat Map.

You can see this image in its dizzying brilliance both in the color section and in the 4thdimen.cdr file in the \Chapt13\ subdirectory on the companion CD-ROM. Load the file and practice selecting an object in a group and recoloring the gargoyles. Try changing the lens shape to make the area inside the chains more or less wild. Also, you can dramatically change the mood by recoloring the vortex shape and the background

---

AS BIG AS THE BIGGEST

When you Export (Ctrl+E) a CorelDRAW file as a bitmap, the page size is determined by the largest object. For this reason, if you create a very large circle shape (as a guide for text, for example), CorelDRAW creates your bitmap as big as this huge, overhanging object, even if that object has no outline or fill attribute. To make an object "invisible" during the printing or export process, stick it on its own layer and turn off the print attribute for that layer, as follows:

1. Choose Window|Dockers|Object Manager to open the Object Manager docker, in which you manage layers.

2. From the Object Manager Options flyout, choose New Layer.

3. Select your object and drag and drop it onto the new layer name in Object Manager.

4. Click on the printer icon to toggle off the Printable value, so that any objects on this layer will not print or export.

rectangle. Go nuts and use the pieces to realize your own twisted visions. That's the advantage of mixing old art in a new, computerized environment: unlimited potential.

Funky Fresh

A recent trend is to incorporate images from the past into a high-tech feel of the present. The logo in Figure 13.20, which looks like a Tide detergent box, has found its way into many contemporary applications, including my own.

This is one of those graphics that you can see from across the room and it always gets noticed. Complete the following steps to incorporate that triple-exploding look into your own design.

Figure 13.20

Bouncing hard and loud, this image borrows from a popular detergent box, producing a bright, happy logo by using the Interactive Fill tool.

1. Draw a perfect circle and then select the Interactive Fill tool. Drag in the circle to start a fountain fill. Click on the Radial button on the Property Bar to change the type of fountain fill. Drag and drop yellow from the on-screen color well onto the center color point. Drag and drop red to the outside control point (the little slider in the middle controls the midpoint setting). This makes a nice, smooth color blend.

2. To get a harsh color transition, drag and drop more color points onto the Interactive Fill control line. Drag and drop another yellow point along the line and then drag and drop another red one. By sliding the points along the line you can change the way the blend works and looks. Moving the points around to get the desired results takes a bit of finesse (see Figure 13.21), but you can master it with practice.

3. Duplicate the circle shape (+ key) and downsize the duplicate about 79% (watch the Status Bar as you drag) by dragging a corner sizing handle inward while holding down the Shift key. Duplicate this

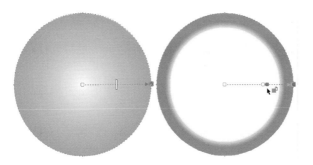

Figure 13.21

Use the Interactive Fill tool to drag and drop color spots from the on-screen palette to create and control a fountain fill.

circle again (+ key) and downsize it about 70%. This places the circles in the right orientation and with about the right shading, but they really aren't quite on the money yet. Use the Interactive Fill tool to move the points along each custom color blend to correct the fill for each downsized circle shape (see Figure 13.22).

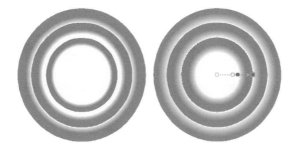

Figure 13.22

Duplicating and downsizing the circle creates the other color rings. To make things look right, tune each color blend with the Interactive Fill tool.

4. Draw a rectangle the size of the page, fill it with the same red as the circle blends, and send it to the back (Shift+PgDn).

5. Use the Text tool to set some thick-looking verbiage. I used a font called Swis721 Blk BT. You can get new fonts from the Property Bar, or select your text and open the Format Text dialog box (Ctrl+T), in which you can control all aspects of your text.

6. Double-click on your text with the Pick tool to reveal the Rotation and Skew handles. Drag the right-center Skew handle upward to tweak the text from its standard layout into something interesting. Give it a thick .153-inch black outline from the Outline Pen dialog box, and then click on OK.

7. Duplicate the text (+ key) and give the duplicate a thinner .111-inch white outline. This produces a thin, black outline around the heavy white one, which makes the main text stand out more (see Figure 13.23).

Figure 13.23

Stack a thinner white-outlined copy of the text on a thicker black-outlined version to produce a multiple-outline look.

8. Use the Text tool again to set the smaller copy. I used the same font that I used for the title, only smaller. Instead of long sentences, set the text as smaller chunks. Click on the desktop, type your word, and then click somewhere else and type another word. Do this so that you can more easily manipulate each word independently of the others.

9. Select one of your text elements and set it up with the correct typestyle, fill, and outline attributes. Give the text a white fill and, from the Outline Pen dialog box (F12), give it a thick .111-inch black outline. Enable the Behind Fill option and change to the squared-off corner option (see Figure 13.24).

Figure 13.24

Use the Behind Fill and squared-corner options from the Outline Pen dialog box to make other text stand out.

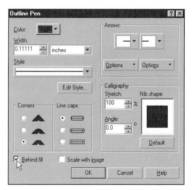

10. After one of your text elements is set up correctly, simply select all the text bits and choose Edit|Copy Properties From (Ctrl+Shift+A). Now, you can enable the Outline Pen, Outline Color, Fill, and even the Text Properties option in the Copy Properties dialog box, and click on OK.

11. Click on the text that you formatted. In a single click, all the attributes of that one text object will transfer to the rest of the text objects.

12. With the Shape tool, you can select an individual letter within a text string. Simply click on the control node below the letter (see Figure 13.25) to modify that letter independently of the others in that text string. (You can also Shift-select multiple control nodes to select more

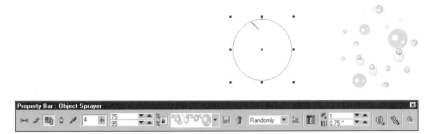

Figure 13.33

You can assign a Spraylist to any existing object (such as the circle on the left) by using the Artistic Media tool in Sprayer mode.

gallery (see Figure 13.33). That's it. Modify the parameters of the current Spraylist (Spray order, spacing, and so forth) on the Property Bar.

Beyond f/x

Mixing media is hardly a new concept. Photos juxtaposed with computer-generated images and other design tidbits make up the majority of desktop publishing projects. The ability to mix up the mood a bit by using the bitmap effects filters opens the doors to more artistic interpretations of otherwise ordinary photos. Instead of actual product shots, make things look a little more artistic by applying one of the Art Strokes filters (Watercolor, Sketch Pad, and so forth). Or, mix the double-vision concept of using the same image twice, but use a muted, artistic rendition of the main image as a background with the original photo lying crisp and clear in the foreground. The potential is staggering!

Mixing real world images with high-tech computer-generated artwork makes the artwork more approachable. Without anything from the real world to use as a reference, a fully computerized design lacks scale or approachability. Designs with computer pieces only might be perfect for some markets, but in general, they seem cold or mechanical, and may alienate a larger audience. Using real-world images to gain instant accessibility and to contrast the hard-edged, geometric feel of the computer creates a nice balance. You don't have to look far to find real-world images to use in your designs. Scan textures from around the house, such as leaves, fabric, your face—whatever—to use as interesting bitmap patterns fills or abstract backgrounds. Today's design climate knows no rules, and mixing technologies just makes you look more skilled and makes your art more contemporary.

Moving On

This chapter explored the ever-evolving world of contemporary design by demonstrating completely computer-generated artwork that uses text, vector, and even 3D images crammed into one canvas. We saw again

FREEHAND OBJECT FLINGING

To use the Object Sprayer in freehand mode, select the Artistic Media tool from the Curve tool flyout and click on Sprayer in the Property Bar. Drag on the screen to scatter the images in the currently selected Spraylist. To choose another Spraylist, click on the drop-down arrow next to the currently selected Spraylist on the Property Bar, and choose another Spraylist from the drop-down gallery.

how to work hand-drawn images into awesome CorelDRAW scenes and how to create unique background coloring. We also saw how to take advantage of new features in the CorelDRAW 9 tool set to create artistically enhanced images.

Working in today's fast-paced world means managing the chaos of clashing technologies. Don't fight it—work with it. Traditional art and design philosophies, techniques, and tools should be a natural part of your modern art studio. Even if you were never skilled with traditional media, you can exploit the look by using the new tools. Sometimes, you'll have to mix media, and CorelDRAW enables you to pull it off brilliantly!

In the next chapter, we look at an even more common design task: creating photo collages. From merging images with subtle transparency effects to stuffing photos into hard-edged geometric shapes, we cover a broad range of techniques. The best part is that these collages involve no paper photos to cut out or glue to spill. On to the montage.

14 PHOTO COLLAGES

This chapter discusses creative ways to merge multiple images and photos into a single eye-catching and appealing graphic.

Mixing scanned photos into computer designs is a staple of the contemporary art diet. It is an amazingly popular method of creating interesting images because you need little illustration talent to mix photos together, and you can get great-looking graphics without too much effort. In addition, a much larger image base exists for photos than for vector-based clip art, with stock-photo companies digitizing their inventory and Corel Corporation offering literally thousands of photos for sale in its photo CD-ROM collections.

In a bit of an oxymoronic twist, a recent trend is to antique images, making them look old and weathered, and then use oh-so-high-tech image-manipulation techniques on the computer to merge these photos together. Ahhh, that great enigmatic era known as the '90s.

In this chapter, we endeavor to mix the old and new, creating collages of old bitmaps in cool, modern ways. In the first example, we use the Interactive Transparency tool to mix photos and hard-edged elements smoothly into a catalog-cover example. Then, we antique images with two-color (*duotone*) effects and merge the images together by using transparency effects. In the third example, we exploit the PowerClip feature and Lens effects to create a photo montage with a strong geometric feel. Finally, we mix and match the lessons learned throughout the chapter in a pastel-colored home-page design. It's fast and fun working with photos, offering quick wins in your design day.

Waves And Grids

Commercial artwork, while the bread and butter of most desktop designers, usually lacks the opportunity for much pizzazz. Typical projects such as product catalogs, brochures, Web pages, and the like, tend to suffer from small budgets and overbearing clients who limit your creative control. Top that off with client math (like when they supply 12 pages of information for an 8-page catalog) and it's nearly enough to make you flip out and go squat by a tree humming show tunes.

Using the Interactive Transparency tool offers a way to help combine the less exciting pieces of a design (such as graphs and charts) with other elements, for a more appealing overall image. The image in Figure 14.1 uses this trick to make the data chart a part of the graphic, and also uses transparency tricks to merge the wave and graph elements. The result is an image that retains the pleasing aesthetics of the curling wave while also literally and figuratively communicating high-tech engineering.

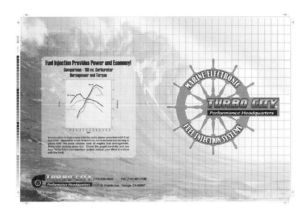

Figure 14.1

The Interactive Transparency tool helps merge individual elements such as the graph, grid, and wave into a uniform design.

This graphic is for the cover of a brochure, with the fold located down the center. So, the back half is on the left, and the front is on the right. It also is only a two-color image (black and cyan), an effort to keep the cost of printing down. Establishing your project parameters at the outset keeps you from backtracking later. Here is how to use the Interactive Transparency tool to merge elements into a single image:

1. Start by locating a graphic that is appropriate for your background. I like secondary images that are interesting but not overbearing. The wave is a photo from Corel's image library, available online or on the Sampler II Photo CD-ROM. Or, you can choose Acquire Image|Acquire and scan a lovely background for your collage.

2. To make the wave a brighter blue and to be in line with my project parameters, I removed all of the yellow and magenta from the photo. First, choose Bitmaps|Mode|CMYK to convert your image. CMYK offers more control than RGB because you can reduce or increase the amount of each color of ink independently of the others.

3. With your bitmap now CMYK, choose Effects|Color Adjustment|Level Equalization. From the Level Equalization dialog box you can control the amount of each color in the image, using the Channel drop-down list box. First, disable the Auto-Adjust option under the Channel area. Then, change to the Magenta Channel and remove all of this color by dragging the bottom-right slider to the left to reduce the Output Range Compression to almost 0 (see Figure 14.2).

4. Change the Channel option from the Magenta Channel to the Yellow Channel. Repeat the process of reducing the yellow ink, again by dragging the bottom-right Output Range Compression slider to the left. Click on OK to remove the magenta and yellow from your wave graphic.

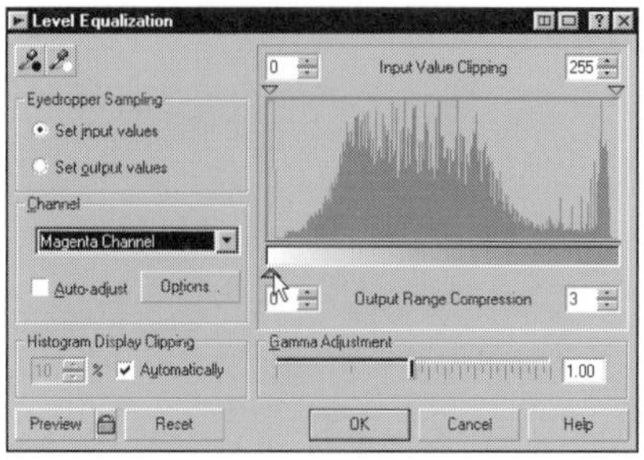

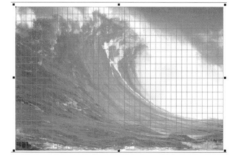

Figure 14.2
Use the Level Equalization dialog box to remove all the magenta and yellow ink from your wave photo.

5. Switch to the Graph Paper tool on the Object flyout. Right-click on the tool and choose Properties to open the Options dialog box on the Graph Paper Tool page. Change the Number of Cells Wide to 40, and the Number of Cells High to 20. Click on OK to close the dialog box.

6. Drag the Graph Paper tool across your desktop to create a 40x20 grid. From the Outline Pen dialog box (F12), give the grid a .013-inch cyan outline. Click on OK to close the dialog box. Now, you should have a nice grid on top of your wave image (see Figure 14.3).

Figure 14.3
The Graph Paper tool makes it easy to create a blue grid across your wave photo.

7. With the graph group selected, choose Arrange|Order|To Back (Shift+PgDn) to put the group behind the bitmap. You can't use the Interactive Transparency tool on a group containing this many objects (800), so instead we use the tool on the single wave-photo object.

8. Click on your wave photo and then select the Interactive Transparency tool from the toolbar. Drag from the bottom-left corner to the top-right corner. This fades the photo gradually from the bottom-left corner toward the top-right, where it fades out entirely to reveal the grid below. You can control how much or how little of the grid you see by moving the control points on the Interactive Transparency tool (see Figure 14.4).

Note: You can circumvent the "Object is to complex" limitation by converting all of the elements in to a single bitmap with the transparent background option enabled. With all of the pieces homogenized into a single bitmap, the Interactive Transparency tool works just fine.

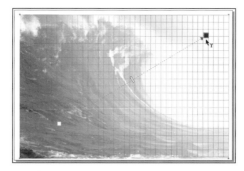

Figure 14.4

The Interactive Transparency tool fades out the wave photo to reveal the graph below.

9. Use the Rectangle tool to draw a square, to designate an area for the comparison chart. Hover the Rectangle tool over a corner node and drag to round out the corners. Duplicate this rectangle (+ key) and down-size the duplicate by dragging a corner sizing handle inward while holding down the Shift key.

10. To get the uniform transparency for the product-comparison chart area, instead of dragging the Interactive Transparency tool, modify the options on the Property Bar. Shift-select both squares and then click on the Interactive Transparency tool. In the Property Bar, change the Transparency Type to Uniform with a Starting Transparency rate of 50.

That's all there is to it. With one square on top of the other, the center area is almost pure white to display the comparison chart, but it's wispy enough to show the wave and other graphic below (see Figure 14.5).

The addition of some text and logos finished off this piece, which isn't worth walking through step by step. The subtle effects created with the Interactive Transparency tool make these otherwise-standalone pieces

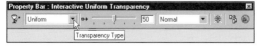

Figure 14.5

The Interactive Transparency tool with the Uniform Transparency Type option enabled creates a semi-opaque area for the comparison chart to sit.

merge into a more continuous graphic element. You can view the finished result in this book's middle color section (hold the book sideways to see the image correctly) and in the \Chapt14\ folder on the companion CD-ROM, in a file called marine.cdr. This is the actual file I used for the catalog project, at full size, so it's really big. I had to scale it down quite a bit to fit into the color section in the middle of this book.

Figure 14.6
Giving each element the same Duotone settings creates a like color scheme, which, in addition to the Interactive Transparency tool, makes for a seamless image collage.

Historic Duotones

Using the Interactive Transparency tool is one way to help multiple images come together in a pleasing composite. Another way to get the images to match together even more is to convert each element to a uniform color scheme. The graphic in Figure 14.6 uses the same Duotone settings for each element and then marries this coloring technique with seamless image transitions by using the Interactive Transparency tool to create a solid composite (see the image in the color section to see how everything is in the same bronze tones).

To really hammer home the idea of an image composite, you can also physically merge all the elements into a single bitmap. Then, you can add an artistic frame effect to the whole thing with a bitmap filter. Here's how to give multiple graphics the same duotone coloring and merge them into a single physical bitmap:

1. Start by collecting images for your photo collage. Scan your own photos (this tutorial presents some techniques that are perfect to make contemporary color photos match the look of antique photos, which can produce cool photo collages for family reunions and so forth). I turned to the online Corel collection for an eagle and Statue of Liberty image, and then searched the CorelDRAW clip-art collection for a flag graphic. You can mix and match vector clip-art and photos, and all will merge together perfectly by the time we are through.

2. Use the Rectangle tool to draw a box to serve as a guide for your final image size. You'll often work with elements that are bigger than or hang beyond the edge of your page, but that's fine at this stage. Just use the boundary box to help you work out the layout of your design, to get a sense of balance and an overall look and feel (see Figure 14.7).

3. With your elements basically in place, it's time to convert them all to the same color scheme. Select one of the photos and select Bitmap|Mode|Duotone. This opens the Duotone dialog box, in which

Figure 14.7
Draw a boundary box to help you visualize how the pieces will fit together for your overall design.

you can recolor your image by using low-color techniques for a very stylized look. The options available in the Types drop-down list box vary the number of colors in your new coloring scheme, ranging from one (Monotone) to four (Quadtone). For this example, change the Type to Duotone and then click on OK to convert the image (see Figure 14.8).

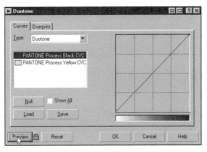

Figure 14.8
Use the Duotone dialog box to convert your full-color graphic to stylized, low-color images.

4. Repeat the process for all of your bitmaps, using the same Duotone settings each time so that they share the same basic coloring scheme.

5. To get the vector artwork of the flag to match the recolored photos, the flag vector image first needs to be converted into a bitmap. Select the vector group and choose Bitmaps|Convert To Bitmap, to open the Convert to Bitmap dialog box. Set the Color to RGB, Resolution to 300 dpi (or whatever you need), and enable the Anti-aliasing, Transparent Background, and Use Color Profile options. Click on OK to convert your object into a bitmap.

6. With your vector flag now a bitmap, you can repeat the Bitmaps|Mode|Duotone process to recolor this image. You may see a Warning dialog box saying that the convert-to-duotone process will result in a loss of the transparent background, but ignore this and do it anyway. In my experience, the background always remains trans-

Note: If you don't like the default colors in the Duotone dialog box, simply double-click on the color chips in the Duotone dialog box to open a color selection dialog box in which you can choose a new color and create any color scheme that you wish.

parent. Use the same colors in the Duotone dialog box as you did in Step 3 for your other images, so that everything is colored the same.

7. Use the Interactive Transparency tool to allow the smaller images to dissolve slowly into the background image. Drag the Interactive Transparency tool from the center of your photo outward. This sets up the default Linear Fountain Transparency. Click on Radial Fountain Transparency on the Property Bar and then reverse the logic of the transparency by changing the color of the transparency control points on the object itself.

8. Drag white from the on-screen color well and drop it on the black center of the Interactive Transparency control line on the object. Drag black from the on-screen color well and drop it on the outside white point of the Interactive Transparency control line on the object. This reverses the default logic of the transparency, making the solid center fade out to clear (see Figure 14.9). Drag the control points around until you get the transition that you like.

9. To get the same transparency effect on your flag object, choose Effects|Copy Effects|Lens From and then click on the bitmap that you were working on in Step 7. The resulting transparency effect probably won't be perfect, but it's faster than starting from scratch. You

BATTLING PRINT TECHNOLOGIES

CorelDRAW can support many coloring schemes for whatever project you may be working on. RGB is useful for on-screen applications, CMYK is good for full-color printing on paper, and Pantone is appropriate when you have spot-color print jobs. However, sometimes you'll want to take advantage of a feature that isn't available to your current coloring scheme. For example, the Duotone coloring option only supports Pantone colors, so you have to choose from this palette to use this feature. Lens and Transparency effects typically are rendered using RGB technology, so this may conflict with other things that you have going on in your design.

Not to worry; you can mix and match all the features and functions within CorelDRAW (within reason). For example, for anything that is destined for on-screen projects you need not worry at all about palette conflicts because CorelDRAW will take care of color conversions during the Export to Bitmap process (or you can always perform a screen capture). If your design is headed for traditional CMYK printing on paper, again, no problem. CorelDRAW will translate any RGB or Pantone spot colors into their CMYK equivalents during the color-separation translation process for printing, if you enable that option.

However, if you have a specialized color need, such as creating a duotone to create specific color plates for printing, keep the color conflicts in mind or you may have more color plates than you bargained for. The easiest way to keep the integrity of a duotone intact, to limit the number of color plates produced, is to simply merge all of your elements into a single RGB bitmap by using the Convert to Bitmaps feature, and then use the Bitmaps|Mode|Duotone command to convert that RGB image back into a true duotone, which produces only the two color plates needed for offset printing.

Figure 14.9
The Interactive Transparency tool, in Radial Fountain Transparency mode, can create a soft, circular transition between your photo and the background.

can easily fine-tune the settings with the Interactive Transparency tool by dragging the control points.

10. When you are satisfied with the layout and look of your photo collage, save a backup copy to disk. Then, shift-select all the individual bitmap elements and the background image and choose Effects|PowerClip|Place Inside Container. Click on the resulting arrow on your boundary box to stuff all the elements inside of it. Right-click on the on-screen x to remove any outline from the PowerClip rectangle.

11. With the PowerClip rectangle selected, choose Bitmaps|Convert to Bitmap to open the Convert to Bitmap dialog box. Change the Color option to RGB, Resolution to 300 dpi, and enable only the Anti-aliasing and Use Color Profile options. Click on OK to merge everything in your PowerClip rectangle into a single bitmap (see Figure 14.10).

Figure 14.10
The Convert to Bitmap feature converts all the individual elements inside the PowerClip rectangle into a single bitmap object.

12. Now that all of your individual elements have been homogenized into a single bitmap, you can frame everything by using a bitmap filter effect. With the bitmap selected, choose Bitmaps|Creative| Frame to open the Frame dialog box. This filter gives your bitmap an artistic frame effect, which you can choose from the Select Frame part of the dialog box. To change the options for the selected frame, click on the Modify tab. On this page of the Frame dialog box you can control the options for the selected frame.

Change the Frame Color to white and modify the Horizontal and Vertical Scale options until your image has the look that you want (click on the Preview button to see how your changes effect the look of the effect). When you are satisfied with the results, click on OK (see Figure 14.11).

Figure 14.11
Use the Frame bitmap filter to get an artistic, ripped-edge look around your bitmap.

That's basically all there is to it. I slapped on some text to create the title, using white text with a drop-shadow to make it stand out against the background. You can view this image in the color section in the middle of this book, and on the companion CD-ROM in the \Chapt14\ folder, in the ushistory.cdr file. All the individual bitmaps have already been merged into a single bitmap in that file, so you probably will want to try this technique on your own stack of digitized photos.

Why Two Kay?

If one more person asks me "Is CorelDRAW Y2K-compliant?" I think I'll scream. Listen up people, your graphics software doesn't care an inkling about the time of day or what year it is. Why would it? I can't think of anything that's time-sensitive about making pretty pictures (unless you are working with acrylics, and trying to finish before the paint dries). The image in Figure 14.12 uses geometric shapes as a vehicle to organize, lay out, and even modify the photo elements into a single theme graphic. And, just to make my point about Y2K hysteria, I set my system date to Jan. 1, 2000 while working on it.

I sometimes prefer strong geometric shapes to the wispy translucence that the Interactive Transparency tool offers when creating a photo collage, as in the previous two tutorials. You may prefer to stick to the soft transitions that the transparency effects provide. Or, if you can't make up your mind (like me), skip to the next tutorial, in which both geometric framing and the transparency transition effects are used. My job isn't to dictate your

---

FAT FRAMES

If you want to increase the size of your bitmap so that less of it is cut away with the Frame filter effect, use the Bitmaps|Inflate Bitmap|Manually Inflate Bitmap command. This adds area around the bitmap, just like increasing the paper size in Photo-Paint. Or, for a more visual approach to enlarging your bitmap, simply draw a larger rectangle around your image, with no outline or fill. Then, Shift-select both the rectangle and bitmap and use the Convert to Bitmap command to merge the two into a larger bitmap with more image area on the edges, so that you have some breathing room when you work with the frame filters.

even Web sites often boil down to simple photo montages. Break things up with interesting geometric patterns and border effects, or use the power and flexibility of a CorelDRAW layout to stack the images right on top of each other by using transparencies. With the addition of layers to Photo-Paint, stacking images in CorelDRAW isn't as critical as it once was, but with all the other design elements coming together in CorelDRAW, and with so many design options available to you there, you might as well create the bitmap effects in CorelDRAW, too.

In addition to being primary design elements, bitmap collages make interesting backgrounds or even abstract patterns for other unique applications. Mix and match the new concepts from this chapter with some of the other concepts that you've learned (adding depth from Chapter 6, double-vision from Chapter 9, and so forth) for your own take on the photo-collage concept. Or, invent your own new ideas—the sky is the limit.

For a unique gift idea, instead of making one of those hideous hand-cut photo collages, create a digital montage. Scan and assemble the photos in the computer and then output the composite image at a service bureau or a high-end color printer. This will cost about the same as having duplicate photos made, is easier than hand-cutting out all of those pieces, and you can use incredible computer tricks to merge the images into one beautiful composite. With a little planning, you can create two unique 8 1/2×11 images on one landscape, tabloid printout. Cut these out, frame 'em, and make your grandmas happy!

Moving On

In this chapter, we looked at creating interesting photo montages mixing a variety of technologies and techniques. Using CorelDRAW, we created drop shadows, manipulated bitmaps, added captions, and even created neat collages with the PowerClip and Interactive Transparency features. With the Duotone option, you can recolor your photos to look alike or to become stylized individual elements. All in all, we looked at some very cool techniques which should come in handy in your virtual studio to create all kinds of projects. You probably won't use these examples verbatim (unless you just happen to be designing a "U.S. History" book cover or assembling your own Y2K-global-disaster graphics) but the techniques will prove to be useful, I guarantee. Unless, of course, you happen to be the only computer artist in the world not using scanned photos....

In the next chapter, we exploit more bitmap features to help us get the campy, pulp feel of sci-fi fiction publications from the first part of this century. Using original and stock images of antique magazine covers, you can produce very cool results with Photo-Paint and CorelDRAW tricks. No need to read under the covers with a flashlight; this pulp fiction is okay out in the open! Leave your high brow tastes behind as we take on the fun and frolic of trashy novels.

15 PULP VISION

This chapter looks at exploiting classic sci-fi pulp images for use in modern designs. Tricks for merging old images with new, how to paint away headlines and add your own, and creating a fun, campy style are all explored.

There was such an emphasis on the future in what is now the past, the combination makes for great contemporary artwork. People were just as wacky about alien invasions back in the '30s and '40s as they are today. With Roswell, New Mexico appearing in daily headlines, why not bank on the trend and add a little sci-fi pulp to your daily design diet?

Using a comic-book style for commercial artwork is not only unique, but it can also be very easy. By working with the volumes of stock images available you can quickly create an easy-to-reproduce piece of art that works great to draw attention. The bold, graphic nature of illustrations coupled with the simplistic use of type almost guarantees good results in any media.

In this chapter, we look at exploiting the campy pulp-fiction styles of yore in modern design applications. In the first example, we take a sci-fi image from the first half of the century and make it feel right at home in a modern computer ad. Then, we manipulate an old comic book magazine cover, painting away the existing copy by using the Clone tool in Photo-Paint. Finally, we generate that signature pulp look by using an original ink illustration and some other tricks.

Computer Bugs Attack!

I have always been a fan of space and comics, and have an eclectic collection that includes such great titles as *True Alien Stories* and the like. (What wonderful drivel to fill a young boy's head with, to keep him looking into the skies in fear!) When I discovered that Time Tunnel (the company that also supplied the pin-up girls from Chapter 12) had a Sci-Fi Pulps collection, I had to have it. (Samples from this collection are also included in the \timetunl\ directory on the companion CD-ROM, and be sure to check out Time Tunnel's Web site at www.timetunnel.com.) This collection is a great source of the kind of campy, girl-in-distress, Buck Rogers art that I so love!

When I get to mix business with pleasure, so to speak, is when I love my job. I have some very cool clients who occasionally let me cut loose and do something different (like in Figure 15.1). This works to our mutual benefit, because when I like what I'm working on I put more effort and time into the project, without charging more, and the client gets great, eye-catching art that usually generates sales—and everyone is happy. This technique borrows heavily from the tried and true Wall Street ad formula; interesting photo+(bold text/catchy slogan)=mass appeal+^sales+repeat business. If you flip through any high-end publication, you won't find a lot of amazing CorelDRAW illustrations (unless it's a computer art mag, of course), but you will find the ad formula at work. So, why not make it work for you?

The beauty of the formula is that, as a contemporary digital artist, you can also draw from volumes of amazing images such as the Sci-Fi Pulp collection, already digitized and royalty-free. In the old days, if you used stock photography you had to pay a fee every time that it ran, and a hefty price tag up front (we once plunked down $10,000 for a one-year contract on an image the client insisted they had to have). Now, for a measly $99 bucks you can score an image CD-ROM with no usage limitations or additional fees. A little image massaging in Photo-Paint, text and layout in CorelDRAW, and even the nonillustrator can make money in the ad game.

I like to try to keep the original look and feel of a period piece as much as possible when using it for a contemporary design. Something is lost if you get too flashy with modern techniques or contemporary fonts. You don't have to be dead on, but if you shoot for close to the original, or incorporate popular techniques of the period (such as having characters block out part of the title, as in Figure 15.1), things look better. If you can nail the original spirit of the design in your makeover, the result is almost like an optical illusion, where your viewer at first thinks they are looking at an antique image. The surprise is things like Web addresses and fax numbers that bring the image into the '90s. Here is how to use a classic stock image in a modern application:

Figure 15.1

Old-time images can be worked into contemporary designs with great success, using Photo-Paint to clean up the images, and CorelDRAW to merge all the design elements.

1. Find an image from the archives that suits your application. Don't try to stretch the reader's imagination too much with images that don't match the ad copy in any way. This can be kind of hard, but I found a workable image in the Time Tunnel collection of this very mechanical-looking monster thing attacking the obligatory damsel, with our hero space-boy coming to the rescue. I've often imagined my computer as an unruly beast, so I decided the image would work. This image has the cryptic title fu-05_50.jpg and is in the \timetunl\ subdirectory on the companion CD-ROM.

2. Load the image, at the largest size available, into Photo-Paint for manipulation (the more image data the better). (The Time Tunnel images are already at 300 dpi, but some CD-ROM photo collections give you a size option when you load. Use the Poster option when you are given an option, which is the largest.)

3. You need to paint away the existing type so that you can add your own, and you need to address some other issues in Photo-Paint to make the image right. First, most PhotoCD images aren't set up for print applications. (Kodak developed PhotoCD technology originally for on-screen applications.) Thus, you need to convert the image from the on-screen version to something that you can use for print (obviously, the parameters are different if you are doing Web-only graphics).

   Select Image|Resample. The Resample dialog box shows the current stats on the selected bitmap. Often, these PhotoCD images have huge physical dimensions (Width: 22 inches, Height: 32 inches, and low 72 dpi resolution). Not exactly useful. To fix this, enable the Maintain Original Size option on the Resample dialog box and then enter the desired resolution—in this case, 300 dpi. Now, with the denser dots, the physical dimensions reflect the size that is appropriate for offset printing, down in the 7x10-inch range. Change the physical settings of your bitmap to what you need, and click on OK. (If you get into the habit of taking control of these kinds of bitmap details, you'll have fewer surprises. This dialog box is also available in CorelDRAW, under the Bitmaps menu.) Now your image is the correct size.

4. Image collections often are in RGB format, which also is on-screen technology. For the kind of control that you need to build this image correctly in CorelDRAW, you need CMYK format, because if you want to match up background objects seamlessly they all need the exact same fill. RGB translates into CMYK automatically from CorelDRAW, but you have no way to guarantee that new objects will translate the same as the bitmap. Eliminate the guesswork and convert the image to CMYK now. Select Image|Mode and then select CMYK Color (32-bit) from the fly-out. The image now is at the correct size and color depth for offset printing. Save the image to disk, only use a nonlossy compression (JPEG will lose info to save space). I use the TIFF format.

5. Start manipulating the image for your application. You may want to adjust the contrast or brightness, or even one of the CMYK levels (like we did with the pin-up, to remove the background cyan). I bumped the brightness and contrast just a hair, because I like high-contrast images.

6. Use the Eyedropper tool to sample the background color. Try in several places, to make sure that you don't sample some strange color mix. My image has a background color of 79% yellow. Left-mouse click on the Eyedropper tool button to select the underlying color as your paint color. Use the Paintbrush tool to replace any of the text with blank yellow area, by brushing over it. Try to get in close to the areas that you know you will crop later with a bitmap color mask, and paint the yellow color right up to the edge. A smooth yellow line around the characters' heads will allow for better results later in CorelDRAW. Use the Selection tool to crop the image to just above the figures' heads, save the cropped image to disk, and then exit Photo-Paint (see Figure 15.2).

7. Open CorelDRAW and import the bitmap (Ctrl+I). Draw a rectangle behind the bitmap at the desired ad size. With the new CorelDRAW 9 Eyedropper tool, it's a snap to give this new background color the exact fill value as the background in the bitmap. Select the Eyedropper tool from the toolbar and click on the yellow background in the bitmap. The tool sucks in the color value of 79% yellow (like a turkey-baster).

8. Move the Eyedropper tool over the rectangle that you just drew and press the Shift key, which toggles between the Eyedropper and Paintbucket tools (and vice versa, if you have the Paintbucket selected). With the tool now in Paintbucket mode, simply click on the background object to fill it with the 79% yellow from the back-

RULE THE PRINTER

If you work in a controlled environment in which you use the same service bureau and the same printer time after time, you can control your artwork to get better results. For example, if in the printing process your images become dark, you can brighten them in Photo-Paint by using the Brightness-Contrast-Intensity dialog box (Ctrl+B). If this doesn't fix the problem, open the dot patterns in your half-tones by using a looser line screen. A typical printing line screen is 133 lpi (this book uses a tight, 155 lpi in the color sections). Drop the line screen to about 100 lpi if printing on less than optimum paper or a press that leaves a lot of ink (newspapers, for example, typically use a loose, 85 lpi to compensate for their printing process and paper).

The same process can be used to fix color problems. If your images consistently seem to turn more yellow, or any other combination of colors, you can tweak the levels of each CMYK color individually from the Level Equalization dialog box (Ctrl+E). Select the desired color channel from the Equalize window and then drag the sliders to increase or decrease the value. Use the Preview window to check your progress. You can use the same process to color-correct before going to print. Generate a match-print or high-end color proof and you can adjust the levels of the images to correct for almost anything. Take control of your printing projects, and you will be much happier with the results.

Figure 15.2

An image from Time Tunnel Sci-Fi Pulps (left) is the starting point for the design. The bitmap is manipulated in Photo-Paint so that it's the right size and color depth. The Paintbrush tool is used to paint away any existing text.

ground of the bitmap. This tool makes color-matching objects in CorelDRAW a breeze. With identical background coloring, no one will ever know where the original bitmap ends and your CorelDRAW box begins (see Figure 15.3).

9. Start to lay out your text elements. I imported a thumbnail of the original cover and placed it next to my artwork to refer to as I worked. This made matching the fonts on my system to those used in the original period piece easier. Back when CorelDRAW 3 shipped with exactly 256 fonts, I probably could have found the fonts used in the original artwork in two seconds, but in today's font-fat design environment I can never seem to locate what I want. Grrr! (See the last tutorial in this section for more on font phobias.)

Figure 15.3

Drawing a box behind the bitmap (on left, in wireframe) creates a seamless background if you fill it with the same CMYK value as the bitmap.

10. Use the Text tool to set your type on the page. I used a font called Faktos for the headlines, which is similar, but not an exact match to the original. The other font is called Futura, which has a clean, simple, retro look to it despite its oxymoronic name. Use a simple, flat color scheme in line with the original (fountain fills are a no-no if you want a period look).

Figure 15.10
The Clone tool removes the unwanted text (inset) and lets you paint an abstract fold of drapes in its place.

8. With the original text gone, you are free to add your own headlines in CorelDRAW. Import the file (Ctrl+I) into a fresh file, so that you can start adding custom text elements in CorelDRAW. Again, I tried to use a font and layout that are similar to the original, which turned out to be Futura Md BT (Bold).

   When these images were originally made, text was added to full-color images in a very low-tech way using manually typeset words and photographic techniques. For this reason, the text is simple, bold, and often one color. Graphic art was used to include additions such as boxes or lines, which were literally cut into the film manually or scraped away with a blade. Feeling spoiled? You should be! Art like this originally took hours to paint by hand, and then quite a bit of additional effort to add text and other details as well as prep for the printing press. Give your computer a hug.

9. Use the Rectangle tool to draw a square, and then duplicate and arrange it to become the Corel Corporation logo (work off to the side, away from your imported bitmap). To distort the logo so that it looks like it's pasted on the round earth, use the Fish Eye lens in the Lens docker. Draw a box over the original logo and then open the Lens docker from the Effects menu (or use the keyboard shortcut, Alt+F3).

10. Click on the drop-down arrow below the preview window, and scroll down to locate the Fish Eye option. Set the Rate at 75% to get the desired roundness. To transform the pieces themselves, and not just how they look, enable the Frozen option and then click on Apply (see Figure 15.11). You now can Ungroup (Ctrl+U) to have actual distorted pieces, instead of just the illusion of distortion created with the lens object.

11. Drop the logo on the globe and then use the Color Add lens on the Lens docker, with the Color box set to red, to achieve the see-through

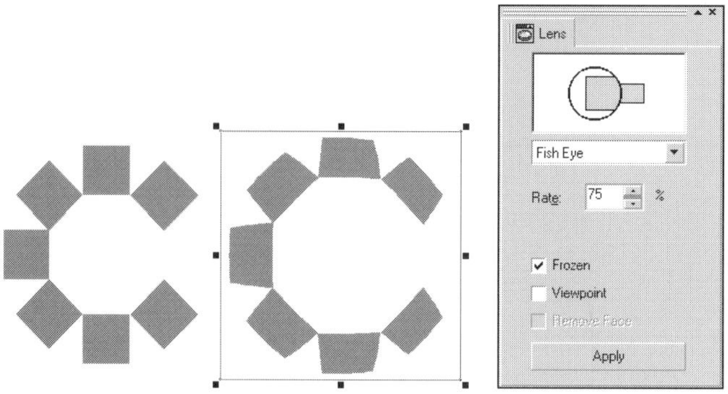

Figure 15.11
Use the Fish Eye lens, with the Frozen option enabled, to distort a Corel logo into a round configuration.

yet vibrant logo on the globe. Trim away the shape in the areas that should be obscured (by the glove, for example). Use the Shape tool to add and delete nodes, to change the shape. Or, draw another shape with the Freehand tool and use it with the Trim feature to chop away areas that should be hidden (see Figure 15.12).

12. To get the logos on the rocket ships, use the Interactive Transparency tool, modifying the parameters on the Property Bar. With the solid-red logo in place, change the Type to Uniform, modify the rate to 15, and set the Transparency Operation to Add. This setting is more convincing than the Normal setting. Again, we will use Photo-Paint to fine-tune this look.

13. To maintain the graininess of the bitmap, you can't just stick new CorelDRAW objects into place without them looking too new and out of place. Achieving a convincing look in CorelDRAW is difficult, but you can do it if you first convert the objects into bitmaps. Select your text, for example, and choose Bitmaps|Convert to Bitmap. On

FREEZE FRAME

Lens effects normally don't change objects at all, only the way in which they appear. This is exactly how an object with a lens effect works in CorelDRAW. The benefit is that you can move the lens (or change the lens effect) to select a different area below to look at with the effect, and the program automatically calculates the changes and displays a new image (like the double-vision example in Chapter 9). The downside to using the lens effect is that the lens object is a live entity that needs constant recalculation to generate the image below. Also, because you never actually change your objects, you create only illusions, not modified objects that you can later select and manipulate.

However, you can change all of this with the Frozen option on the Lens docker. With this option enabled, the program not only changes the way that objects appear, but also builds an entirely new set of objects from which to create the illusion. This way, you don't have live elements, and have objects that you can Ungroup and manipulate. Getting a Frozen lens group to calculate may take a few compute cycles, but the end results can be very handy, as demonstrated in this tutorial.

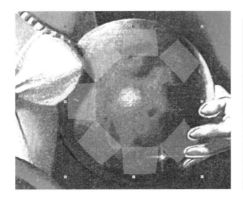

Figure 15.12

Use the Color Add lens to add the logo to the globe.

the Convert to Bitmap dialog box, set the Color option to RGB, unless you are really trying to match some particular CMYK color, in which case you should choose CMYK. (Many bitmap filters, unfortunately, support only RGB, so you might be forced to use this Color setting. However, RGB has the benefit of using less memory.)

Still in the Convert to Bitmap dialog box, enable Anti-aliasing, enable Transparent Background, and keep the default Use Color Profile enabled. (The Use Color Profile feature either cross-references the conversion to whatever color profile you have set up or uses a default setting. Either way, you should be fine.) Choose a suitable Resolution (300 dpi for print; lower for on screen), and click on OK to convert your objects into a uniform bitmap (remember, you may want to save a copy to disk first because you can't ever modify the contents of the text after it is converted).

14. After you convert all the individual objects into a single bitmap, you can modify it with the bitmap filter effects. The Add Noise dialog box (see Figure 15.13) from the Bitmaps|Noise fly-out, for example, enables you to add random dot patterns (visual noise), to help make the text weathered-looking rather than sparkly new. Or, experiment with the Dust and Scratch filter, also available from the Bitmaps|Noise fly-out, to get your new text to match the old, antique look of the original image.

You can convert bits and pieces of your object to bitmaps in CorelDRAW or export the image as a composite bitmap and manipulate things further in Photo-Paint (or another bitmap-manipulation program). The point is that you aren't limited to the hard-edged results that CorelDRAW objects afford, but can use them as a starting point and then move on to other effects that bitmaps offer. You can mix and match objects and bitmaps to get the exact look that you are after.

Figure 15.13

Use the Add Noise dialog box to make your new additions to the old graphic seem weathered.

Figure 15.14

The original stock image with all remnants of the cover removed, awaiting your own custom application.

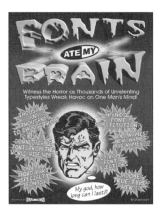

Figure 15.15

Electricity sparks can add an interesting glow behind objects to draw attention to them and pull them away from the background.

You can view this image in the color section in the middle of this book, or by loading spacegrl.cdr from the \Chapt15\ section of the companion CD-ROM. I waffled back and forth with this image, at times laughing hysterically at the original *Thrilling Wonder Stories* magazine title, and then the next moment thinking I might come up with a different title. Well, I didn't come up with a title that made me laugh like the original, but I went ahead and painted out the headline anyway. It is called spacegrl.tif and I stuck it back in the \timetunl\ directory on the CD-ROM. If you come up with a better title, let me know (see Figure 15.14).

Fonts Ate My Brain

The image in Figure 15.15 was supposed to accompany an article I did ranting and raving about a big font fiasco in an earlier CorelDRAW version upgrade. When CorelDRAW first hit the market it used copycat fonts, which looked similar to Adobe PostScript fonts, but without having to license them (like Brooklyn instead of Bookman). Well, somewhere along the line, the copycat fonts were replaced by the real ones and I ended up with both versions on my poor, choking computer and I just went nuts. Although *Corel* magazine didn't print my rant, I still love this artwork and it fits in nicely with our pulp theme.

Here is how to get a campy graphic with electric sparks, a 3D Saturday afternoon matinee horror marquee headline, and exploding type balloons:

1. Duplicate the objects for which you want to create a fuzzy background and drag them off to the side to make working on them easier. Assign a black fill and outline for these objects. To control the area occupied by the sparks, use a thicker or thinner outline. A thicker outline results in a more dramatic, wider spark area.

2. Draw a box the size that you want your bitmap to be, with no outline or fill. Select all the objects and choose Bitmaps|Convert to Bitmap. In the Convert to Bitmap dialog box, set Color to Grayscale,

FONT HELL

Back when all of this font lunacy started with CorelDRAW 1, you got a much, much smaller box. It had a handful of 5 1/4-inch floppy disks, a smattering of clip art, a VHS training tape, and a bunch of fonts. Well, it seemed like a bunch of fonts, but compared to today's giant box-o'-draw goodies, with a handful of *CDs*, it doesn't seem like that many fonts at all. Ah, those simple bygone days of CorelDRAW 1 and 2. (Even CorelDRAW 3 had only 256 fonts total, with a handy chart to stick on the wall to find them all.)

How is it that back then I had only a quarter of the fonts, yet I always found exactly what I wanted, and now, with thousands and thousands to choose from, I am never satisfied? Power corrupts, I suppose. Fonts also eat up system resources, big time. If you ever want to commit computer suicide, install all the fonts that come on those shiny CorelDRAW CDs. Forget about it! You'll never recover your system again! (The sad but true tale of a total Corel geek like myself that actually decided to try it one day.)

As a general rule, try to have fewer than 400 fonts actually installed on your machine at any time. This seems like a paltry few, but any more than that and Windows chugs, taking longer to boot up and run any application that uses fonts. (Hmm. Reality check—that would be all of the programs that you use.)

The best way to keep your font choices wide open—while minimizing the number of installed live fonts that are system hounds—is to use a font management application. CorelDRAW ships with one called Bitstream Font Navigator 3.0, which offers a quick and easy way to find and install fonts, organize fonts into manageable groups, and view and print font samples. It beats the heck out of the Win95 font management tools. If you are trying to glean more performance out of your system, limit the number of fonts installed. Then, use a program such as Font Navigator to keep your font options open. The best of both worlds. How often does that happen?

Figure 15.16
Color all objects black, draw a boundary box around them, and then convert to a grayscale bitmap.

set Resolution to 300, and then click on OK to convert them (see Figure 15.16).

3. Fuzz the grayscale bitmap with the Gaussian Blur effect located on the Bitmaps|Blur fly-out. The more blur, the larger the area of your sparks. Predicting the appropriate line weight and level of Gaussian Blur takes a little practice, but is easy to experiment with.

4. To convert the soft-gray fuzz into a harsh set of dots use the Mode option on the Bitmaps menu. Choose Black and White from the Mode fly-out to open the Convert to 1 Bit dialog box. *1 bit* simply means that a pixel is either on (black) or off (white). The default Conversion method and options work fine for this technique, or you can experiment with this dialog box (see Figure 15.17). For bigger chunks, use a lower DPI setting when converting to grayscale, such as 200 or 150 rather than 300.

5. Give the black-and-white bitmap a yellow outline and no fill, and arrange it behind the original objects to create a glowing effect (see

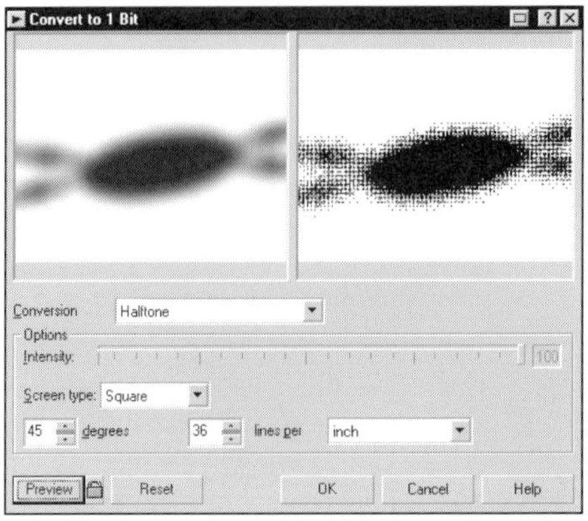

Figure 15.17

Use the Convert to 1 Bit dialog box to experiment with different conversion techniques, to convert your artwork into unique dot patterns.

Figure 15.18). With a 1 bit bitmap, you can assign any color value for the black pixels in the same way that you would assign the outline color to an object: either from the Outline Pen dialog box (F12) or by right-clicking on an on-screen color chip. Color the white background of a 1 bit bitmap in the same way that you would assign any normal Fill value: either with the Uniform Fill dialog box (Shift+F11) or by left-clicking on an on-screen color chip.

Figure 15.18

The grayscale is converted to a black-and-white bitmap then colored yellow and arranged behind the original objects.

6. You can use this effect on any group of objects, such as the colorized comic face in this graphic. Select the objects that make up the face, duplicate, and move off to the side. Color these objects black, draw the boundary box, and repeat the Convert to Grayscale, Gaussian Blur steps as before (see Figure 15.19).

Figure 15.19

Anything can be fuzzed, even object groups containing bitmaps.

7. Convert the bitmap to black and white to create the electricity, as before, and assign a magenta outline with no fill. For a twist, enlarge the bitmap 120% by dragging outward on the sizing handles with the Pick tool, while watching the Scale value on the Status Bar across the bottom of your screen. Duplicate the bitmap, reduce it 90% by dragging inward on the sizing handles with the Pick tool, and change the outline to yellow.

8. Duplicate and reduce again, with the small center having a white outline. This way, you can create electric bursts, much like the explosion blends, except that you can't use the Interactive Blend tool on bitmaps so you have to create the interim steps by hand (see Figure 15.20).

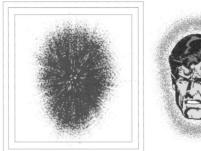

Figure 15.20
To create an electric blend, duplicate and downsize the bitmaps manually, changing the outline color each time (shown in wireframe on the left). By using color changes in this way, you can create a glow effect behind your original objects.

9. The 3D headline text at the top of the page looks complex but it's no sweat in CorelDRAW 9. Use the Text tool to set the words FONTS and BRAIN on the page, using a font called Horror, in a green color. Split the single text object into two individual words with the Break Apart (Ctrl+K) command. This way, you can independently manipulate each word, to tweak each slightly with the Interactive Envelope tool. In the Single Arc mode, distort your words into a creepy, twisted layout (see Figure 15.21).

Figure 15.21
The Interactive Envelope tool distorts the text.

10. After you distort and arrange your individual text objects as you wish, Shift-select them both and Convert to Curves (Ctrl+Q). With a single object, you can get some cool depth with the Interactive Extrude tool.

11. Drag on the text to create an extrude group, which you can then modify by using the options on the Property Bar. Click on Bevels, enable the Use Bevel option, and set the width to .05 inch. Click on

the Lighting button (the light-bulb icon) and then click on the 1 light-bulb button on the pop-up dialog box to enable a light source. That's all there is to it! (see Figure 15.22).

Figure 15.22
Use the Interactive Extrude tool to transform flat text into a 3D-looking headline.

Witness the cerebral carnage in the color section in the middle of this book, and in the fonts.cdr file nestled in the \Chapt15\ subdirectory of the companion CD-ROM. Open the file and create a blended electricity blur by duplicating and downsizing the black-and-white bitmap behind the comic face. It's not as automated as using the Interactive Blend tool on vector objects, but with a little effort you can get some unique exploding effects this way.

The balloons around the words are symbols from a library called Balloons. Use the Shape tool to move around the spikes in each balloon duplicate to make it look unique.

Using the Bitmap menu to create low-resolution, chunky sparks is a quick and easy way to get a very unique effect. Manually blending a bitmap can expand the concept into explosions or bursts. Don't hesitate to experiment by mixing and matching effects in this book, or any other CorelDRAW effects. For example, instead of using a Gaussian Blur, create a white to black blend in CorelDRAW and then convert it to a black-and-white bitmap, to get some nifty variants (see Figure 15.23).

Figure 15.23
Start with CorelDRAW objects instead of a grayscale bitmap, and then convert to a dithered, black-and-white bitmap.

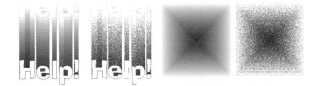

dium to cut corners and speed things along. For example, all the objects on the left side of this robot are mirrored duplicates of the pieces on the right, which cuts your design time in half. You can easily reposition modular art objects, such as the robot's limbs, to create different poses. You could even duplicate the whole robot, creating an army of invading beasts, making each duplicate unique by repositioning arms or changing other details. With "CorelDRAW-aided design," you have many options.

This exercise first discusses the tentacle technique and then shows how to make Brian the BrainBot with movable limbs:

1. With the Ellipse tool, draw a circle. Open the Fountain Fill dialog box and use the Cylinder - Green 03 (or similar) Preset. The key to this technique is to use a custom color blend that has dark edges and highlight in the middle (see Figure 16.2). You can create this color blend manually or use a Preset blend that is similar. For the hydra octopus arm, my custom blend went from black to red to white to magenta. Change the Angle setting in the Options area to get the gleam in one of the top corners, and then click on OK.

Figure 16.1

Using a high-step blend technique you can create movable tube and tentacle objects.

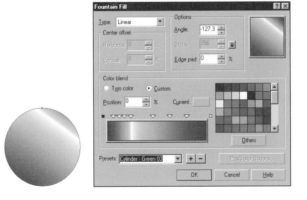

Figure 16.2

A custom color blend is critical to the success of this effect. The idea is to have shadow, highlight, and then shadow again in the color scheme.

2. Duplicate the circle (+ key) and reduce the duplicate by dragging a corner sizing handle inward with the Pick tool. Use the Bezier tool to draw an *S* curve (or any other shape), which you'll eventually run the blend along. Move the two circle objects to the start and finish of the curve and drag between them by using the Interactive Blend tool. Change the Number of Steps to 300 on the Property Bar (see Figure 16.3).

3. On the Property Bar, click on Path Properties, click on New Path, and then click on the curve along which you want your objects to blend (see Figure 16.4). Click on Miscellaneous Blend Options and enable the Blend Along Full Path radio button, which generates a twisty, curving tentacle.

Figure 16.3

Although you draw a curve for the blend to follow along initially, you must blend to objects directly by using the Interactive Blend tool.

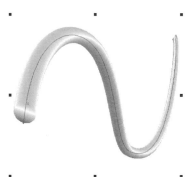

Figure 16.4

Blending along a path transforms the straight tube into a wiggly tentacle shape.

4. Select the control curve and right-click on the on-screen *x* to remove the outline color. That completes your tentacle.

5. To change the orientation of the tentacle, simply change the order of the parent shapes. For example, select the right control curve and send it to the front (Shift+PgUp). The blend redraws, changing how the tentacle looks; instead of looking like it's going away from you, it looks like it's coming toward you (see Figure 16.5). Essentially, this effect is all an optical illusion, but it works great.

Figure 16.5

Sending a control curve to the front or to the back changes how the blend redraws itself, making the tentacle seem like it's either going away from you or coming toward you.

The tentacle process produces flexible, movable limbs, either as gooey octopus arms or as straight rigid tubes. Here is how I made the main robot character with tube arms:

1. For the robot's brains, I used, er, brains. From the \medical\organs\ directory on CorelDRAW's clip-art CD-ROM, import (Ctrl+I) a nice, squishy, pink brain. Starting with this clip-art, add details to get the look of a mechanical creation. (I tend to get carried away adding details, so if you prefer to create a less-complicated robot, skip to Step 7, where the tentacle technique begins.) Use the Bezier tool to draw a metal plate over half of the exposed frontal brain area, and give it a shiny metallic fill with the Presets Cylinder - Grey 02 custom color blend in the Fountain Fill dialog box (F11).

2. Duplicate the metal-plate shape (+ key) and downsize it. Use the smaller duplicate (with fill and outline removed) as the reference path to for the rivet blend. This creates the illusion that the plate is bolted into the brain. (The rivets are simply circles with black-to-white radial fountain fills and the centers offset to create a gleam, similar to the metal studs from Chapter 5.)

3. Use the Interactive Blend tool to create an active blend group. On the Interactive Blend Property Bar, click on the Path Properties button, click on New Path in the quick menu, and then click on the duplicate metal-plate shape to place the rivet blend there. Click on Miscellaneous Blend Options and enable the Blend Along Full Path radio button.

4. Duplicate (+ key) and flip the plate-and-rivets shape for a symmetrical look. Draw more fountain circles around the brain for sensors, and use the Freehand tool to draw wires connecting them to the plates. If you draw a fat line and then blend it with a skinny one on top, you can create rounded wires, just like the lasers from Chapter 10 (see Figure 16.6).

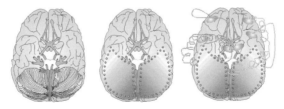

Figure 16.6

A clip-art brain is wired with sensors and metal plates.

5. Use the Rectangle tool to draw a base on which to rest the brain, and then use the Bezier tool to draw a pointy support object. Give this a black fill and then duplicate it (+ key). Downsize the duplicate support object by dragging on the sizing handles inward the Shape tool, and fill it with white. Blend it with the original, thus creating a

rounded, pointy, brain support. Duplicate the support to create a total of four, downsizing two for the distant pair.

6. To create eyes, fill circles with custom color radial fountain fills. Drag with the Ellipse tool, holding down the Ctrl key to make a perfect circle. Then open the Fountain Fill dialog box and change the Type to Radial. Change the From color from black to a light blue by clicking on it and selecting a new color. In the small preview window at the top right of the Fountain Fill dialog box, drag the cursor up and to the right to change the center of the fountain fill, creating a sphere illusion. Click on OK to close the dialog box. Draw rectangles connected with spheres for articulators on which the eyes will rest.

7. Use the Ellipse tool to draw ovals to use for the glass dome shape and the beehive ear electrodes. To make the bottom of the glass dome flat, draw a rectangle and use the Trim function to cut away a uniform base. Place all the objects behind the glass dome shape, except the eyes.

8. Give the dome a semi-opaque look with the Interactive Transparency tool. To assign a uniform transparency, click on the Transparency tool, but instead of dragging on the object change the parameters in the Property Bar. To heighten the glass look, draw a reflection shape with the Bezier tool and fill it white (see Figure 16.7).

Figure 16.7

Place the brain on a stand, level it, and give it eyes. Then, place everything under glass, which is an egg-shaped object with a 50% uniform transparency.

9. Create another rectangle, to rest the head shape on, and make it look cylindrical with the Cylinder - Green 03 Preset in the Fountain Fill dialog box (F11). Create another rectangle, and then a third rectangle, which you make into a double parallelogram with the Interactive Envelope tool. Give each of these objects the look of a cylinder by using one of the Preset cylinder fountain fills.

10. Draw circles for the shoulder, elbow, and hand and use a custom color radial fountain fill to make them look round (load branvshydra.cdr from the \Chapt16\ subdirectory on the companion CD-ROM to see all the custom color blends). Use the same technique to create round casters underneath the robot, for it to roll around on.

11. To create a grid for the speaker grill, first right-click on the Graph
     Paper tool (located on the Object flyout, along with the Polygon and
     Spiral tools) to open the Properties dialog box, in which you can
     change the values for Number of Cells Wide and Number of Cells
     High. Drag the Graph Paper tool to create a grid, and give it a white
     outline to become a speaker grill. Stuff the grill into an oval shape
     using the Effects|PowerClip|Place Inside Container command.

12. Draw a circle on the left center of the shoulder shape, and give the
     tentacle a custom color blend from the Fountain Fill dialog box
     (F11), such as the Cylinder - Green 03 Preset. Duplicate this shape (+
     key) and move it to the center of the elbow circle. Duplicate again
     for another elbow shape, and then once more for the hand. These
     four shapes will connect with blends to create the arm. Duplicate
     and reduce the shape three more times, once for each finger (see
     Figure 16.8).

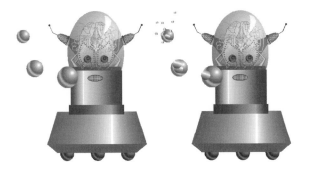

Figure 16.8
Simple geometric shapes, given
life with fountain fills, stack up to
become the body of the robot.
Control curves are put into place
to create the arms and fingers in
the blend steps to come.

13. Select the small circles in the shoulder and elbow and connect them
     with a 40-step blend, using the Interactive Blend tool. Repeat this
     process to create the other arm section and the fingers. Arrange the
     objects with the blend groups so that they start in front of a joint,
     such as the shoulder, and end behind the next joint, such as the
     elbow. This creates an arm group, which you can duplicate and flip-
     flop for the other side. To make all the gleams and shadows alike,
     right-click on the fill properties from the left arm pieces and use the
     popup menu to copy them to the right arm pieces (see Figure 16.9).

14. Switch to Simple Wireframe view, which displays only the control
     objects in a blend, making it easier to select and move the end of a
     finger, for example. When you switch back to Normal view, the live
     blend rebuilds itself to reflect the new position of the control object.
     You then can easily place the limbs of your character in any position
     (see Figure 16.10).

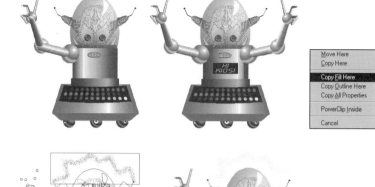

Figure 16.9

Use the Interactive Blend tool to connect the small circles into solid arm shapes. Arrange the blend groups and the joints to create a dimensional arm, and then duplicate them for the other side.

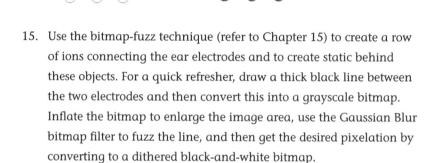

Figure 16.10

You can select and move the control curves in Simple Wireframe view (shown on left), and the limbs automatically rebuild themselves in Normal view, thanks to the live blend groups (right).

15. Use the bitmap-fuzz technique (refer to Chapter 15) to create a row of ions connecting the ear electrodes and to create static behind these objects. For a quick refresher, draw a thick black line between the two electrodes and then convert this into a grayscale bitmap. Inflate the bitmap to enlarge the image area, use the Gaussian Blur bitmap filter to fuzz the line, and then get the desired pixelation by converting to a dithered black-and-white bitmap.

16. For additional bits of animation, add blends of circles to create rows of lights. The great part about these blends is that you can drag and drop a new color on any of the control curves to change the interim light colors. These simple circles also help show emotion and mood for each frame. (If you were animating a multimedia character, this section could be its own film loop, with the circles advancing like lights for each cell.)

17. To add the final touches to the robot, add a little screen for it to speak, using a font called LCD.

You can view this robot in this book's color section and in the brainvshydra.cdr file in the \Chapt16\ subdirectory on the companion CD-ROM. Open the file to see how the custom color blends give the circles depth, and move the control curves around to watch the limbs rebuild themselves.

Geared For Success

Everything I needed to know about mechanical engineering I learned from LEGOs. I still have quite an impressive collection of these plastic wonder-bits from which I fashion all kinds of strange things in my spare time.

I always liked the LEGO gears. I still tend to be fascinated with gears and I find that they make great design elements (see Figure 16.11). They're visually interesting geometric shapes, are easy to render, and have a great deal of connotative meaning in our society (precision, constancy, high technology, and so on). Gears are also easy to animate, which we will seein my sample Web site (see Chapter 20). Gears serve as all kinds of visual vehicles in art, as both primary and secondary design elements. The next three tutorials show how to create gears and how to use them in artwork.

Figure 16.11
The Interactive Blend tool and the Weld command make gear shapes in any size. You can use these objects for the background blueprint image, or you can make them into 3D objects with the magic of the Interactive Extrude tool.

Gears, Gears Everywhere

CorelDRAW is an awesome tool for creating images that are both geo-metrical and mechanical in nature. The Interactive Blend tool creates such nice and even-spaced duplicates that it's a natural choice for creating such things as rivets, bolts, and even the teeth in a gear. After you create your basic gear shape, you can use it as a 2D design element or add a third dimension with the Interactive Extrude tool. Here's how to create gears of any size and then make them look three-dimensional:

1. Start with a rectangle and round the edges with the Shape tool. Use the Envelope function to squeeze the top closer together. Duplicate this gear tooth and set it aside for use later.

2. Double-click on the gear object to reveal its axis of rotation (it looks like a bull's-eye in the center of your object). Drag this center of rota-tion downward while holding down the Ctrl key to snap the axis of rotation to the bottom center of your object (see Figure 16.12).

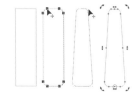

Figure 16.12
A rectangle becomes a gear tooth when you round the cor-ners with the Shape tool and distort the object with the Inter-active Envelope tool.

3. Duplicate the object (+) key and move the duplicate off to the side. Use the Interactive Blend tool to drag between the two objects. Shift-select both control curves and align them to horizontal and vertical center, using the C and E keys.

4. After you neatly stack your blend group of gear teeth on top of each other, you are ready to spin them into a round gear. Press the Esc key to deselect anything that is selected, and then drag-select around the blend group to select all the elements (if you click on the group, you select only the top Control Rectangle, which is not what you want to do).

Note: *With the Blend docker now defunct, you can't easily use the Interactive Blend tool to create a Blend group using two objects directly on top of each other. You have to move the objects apart, create the blend, and then align them, as in Step 3. See Chapter 1 about customizing the workspace and on hiding the Blend and other dockers.*

5. On the Property Bar, change the Blend Direction value from 0 to 360. Because we changed the axis of rotation on the Control Rectangles, the result is a perfect circle of spokes (see Figure 16.13). If the spokes aren't perfectly spaced, click on the Object and Color Acceleration button on the Property Bar and move both Acceleration sliders to dead center.

6. Choose Arrange|Separate and then choose Arrange|Ungroup All so that you can manipulate the objects individually. First, select and delete the extra, redundant gear object at the top center of the once-active blend group.

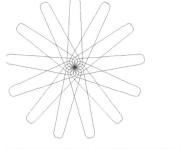

Figure 16.13

With the axis of rotation moved in the Control Rectangles, when you change the Blend Direction value to 360 degrees in the Property Bar the objects spin around in a complete circle.

7. Select All (Ctrl+A) gear objects and choose Arrange|Shaping| Weld. Disable both Leave Original checkboxes, click on Weld To, and then click on the selected group. You now have a giant asterisk (see Figure 16.14).

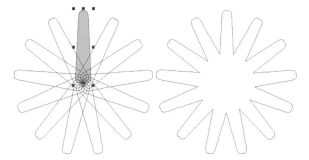

Figure 16.14

After you separate all the blend objects and delete the extra gear shape (in gray), you can merge all the objects into one using the Shaping|Weld command.

8. Draw a perfect circle. Shift-select both the circle and the star shape and choose Arrange|Align and Distribute. In the Align and Distribute dialog box, enable the top Center and the left Center radio buttons. (Note the underlined letters in this dialog box because these are the single-key keyboard shortcuts for these commands.) Click on OK to align your two objects.

9. Select your circle shape and choose Arrange|Shaping|Weld. Disable the radio buttons, click on the Weld To button, and then click on your star object. This should result in a nice, gear-looking object (see Figure 16.15).

10. Duplicate the gear shape (+ key) as many times as you wish and arrange the duplicates so that they mesh nicely together. After you configure the gears as you like, Shift-select them all and combine them into one curve (Ctrl+L).

11. With all the gears combined into one curve, you can use the Interactive Extrude tool to add depth, a bevel, shadows, and highlights, and even to rotate them in 3D space. Drag on the gear curve with the Interactive Extrude tool to create an active extrude group and then modify things to your liking by using the Property Bar.

12. Click on the Lighting button and then the number 1 bulb to enable a light source, which results in the automatic highlight and shadow effects. Click on the Bevels button and enable the Bevel feature with a click in the Use Bevels checkbox. To spin your gears in virtual space, simply double-click on the extrude group and drag the 3D rotation arrows (see Figure 16.16).

That's essentially all you need to do to create any kind of gear shapes. I went a little nuts in my example, located in the color section and on the companion CD-ROM's gears.cdr file in the \Chapt16\ subdirectory. I

RACK 'EM UP

The Align and Distribute dialog box has many handy options that aren't available as keyboard shortcuts. The Align to Center of page and Align to Edge of page options are very useful. Click on the Distribute tab to reveal many heretofore unavailable ways to arrange your objects predictably. Sometimes you want to align and distribute your objects with more precision than eye-balling it affords, and this tab is where you can do so.

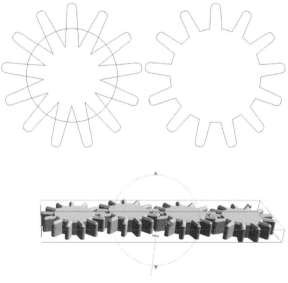

Figure 16.15
Using the Shaping|Weld command on the circle and star shapes results in the final gear object.

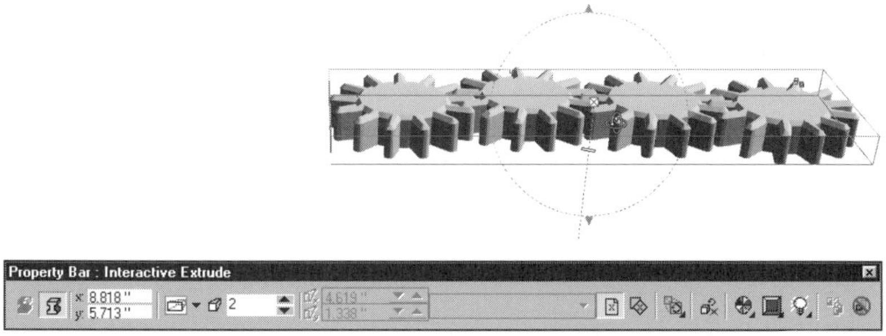

Figure 16.16
The Interactive Extrude tool converts a gear curve into a set of dimensional objects with shading and even a bevel.

Figure 16.17

Gears can be interesting design elements that suggest motion or machinery. When all the gear shapes are combined into a single object, the Interactive Extrude tool creates depth with shadows, highlights, and a shared vanishing point.

made gears of all shapes and sizes and then used them in both their original flat state as a background design and with 3D effects, using the Interactive Extrude tool on a duplicate of the shapes. I spent way more time on this image than any sane person would, but like I said, I love gear shapes!

The Imagination Machine

Ever found something that you created a long time ago and said to yourself, "What was I thinking?" The image in Figure 16.17 (well, only pieces of it now) is something that I submitted to the Corel International Design Contest many moons ago (and didn't win). When I first opened the file recently, I was so aghast at some of the amateurish techniques that I immediately closed it again, too embarrassed to look. Many weeks later I remembered that the image used gears, so I opened it again for potential inclusion in this chapter. I liked the layout, but spent so much time fixing the artwork I probably would have been better off starting from scratch.

Gears work well in advertising or other commercial artwork on both a visual and connotative level. In Figure 16.17, the "Grease the Wheels" and "Imagination Machine" concepts are reinforced by the gear image. Of course, this machine would produce nothing but noise and static if you could turn it on, but the laws of mechanical engineering don't apply to the art world. As an interesting visual vehicle it rolls along just fine.

This tutorial introduces a totally different way to create gear shapes. In addition, these gear objects look different than the ones in the previous tutorial because they have big cutout areas in the centers for a more stylized, less realistic look. The electric static is created by using the exact process outlined in Chapter 15, and the metallic fills are produced just like the piercing pieces in Chapter 5. (This tutorial does, however, introduce some new techniques, so read on.) Here's how to create gear shapes by using the Polygon tool, and then make them stylized design elements:

1. Select the Polygon tool from the Object flyout. Before you use the tool, right-click on it and choose Properties. In the Options dialog box, enable the Polygon as Star radio button, increase the Number of Points value to 8, increase the Sharpness to a whopping 75, and then click on OK.

2. Use the Polygon tool to create a perfect star by holding down the Ctrl key while dragging. Remember, you can drag with the Shape tool on the inside or outside nodes in a symmetrical polygon to fine-tune it.

3. Use the Ellipse tool to draw a perfect circle by holding down the Ctrl key while dragging. Shift-select both the circle and the star and use the C and E shortcut keys to align them perfectly, both horizontally and vertically.

4. Select the star shape and choose Arrange|Shaping|Intersect. Disable both Leave Original checkboxes and then click on the circle. The result is the beginning of a gear shape (see Figure 16.18).

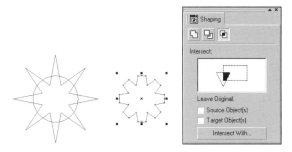

Figure 16.18
Use the Shaping|Intersect command to chop away the star points.

5. Draw another perfect circle, aligned with the gear shape, to get rid of the inside star points. Choose Arrange|Shaping|Weld, disable both Leave Original checkboxes, click on the Weld To button, and then click on your star object (Figure 16.19).

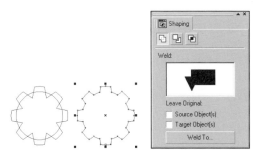

Figure 16.19
Use the Shaping|Weld command to remove the inside star points.

6. Draw two more perfect circles, aligned and inside the gear object. When you select all three objects and combine them (Ctrl+L), you create the stylized gear object. Use the Cylinder - Gold 07 Preset in the Fountain Fill dialog box (F11) to give this a nice metallic shading (see Figure 16.20).

7. The addition of the custom color blend to your gear shape results in some very nice shading effects when you modify the shape with the Interactive Extrude tool. Just as before, drag the Interactive Extrude tool on the curve and then change the parameters in the Property Bar to include Bevel and Lighting options. The result is an

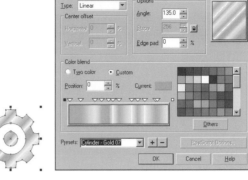

Figure 16.20
Combining two circles with the gear curve results in a stylized shape with a ring of clear, open area through it. A custom color blend Preset creates the look of metallic shading.

Figure 16.21
The Interactive Extrude tool works on the complex gear curve to create dynamic 3D objects with shared shading and a shared vanishing point.

> **Note:** The imagine.cdr file has handy little screw heads that you can load and steal for your own designs later on. Why build when you can pilfer these?

interesting set of gears that share a common light source and vanishing point (see Figure 16.21).

However you choose to make your gears is fine with me. Heck, you could forget the whole custom gear idea altogether and find some very useful gear shapes in the Symbols and Special Characters dialog box (GeographicSymbols has a nice set, for example). The included clip-art library that ships with CorelDRAW also has some fine gear shapes for you to exploit, so weigh your choices and do what you like. Personally, I like making my own gears.

That's all of the real magic behind this piece. My secrets all are basically yours now (and a huge portion of my personal artwork, to boot). You can see this piece in this book's color section and on the companion CD-ROM's imagine.cdr file in the \Chapt16\ subdirectory.

Belts And Pulleys

You can create belts and pulleys in the same way that you create gears. Connecting objects with a belt or other visual vehicle can be a useful design element to guide the reader's eyes around the page (see Figure 16.22). Like gears, belts and pulleys have high-tech and mechanical connotations, but they aren't as obtrusive or harsh as the toothy gears. Unlike gears, belts and pulleys are perfect for borders, because they aren't as "busy" as gears.

This same type of graphic works for the printing industry. Big printing presses that print newspapers and other big publications print onto giant rolls of paper that weave through many rollers, just like the belts and pulleys. For the printing-press look, add more depth to the rollers and pulleys and decrease the thickness, to look more like thin paper instead of a thick belt. Here is how to connect pulleys with a belt:

Figure 16.22

Like gears, belts and pulleys make interesting mechanical additions to a design, to add a sense of motion and a high-tech edge. The pieces can also work to unify a logo or act as a border element.

1. Use either the gear-tooth blend technique or the Polygon as Star option to create a multitoothed pulley object. Or you can use the Interactive Blend tool and small circles (rather than gear teeth) to blend along a round path (see Figure 16.23). When you use the Arrange|Shaping|Weld command on all of these objects you get a nice round-toothed pulley shape.

Figure 16.23

Use the Interactive Blend tool to scatter circles along a round path; merge them into a pulley shape by using the Shaping|Weld command.

2. Use the Polygon tool to create a six-sided shape and then center it with the outside circle. Combine the shape and circle (Ctrl+L) to finish off the hollow-centered pulley. Arrange any duplicates that you want to include and then add depth with the Interactive Extrude tool (see Figure 16.24).

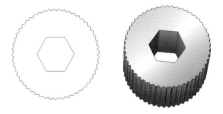

Figure 16.24

Use the Interactive Extrude tool to add depth and shading to the pulley wheel.

3. As you did with the gears, you can duplicate and arrange multiple pulley curves and then combine them into one curve (Ctrl+L). Use the Interactive Extrude tool again to add depth and shading to the curve. Draw a shape with the Bezier tool to connect the pulleys with a belt (see Figure 16.25).

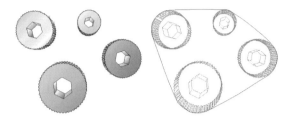

4. With the belt curve selected, duplicate it (+ key). Enlarge the duplicate symmetrically by holding down the Shift key as you drag a corner sizing handle outward.

5. Shift-select both belt pieces and make them into one solid piece by using the Combine command (Ctrl+L). Click on 50% black to give the belt some color.

6. Now that you have a solid belt object, you simply need to copy the Extrude tool settings from your pulleys. Choose Effects|Copy Effect|Extrude From and then click on the pulley extrude group (see Figure 16.26). Modify the extrude group for the belt on the Property Bar to increase the Depth value, if you want more depth.

7. Send the belt group To Back (Shift+PgDn).

You now can place gears and pulleys in, around, and through your next design.

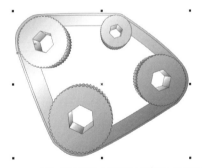

Beyond f/x

Gears, mechanical elements, and modular designs have a ton of design potential. From logos to animations, these art elements have many uses. In fact, we animate gears in Chapter 21, to enhance a Web site design that you create in Chapter 20.

The pulleys can pull a belt through a design, guiding the reader and directing attention throughout a publication. Or, you can connect parts of your page by using the tubes and tentacle shapes, creating a pattern similar to a road map to direct readers through your page.

Gears add that sense of action and mechanical feel that are right at home in the corporate logos of many industries. Animated gears (as in my Web page demo) also make interesting button elements, adding a sense of danger. Sticking your finger (or in this case, the cursor) into the intermeshing and rotating gears is against your better judgment, so it's kind of a reverse-psychology design trick. Because the virtual experience is safe you can create all kinds of moving, dangerous, sharp machines for your viewers to interact with. By using modular design tricks, or the blending techniques used with the robot arms, your Web machines can easily become animated when you click on them.

In advertising you can play off of the mechanical nature of these graphics, with tag lines such as "Put us to work," or "Working to bring you the best deals," or "Geared for success," or any of a gazillion phrases. Now get in gear and get to work!

Moving On

This chapter showed how to create robotics and mechanical-looking designs. The robot image used symmetry to cut design time in half and added tricks to make moving and animating the limbs easy. The gear sections showed how to create gears of any size and shape with the Interactive Blend and Polygon tools. We also saw how to add depth to the gears by using the Interactive Extrude tool, and how to use gears as interesting design elements in their flat state, in three dimensions, and even as a frame element.

In the next chapter, we use grids and lines (rather than the Interactive Extrude tool) to create dimension. The great thing about the human mind is how easily it is fooled, and we will endeavor to trick readers into seeing depth and dimension where none exists. So, let's leave robots and machines behind for now and head into the mysteries of grids and black holes.

GRIDS, BLACK HOLES, AND BENDING LIGHT

17

In this chapter, the illusion of depth, dimension, and structure is created by using lines, the Graph Paper tool, the Perspective feature, and Interactive Envelope effects.

In the vein of idealized reality, it is often advantageous to simplify your designs even further by using grids and lines to suggest depth and substance. Sometimes, to create a dimensional environment in a universe that has little definition, you have to include a man-made object such as a grid to give the vast blackness of space tangible dimensions. Grids and lines are excellent visual vehicles to create a dimensional universe that the reader can comprehend and explore.

In this chapter we create universes by using the powerful illusions created with grids and lines. Using the mathematical accuracy afforded by CorelDRAW's functions, you can easily create perfectly spaced lines that suggest depth and substance. We use the Graph Paper tool to create grids of all sizes and shapes, add depth with the Perspective function, and then add some special effects with a light-bending lens. Next, we create a spinning light show with the Interactive Blend tool, using the rainbow coloring options and object-acceleration features. We then add the illusion of depth to create a multicolored black hole or tunnel into another dimension.

We'll combine the techniques of the grid and light show and work them into a practical design example. Finally, we create evenly-spaced patterns with the Interactive Blend tool and use some low-tech design tricks to create a high-tech image of a black hole that appears to bend rays of light. This chapter uses our powers of imagination to fill in the blanks, with images that trick the eyeballs and scream "Neat-o" at full-volume into your voice mail.

Grids In Space

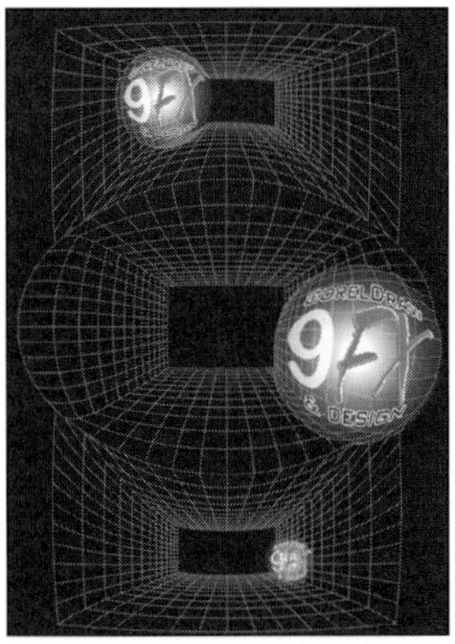

Believe it or not, Figure 17.1 was the first graphic I created for this book. Before I signed any contracts or made any deals, I spent a few days just brainstorming, trying to put my finger on the pulse of what a book titled *CorelDRAW f/x and design* should be about. This image went together so easily, and the results were so cool, that I made it into an animation and sent it to the publisher. Within a week, we agreed to do the project and even hammered out the table of contents (which is now this book in your hands). This image represents exactly the kind of cool—but not insanely difficult—type of effect that I was after.

Grids provide a great way to tie images together in a design. They can add depth when placed in perspective, add structure when left flat, and even suggest shapes when distorted. Grids can foster other designs, too, such as art that looks like video games or menacing target-acquisition-

Figure 17.1
The Graph Paper tool easily manufactures grids, which are given 3D effects with the Add Perspective feature and distorted with the Interactive Envelope tool.

INSTANT INVOICES

If you're ever stumped on a design, start with a grid and go from there. At the ad agency where I used to work we used to have a generic formula for generic clients, and it worked every time. Set a row of type in a brush font, set it on top of another row in a sans-serif font, and then float them both over a grid. Bang. Instant graphic, happy client, job done. Works every time (see Figure 17.2).

Figure 17.2
Grids are a universal design element that add interest to almost any design.

type displays for fictitious weaponry (such as in the "sword girl" images from Chapter 11). Grids and line art hearken back to simpler times when computer graphics weren't as insane as they are today. My favorite video game from my misspent youth, *Battlezone* by Atari, uses simple vector graphics and grids to build a 3D world. This same kind of imagery, in which you simply suggest objects and space, can be more dramatic than photos of the real thing.

Here's how to create grids with the Graph Paper tool and give them depth with the Perspective function:

1. Right-click on the Graph Paper tool icon on the toolbar to open its Properties dialog box (the Graph Paper tool is on the Object flyout, with the Polygon and Spiral tools). Change both the Number of Cells High and Number of Cells Wide values to 12 and then click on OK (see Figure 17.3). Drag the Graph Paper tool to create the grid, while holding down the Ctrl key to create a perfect square.

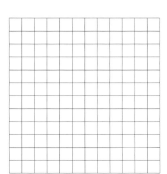

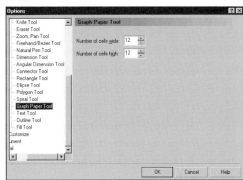

Figure 17.3
A setting of 12 cells across and 12 down creates a 12x12 grid when you drag the Graph Paper tool on the desktop.

2. With the grid selected (incidentally, the grid is nothing more than a group of identical rectangle duplicates, in case you want to ungroup and manipulate the objects), choose Effects|Add Perspective. With the Shape tool, drag the top-right node inward while holding down both the Shift and Ctrl keys, which pulls in the opposite node simultaneously. Release when finished to place the grid in the distance. Drag down the top-center sizing node with the Pick tool while holding down the Shift key to squash the grid vertically (see Figure 17.4).

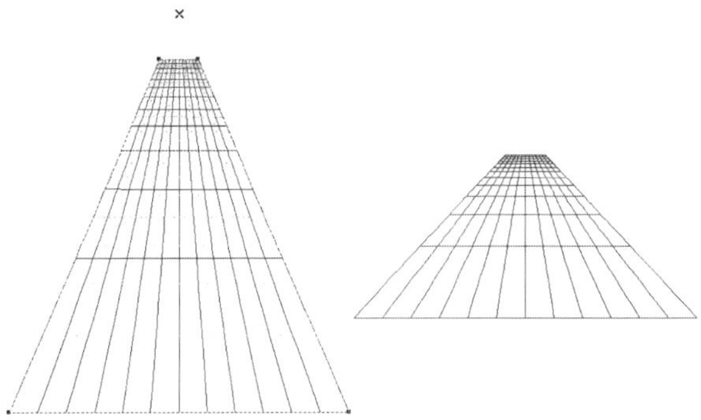

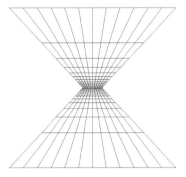

Figure 17.4

The Perspective tool places the grid in what appears to be a 3D orientation; reducing the grid's size vertically makes it look less stretched out.

3. Duplicate the grid (+ key) and flip it vertically by grabbing the bottom-center sizing handle and dragging upward while holding down the Ctrl key. This creates two planes that disappear at the same horizon line, which is a quick and convincing way to add depth to a design (see Figure 17.5).

Figure 17.5

Simply duplicating and flipping a grid vertically instantly creates an illusion of depth.

4. Matching up all the lines to create a grid box is a bit tricky, but not impossible. (Before you do so, delete the vertically flipped duplicate from Step 3—I was just showing you how easily you can produce a 3D effect with a grid.) Start with the bottom grid element and duplicate it, but this time rotate it –90 degrees by dragging a corner rotation handle while holding down the Ctrl key.

5. Shift-select both grids and choose Arrange|Align & Distribute. In the Align & Distribute dialog box, select the Bottom and Left checkboxes and click on Apply. Select the left grid and using the Pick tool, align it perfectly to the original by resizing horizontally and vertically (see Figure 17.6).

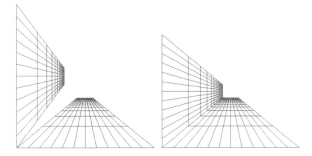

Figure 17.6
Duplicate and rotate the original grid to create a side. Stretch the object with the Pick tool and align the side with the bottom grid.

6. With the left side in place, Shift-select both grid groups and choose Arrange|Transformation. Click on the Scale and Mirror button, enable both the Horizontal and Vertical Mirror options, and then click on Apply to Duplicate. Now you have a 3D-grid hallway that you can twist and distort at will (see Figure 17.7).

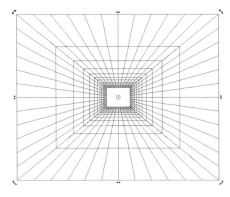

Figure 17.7
Duplicating and flipping the left and bottom sides horizontally and vertically results in the right and top side of a grid tunnel.

7. Select all the grid elements and group them (Ctrl+G). I gave my grid a thin .015-inch magenta outline and no fill. (Remember that these are actually rectangles, so you can also assign a fill attribute, such as a radial fountain fill, for a totally different look, as in the example on the left side of Figure 17.8.) Place the grid on a solid-black rectangle to suggest the bleakness of space.

8. Because the grid consists of vector objects, it is the perfect design element to tweak with the Fish Eye lens. Draw a circle, open the Lens docker (Alt+F3), and change to the Fish Eye option. Change the rate to 100% and then click on Apply. This distorts the lines behind the circle to make the circle look like a glass orb (see Figure 17.9).

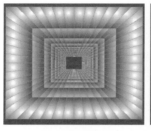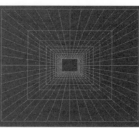

Figure 17.8

The grid groups are rectangles and thus can be given a radial fountain fill for a patterned look (on left) or no fill (on right) to emphasize the outline-grid look.

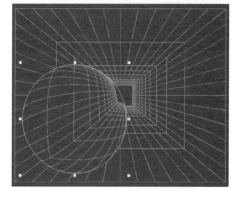

Figure 17.9

The Fish Eye lens distorts the lines behind it to make a circle appear to be a solid-glass orb.

9. Because a lens doesn't change any of the objects underneath it (it only changes the way that they appear), you can move the circle around to make it look like it's dancing through the grid tunnel. For a glass ball, use the Interactive Transparency sphere illusion from Chapter 7, or just steal the sphere directly from that chapter and use it here. You can move the orb anywhere, and the Fish Eye lens will redraw each time to create the new illusion (see Figure 17.10).

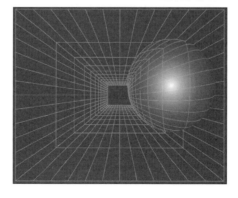

Figure 17.10

Moving the live lens creates a new illusion wherever the ball is placed.

10. To add even weirder illusions of bending space, use the Interactive Envelope tool on your grid group. Select the Interactive Envelope tool from the Interactive tool flyout and then click on Envelope Single Arc Mode on the Property Bar. Drag upwards the top-center control node of your envelope while holding down the Shift and Ctrl keys,

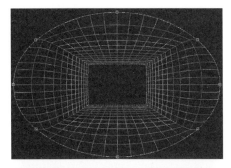

Figure 17.11

The Interactive Envelope tool, in Single Arc Mode, creates a round distortion shape.

which moves all four center control nodes outwards simultaneously, creating a round distortion envelope (see Figure 17.11).

That's really all there is to it. Instant grids and automatically redrawing lens effects—heck, what more could you ask for? You can see this file, in various stages of animation, in this book's color section and in the grids.cdr file in the \Chapt17\ subdirectory on the companion CD-ROM. An animation, grids.avi, is included on the CD-ROM, too. This is a great example of how a good-looking, versatile graphic need not be incredibly difficult to create. Also, because of the nature of lenses, you can move around and resize the orb at will, and CorelDRAW will dutifully re-create the appropriate illusions for you each time.

Black Hole Light Show

During a moment of experimentation—trying to perfect a look for the black hole section of this chapter—I discovered the very cool technique displayed in Figure 17.12.

This brilliant, colorful design, which is used in the book-cover example in the next tutorial (see the middle color section for the full impact) is another one of those really fun and easy techniques. It's actually a simple blend between two shapes, but those two shapes are key to this design. Unlike other blends, this one starts with a distorted, spoked curve that, when blended to a reduced duplicate, creates a very unique design. Depending on how tight or how loose (lower rotation and fewer steps) you make the blend, you can produce a solid mass or a gridlike design. When you offset and reduce the center control curve (shown in the bottom two examples in Figure 17.12 and in the color section), the blend builds as a spiral that is sucking down into the center, which could become a black-hole variant.

Figure 17.12

Blend a spiraled set of spokes to a smaller duplicate to result in an impressive light show. Change some of the blend parameters to create colorful black holes.

CONSTRAIN THIS

The default Constrain angle value is 15 degrees. You can change this to any value that you want, for more or fewer spokes in your wheel. From the Options dialog box (Ctrl+J), click on Edit to display the Edit page, in which you can change the Constrain angle. To double the number of spokes in your wheel, halve the value to 7.5 degrees. To decrease the number of spokes, increase to 30 degrees. Click on OK to close the dialog box.

Here is how to create spinning light-show blends:

1. First, you need a collection of lines for a spoked wheel type shape. This is easy. Draw a straight line with two clicks of the Bezier tool while holding down the Ctrl key. Double-click on the line to reveal the rotation arrows. Grab the corner rotation arrow and drag while holding down the Ctrl key. This constrains the movement to 15-degree increments. Before you let go of the line, right-click to create a duplicate. Now, simply repeat (Ctrl+R) until you get a spoked-wheel shape.

2. Select all of your objects (Ctrl+A) and combine them into a single curve (Ctrl+L).

3. Select the Interactive Distortion tool from the Interactive tool flyout. On the Property Bar, click on the Twister Distortion button and change the Additional Degrees value to 350. Choose Arrange|Convert to Curves to "freeze" the effect (see Figure 17.13).

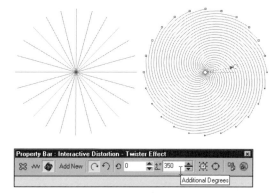

Figure 17.13

A straight line, duplicated and rotated, becomes a spoked-wheel object. Using the Interactive Distortion tool in Twister mode on this object creates a dizzying swirl pattern.

4. Give this curve a .023-inch yellow outline and duplicate it (+ key). Downsize the duplicate until it's about 30% smaller than the original. With the Interactive Blend tool, drag between both objects to create a blend group.

5. On the Property Bar, change the number of steps to 75 and set the rotation to 360 degrees again; then, enable one of the Rainbow options. Click on Apply to watch the show begin (see Figure 17.14).

6. To achieve the image used in the book cover, downsize and move the center vortex curve. Then, select the big curve and change the Outline Color value to cyan. Increase the number of steps to 125 but reduce the rotation to 180 degrees. These settings produce an image that could be a cornucopia of light or even a stylized black hole (see Figure 17.15).

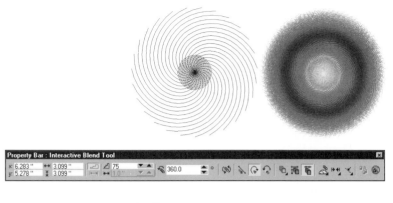

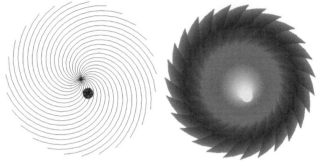

Figure 17.14

Blend the two vortex curves (on the left in Wireframe view) and enable the Rainbow option on the Interactive Blend tool to produce a dizzying color show.

Figure 17.15

Change the size and location of the center control curve, increase the number of steps, and reduce the rotation to 180 degrees to produce a unique result.

"These sure are pretty, but what the heck would I use them for," you ask? Well, read on.

Physics

The book-cover design in Figure 17.16 uses (surprise, surprise) the light-show twirls from the last tutorial and, yes, the multipurpose, all-season, multilingual, nonstick grid, available in all colors, shapes, and sizes.

To suggest depth, we again turn to the trusty Perspective function, and we also take advantage of the computer medium to duplicate and mirror the image almost effortlessly. The impact of the final image again defies the simplicity of using the power and automation of CorelDRAW. Here's how to combine the twirly blends with a grid for an artistic but spacey design:

1. Use the Graph Paper tool to create a grid, as before, and again distort it with the Perspective tool. Use the Pick tool to drag the top-center sizing handle, as before, to squash the grid vertically.

2. Create (or better yet, just borrow) the light-show blend from the previous example. Before you can alter the object with the Perspective tool, however, you must disable the live blend. Choose Arrange|Separate, choose Arrange|Ungroup All, and then use the group (Ctrl+G) command routine to freeze the blend and produce a group of some 127 objects that you can now distort.

Figure 17.16

Combine the grid and light-show elements to create a bright and interesting book cover.

3. With the colorful swirl group selected, choose Effects|Copy|Perspective From and click on the grid shape. This places the black-hole light show in the same perspective as the grid, giving you a more convincing graphic with all the elements sharing a like orientation (see Figure 17.17).

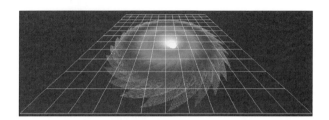

Figure 17.17
The Perspective tool places a grid in the desired 3D-like orientation; then, the same perspective is copied to the black-hole-swirl object group.

4. Select both the swirl and the grid, and choose Arrange|Transformation to open the Transformation docker. Click on the Scale And Mirror button to activate that page of options. Toggle just the Vertical option on and then click on Apply to Duplicate. Who said design has to be hard?

5. To make the arrow spin both behind and in front of the objects, use duplicates of the same curve. First, draw an oval with the Ellipse tool and then duplicate it. Use the Shape tool to drag the control nodes of the ellipse around (on the outside of the ellipse) to create the curve for the area in front of everything. Then, use the Shape tool on the other copy to drag the nodes of that ellipse around to create the curve that will be placed behind everything and that will match the other curve.

6. Choose Arrange|Order|In Front Of or Arrange|Order|Behind, respectively, to place the arrows correctly within the image stack. Select the front arc, open the Outline Pen dialog box, and assign an arrow for the start of the curve (see Figure 17.18).

That's the whole shebang (or in this case, the big bang). The image is in this book's middle color section, and the corresponding file, physics.cdr, is in the \Chapt17\ subdirectory on the companion CD.

I love designs like this, which seem simple yet are visually engaging. When I show other people this artwork, "simple" never enters their minds because they are just dazzled by the image. That's a good thing; sort of the wizard-behind-the-curtain illusion.

I love book-cover designs. I think I'll just retire and do nothing but scholastic book covers. Problem is I wouldn't be able to resist the urge

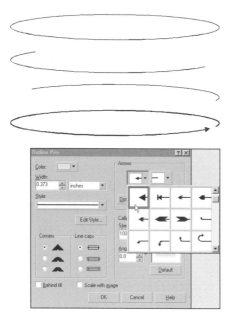

Figure 17.18

Use the Shape tool to transform an ellipse into a graceful arc. Repeat the process on a duplicate behind the objects to create the illusion of an arc behind and in front of the grids. Assign an arrowhead end from the Outline Pen dialog box.

to put in hidden graphics or subliminal messages to mesmerize students as they sit in class...on second thought, I probably should steer clear of those projects.

Black Holes

I'm so thrilled with the image shown in Figure 17.19 because it represents the eventual solution to my black-hole design problem: how do you draw something that, in essence, is nothing and is so dense that even light can't escape?

I spent much time staring off into space (uh, figuratively, not literally) and trying to come up with some kind of interesting and unique solution (some attempts went into the old Windows Recycle Bin).

This image is a series of lines and circles blended together to create the illusion of bending space and light, such as might take place around a black hole. I came up with the idea when I blended two ovals together with the Acceleration option enabled. This created a funnel shape, made from the stacked wireframe circles.

As you have seen, grids provide a great way to suggest depth and dimension, especially to things that don't exude those properties on their own (such as the blackness of space or bottomless oceans). With grids on my mind, and the subject being black holes, combining the two ideas naturally occurred to me, because a grid suggests both depth and dimension and can be distorted into the shape of a black hole. The design also lends itself to bending light, which also is associated with black holes. It's a

Figure 17.19

The Interactive Blend tool can create the illusion of space by using lines to represent bending space and light.

SHUT UP AND CASH THE CHECKS

Remember, it's the results that are important, not the process. Even if a design is very easy to create, never confirm that it is, especially to a client. Only you should know what actually goes into a job, and a client will just be annoyed if you proclaim how easy the job was or brag about the amazing shortcuts that you took. Even the most generous customer wants to feel like their job was special and that you worked hard on it. Most clients perceive "hard work" as spending a lot of time on their project, not realizing that experience and ability often enable you to take *less* time. So, to bill at a rate commensurate with your expertise, don't discuss your time-saving techniques with customers.

Half of the computer graphics game is politics, and learning to cater to the client is just as important as how to wield your computer graphics software efficiently. To make any money, your artwork needs to look incredible and unique, be quick and easy to create, and yet be worthy of big-ticket invoices. I have the technical aspect of the equation down, where I can quickly and efficiently create aesthetically appealing images that match the project parameters. Now I just have to learn how to stop rolling my eyes when clients make idiotic requests....

great graphic to illustrate an entity that is very enigmatic from a design perspective, insofar as it's literally a black hole, so dense that even light can't escape.

This isn't the only solution to this design problem, but as they say, "I may not know much about art, but I know what I like." The best part of this design is that the majority of the work is pretty easy, although it involves a section of mundane manual labor that I simply couldn't get around. Here is how to blend lines to create a 3D black-hole grid:

1. Draw an oval with the Ellipse tool and use the Skew arrows to tilt up the right side. Duplicate the oval, move the duplicate down, and reduce it.

2. Drag the Interactive Blend tool between the two objects to create a blend group. On the Property Bar, click on Object and Color Acceleration, and then drag the Object Acceleration slider to the left to create a black hole funnel (see Figure 17.20).

3. Select the funnel blend and perform the familiar separation dance (choose Arrange|Separate and then Arrange|Ungroup All). The first blend creates the funnel part perfectly, but it also results in some gaps, with far-apart ovals on the bottom end. With the objects all separated into individual ovals, you can select the oval on each end of a gap and fill them in with the Interactive Blend tool. Be sure to disable Acceleration for these in-between blends. Vary the number of steps (sometimes only 1 or 2) to keep the spacing about even for all the objects, to create a long-neck funnel out of ovals (see Figure 17.21).

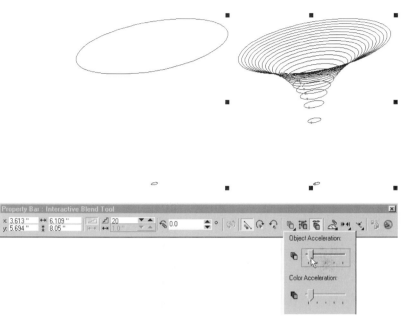

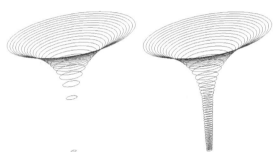

Figure 17.20
Use the Interactive Blend tool with the Object Acceleration slider to create a funnel-like illusion.

Figure 17.21
The original blend pieces are broken up so that the gaps can be filled in with even more blends.

4. Draw a rectangle to represent the page frame so that you can begin to position the funnel object. Choose the Zoom tool and right-click twice on your page to zoom way out. Select and duplicate the largest funnel oval and enlarge it 630% by dragging outward on a corner sizing handle. Position this huge circle so that its top is closer to the top of the funnel than the bottom is.

5. Shift-select the huge circle and the largest funnel circle and use the Interactive Blend tool again to create 22 duplicates between them. You may need to fiddle with the number of steps on the Property Bar and with the Object Acceleration slider to get evenly spaced circular rings. Select all of these grid rings, group them, and give them a yellow outline and no fill (see Figure 17.22).

6. With the Bezier tool, draw lines along an imagined X- and Y-axis, with the ends sucked into the black hole. Use the Shape tool to simplify the lines and to ensure that each line consists of only three

Figure 17.22

The Interactive Blend tool creates rings between the funnel and a huge circle enlarged way beyond the page size.

nodes. You don't need more than three nodes for a line like this, one at each end and another about midway down the funnel. You need the same number of nodes in all the lines to ensure that the blends work smoothly in the next step. The top-right and bottom-left lines are magenta, and the other two are cyan. All have a line weight of .013 inch (see Figure 17.23).

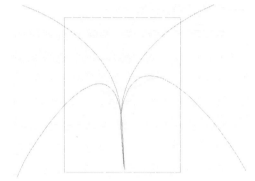

Figure 17.23

Draw lines with the Bezier tool, criss-crossing the page in an *x* orientation, with the ends sucked into the black hole.

7. With the Interactive Blend tool, drag from the top-left to the top-right line. Make sure that no Acceleration or Rainbow effects are enabled on the Property Bar, and change the number of steps to 22. Select the top-right line and drag the Interactive Blend tool to the lower-right line to create the blend between them. Continue to drag the Interactive Blend tool between the line pairs until you have blends connecting all the lines. Now our beams of light are being sucked into one spot (see Figure 17.24).

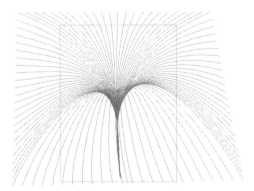

Figure 17.24

Blend the lines to create the illusion of light and space being sucked into the black hole.

Houston, we have a problem. (Or, should I say Ottawa, which is where Corel is located?) If you are particularly detail-oriented, you may notice that the illusion begins to break down because the front light-beam blend needs half of the lines to go into the vortex and the other half to lie on top. This presents a nasty problem that you've seen before, in which an object needs to be both in front of and behind another. Well, as you know, you can't bend CorelDRAW objects across layers, so you need to fool the eye manually.

Rather than explain the mostly manual-labor process, I'll just hit on what you need to do if you're also a perfectionist. You need to create three pieces to make the illusion work. From back to front, you need the cyan-magenta light beams to appear to be sucked into the vortex, and then you need a half copy of the vortex itself, to place on top of the objects inside it. Finally, you need the light-beam blend on top of the grid, bending into the vortex (see Figure 17.25). For an accurate 3D illusion to work, the blend elements need to be broken up so that they can be stacked in front of and behind each other, to create the illusion of bending light and space. The easiest solution is simply to open the blckhole.cdr file in the \Chapt17 subdirectory on the companion CD-ROM and steal the finished image. Feel free to use the artwork on the companion CD any time that you want to solve a design problem or take a shortcut.

You can see this image in this book's color section, with some text added to finish off the book-cover example. If you load the file from the companion CD-ROM to pick it apart, you have to choose PowerClip|Extract Contents to work with the pieces.

Beyond f/x

Grids and vector-type graphics can work into many design applications. You can create interesting and fantastical computer screens for video games or graphics in which you want to suggest some sort of automated target tracking or what have you. (Remember the weapons system on the *Millennium Falcon* from *Star Wars*? It's a grid!) The funnel grid can be used to suggest twisters, or you can work in a drop at the tip of the funnel to represent a digital version of a water droplet hitting a puddle (it has that

Figure 17.25
The pieces that you need to stack to create the light-beam blend into the vortex.

unique shape of the inverted funnel). Or, with a few changes, the funnel can be transformed into a bowl which, when duplicated, becomes a sphere (see Figure 17.26). The only limit is your imagination.

Grids work well to organize information for easy consumption, such as a hierarchy chart for data. Or, you could map out sales territories with a grid over a map. Or, create a Web navigation scheme in which each page is part of a grid and visited pages go black. The uses are endless, because grids are such a design staple. Remember the grid-design formula if you want to appease a generic, waffling client. Place brush script text over Eurobold text, hovering over a grid background. If that doesn't do it, toss in a drop shadow and a few palm trees.

Moving On

In this chapter, we created a lot of eye-popping artwork by using ordinary lines. We used the Graph Paper tool to create simple grids, which we tweaked and twisted into new configurations, and then called upon the Interactive Blend tool to perform its magic. The even spacing that the Blend function affords can also create very interesting gridlike elements, as we saw in the last example.

Grids and line-based artwork have myriad uses. We saw how flashy color patterns and fancy gridwork can become book-cover designs, just one of an unlimited number of uses. Grids and line art are just too versatile to ignore. If you haven't already, you'll encounter many situations in which a simple grid can jazz up a boring logo or page layout, or even aid as an organizational tool. (Whenever you can divide a full-page image into smaller, more easily digested chunks, you'll make the page more appealing to your audience.)

In the next chapter, we continue on the theme of illusions, only this time we add the concept of speed and motion. Once again, we'll trick the eye into seeing motion that isn't there (unless you happen to read by flinging the book past your face). Fasten your seat belts, because we're going to move into the fast lane, hit the gas, and taste some speed!

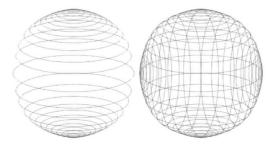

Figure 17.26
Blended circle shapes create the illusion of a 3D sphere.

18 SPEEDY THINGS

This chapter examines techniques to suggest speed and motion, using the Interactive Blend tool and bitmap blurring effects.

These days, with multimedia and the Web, designs can be much more than simple, static images. Animations, jumping and dancing icons, sounds, music, streaming video—you name it—all make the modern electronic-design experience very energetic and interactive. A side effect of this new media avalanche is that it also raises the bar for traditional print applications. No longer is the playing field level, with the flat, 2D page directly competing with all kinds of other media for the reader's attention. Somehow, your printed pages must gain and hold a viewer's attention without the benefit of sound or animation. It's downright unfair!

In this chapter, we level the playing field by looking at a few techniques to get your images to pop off of the page and look like they are moving and alive. In the first example, three variations of the same theme suggest motion in a racing buggy, using the Interactive Blend tool and a bitmap blur effect. In the second example, a jet fighter is given speed trails with the Interactive Transparency tool, making it speed across the page. Then, a combination of effects is used to create a blurry background for a speeding motorcycle. Finally, we create the unnerving dizziness of an adrenaline rush by using the Radial Blur feature. It's a fast ride, guaranteed to blur your vision, but you can handle it.

Bouncing Buggies

The graphic in Figure 18.1 is from a piece that I was going to use to illustrate an article that I wrote about racing remote-controlled model cars. The magazine that I was working for sent me a car to build and review. Well, I ended up smashing the test car into a gazillion little bits when it crashed in an empty swimming pool, which really annoyed my contacts at that magazine and quickly ended my career as a model-car journalist.

Figure 18.1

By using the Interactive Blend tool you can suggest movement by blending either just the object outline or the entire image (top and center). With a bitmap of the image, you can exploit the motion blur effects to create some zip and zoom (bottom).

Getting an image to look like it's moving isn't really that difficult. Using comic-strip-like motion-trail images, both straight and strewn along a path to suggest rotation, and then blurring a duplicate of the image are universally understood ways of showing motion. In the next sections, we look at a few tricks to add motion to my bouncing buggy illustration. Each technique suggests a different kind of motion and speed so you'll have to choose the one that is right for your fast designs.

Green Ghost

One way to suggest motion is to leave a ghostly trail of color behind the speeding object. Like the effect that it creates, this trick is also quick and easy. The primary object is blended to a duplicate, which has been placed to the back and behind and filled with the background color. The blend fades the original into the duplicate, which is the same color as the background so that it appears to fade away altogether. Here is how to make a fade-out effect from the buggy to the background:

1. The buggy started as an ink illustration, which I converted into vector artwork by using the Corel Trace program. The CMX trace file was imported into CorelDRAW, where it was easy to colorize the pieces. This kind of file consists of a lot of smaller objects resting on a big black shape. By selecting the smaller objects and combining some of them (such as all the pieces that make up the main body), you can assign a fountain fill that flows across the entire car body (I used the exact same process on the Land Rover in Chapter 9, making it really easy to recolor these vehicles). If you don't select and combine these individual objects first, and then fill them with fountain fills, they won't line up correctly (see Figure 18.2).

Figure 18.2
An ink illustration is converted into CorelDRAW objects by using Corel Trace. After you import them into CorelDRAW, you can select the pieces and give them outline and fill attributes.

2. Because an image like this one is a bunch of smaller objects on a big black main outline shape, you can easily select and duplicate this outline shape for the blur effects. Duplicate the big black outline pad, give it a solid-white outline with no fill, and move it up and to the right. This is the point at which your speed blur will fade to solid white. Send this white outline to the back (Shift+PgDn). See Figure 18.3.

ROAD MAPS FOR PAINTERS

One thing that I have used illustrations such as this buggy for is to work out color and graphics schemes for the real world. You don't need much more than a simple line-drawing of a car, motorcycle, or jet ski, for example, to work out really cool graphics schemes.

You can then give this road map to the people who actually paint the graphics onto the vehicles, for them to use as a reference. Or, you can go one step further and design the graphics to scale, and then use the artwork to create the actual masks used when painting. Most computerized sign companies will cut paint masks for you right from your CorelDRAW files, using big sheets of masking-tape material instead of vinyl. If paint isn't your style you can also find places that will print full-color, sun- and weather-proof images on vinyl, for stickers of all sizes—again, right from your CorelDRAW files. A dull-looking vehicle is simply unacceptable.

Figure 18.3

A bitmap converted to vector artwork in Corel Trace, using the default Outline mode, consists of many small objects on a big outline curve (shown in Wireframe view). For the blur effect, select and duplicate the outline shape and move it behind and in back of the original.

3. With the Interactive Blend tool drag between the original and the white outline to create the speed-blur effect. For control over the beginning and ending colors in the blend, select the black control curve and duplicate it. Now, the black outline is on top of the black control curve.

4. Press the Tab key to select the next most recent object (the duplicate is the newest object, with the original behind it being next in line). With the control curve selected click on an on-screen color well to change the fill to any color, such as the green that I chose for the color page (see Figure 18.4).

Figure 18.4

Blending the black outline curve to a white duplicate creates a stark motion blur. Duplicating the control curve enables you to change the colors in the blend to soften the speed blur.

This is a quick and easy way to get your objects moving.

Motion Steps

To offer a path of travel, you can blend an all-white copy of the buggy along a path. This not only shows motion, but also shows both where the buggy has been and its direction of travel. Here is how to do it:

1. Start with a colorized version of your buggy, drag-select all the pieces in it, and group them. Duplicate the group and give the duplicate a white fill and outline by clicking both the left and right mouse buttons on the white on-screen color well. This fills all the objects within the group with white and also changes the outlines, if any, to white. Move the duplicate to where you want the speed blur to fade out entirely, and rotate the buggy in an upward angle.

2. Draw a line with the Bezier tool, to show a range of motion. Shift-select both the colorized and white-only buggy groups and prepare them for blending by choosing Arrange|Order|Reverse Order (we need the colorized version in front). See Figure 18.5.

Figure 18.5
A colorized buggy (on the right, in Wireframe view) and an all-white copy (on left) will be blended along the curve to show a range of motion.

3. Drag the Interactive Blend tool between the two shapes and then use the Property Bar to modify the blend parameters. Click on Path Properties, and then click on New Path, and then click on your range-of-motion line drawn in Step 2. Vary the number of steps to as few or as many as you wish. Be sure to enable the Blend Along Full Path option by clicking on Miscellaneous Blend options and clicking on the corresponding checkbox. If you like, try the Rotate All Objects option, as well (see Figure 18.6).

Figure 18.6
Blend the buggies along the path to create a trail of image duplicates.

4. To make all the blended objects more ghostly white, use the Color Acceleration slider on the Interactive Blend Property Bar. Dragging to the left makes the duplicates favor the white end of the blend, so that they all become more pale (see Figure 18.7).

That's all you do to give your objects a trail of motion that indicates rotated movement (as opposed to simple, linear movement). Vary the number of steps for more or fewer ghostly images.

Figure 18.7
Use the Color Acceleration slider to change the blend duplicates into a paler set of objects.

Transparent And Blurry

The last technique uses a duplicate of the buggy to create a bitmap and then uses a motion blur. Like the first example, doing so leaves a ghostly trace where the buggy has been. In this section, however, the entire sub-dued image is in the speed blur. Here is how to get blurry eyed:

1. Select your buggy group again and draw a rectangle around it. Give the rectangle no outline or fill attributes because its function is to provide a transparent background for the bitmap. Shift-select the outline rectangle and the buggy group and duplicate them. Move the duplicate to the side and convert the image to a bitmap from the Bitmaps menu. Choose whatever color depth and resolution are appropriate for your project (72 dpi RGB for on screen, 300 dpi CMYK for print) and make sure that the Anti-aliasing Transparent Background option is enabled before you click on OK (see Figure 18.8).

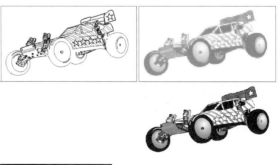

Figure 18.8
Use the Convert to Bitmap option to convert the vector art into a bitmap. The top row (in Wireframe view) shows the no-fill, no-outline rectangle used to assign the area for the transparent background.

SEE THROUGH IT ALL

When you use the Convert to Bitmap function's transparent background option, the transparent background remains transparent through any bitmap effects that you may apply to the object, so that only the image itself shows through. This is cool, because you don't have to worry about certain colors being see-through as you do with the bitmap color mask.

If you had created a bitmap with a white background and then used a bitmap color mask to make the background transparent, the stars and stripes would be transparent as well. Although this could be a cool effect, it generally isn't what you are shooting for.

2. Select the bitmap and choose Bitmaps|Blur|Motion. Crank the Distance value up to 50 pixels and change the Direction setting to hit your object head on. Click on OK to fuzz the image (see Figure 18.9).

Figure 18.9

Use the Motion Blur bitmap filter to add a speed-blur effect to the bitmap.

3. You can repeat the Motion Blur filter as many times as you want, to make the image super fuzzy. To soften the image further, choose Effects|Color Adjustment|Brightness-Contrast-Intensity. Increasing the Brightness value while decreasing the Contrast mutes the image (see Figure 18.10).

Figure 18.10

Use the Brightness-Contrast-Intensity dialog box to mute the blurred bitmap to become a background image.

4. Place the original buggy objects on top of the bitmap, to contrast the light, fuzzy blur with the crisp, high-contrast vector objects. Remember, the bitmap background is transparent so you can place objects behind the racing buggy, such as this checkerboard, to add depth to the design (see Figure 18.11).

For even more versatility, instead of using the Brightness/Contrast values on your background blur bitmap use an interactive transparency, to give it a semi-opaque look. Use the Uniform mode or a fountain fill for different looks (see Figure 18.12).

Figure 18.11

Stack the bitmap and original artwork on top of other background elements, to exploit the transparent background of the bitmaps.

Figure 18.12

Use the Interactive Transparency tool instead of modifying the Brightness setting on the bitmap, to get a softer background image.

Adding speed or motion to an image might not immediately seem very practical, but the process has many uses. For example, the blending technique is a great way to add both depth and a sense of energy to a logo (view the image in the color section to see how I used this technique on my racing logo, to give it a sense of speed).

That's enough of the bouncing buggies. The race continues in the color section and in a file called rccars.cdr, at a pit stop in the \Chapt18\ subdirectory on the companion CD-ROM. Open the file and experiment with the blend steps and the Acceleration options for the live blends in the racing logo and bouncing buggies. The logo is especially interesting to toy with. A few changes in the Acceleration options and you get a totally different set of results.

Jet Trails

Motion trails are great for adding a sense of speed and motion to an object, as we just saw. The buggy examples, however, don't have a busy background to contend with, which poses some new problems. You'll want to create a sense of motion that is appropriate, and also transparent so that background details still shine through, as in Figure 18.13. This is a great use of the Interactive Transparency tool.

This same kind of technique can be given more finesse in CorelDRAW using the Interactive Transparency tool to create subtle but convincing vapor trails for a screaming jet (or any other object that you want to give motion to). You could use the same technique, for example, on an arrow

Figure 18.13

By using the Interactive Transparency tool, a jet is given a sense of speed by leaving clear vapor trails in its path.

that points to how to put together pieces in an instruction booklet or installation guide. Motion effects pop up in many design projects. Transparency effects hint at motion without distracting too much from the overall design. Here is how to make a jet scream across the sky:

1. Once again, I turned to the versatile art archives of the CorelDRAW clip-art CD-ROM. Import a cool plane from the \clipart\aircraft\jets\ subdirectory. To give the entire plane a fat outline, group all the plane objects, duplicate them, and give the duplicate a thick .05-inch black outline. Enable the round Corners option from the Outline Pen dialog box (F12) and then send this thick-outline group behind the original objects. This is an old line-art illustration trick that I still like to use to isolate images from the background (see Figure 18.14).

Figure 18.14
A clip-art jet is given the thick-outline treatment by assigning a heavy outline to a duplicate group of the objects sent behind the originals.

2. Draw a rectangle the size of the desired page and send it to the back. Use a texture fill called Aerial Clouds from the Samples Library to fill the rectangle, or any other fill that you wish for the background. Using guidelines is helpful when mapping out a project such as this, for which you need to draw objects (in this case, the motion trails) by hand. To create a guideline, move the mouse pointer over the ruler at the left or top edge of your picture area and drag inwards. A guideline is a nonprinting, nonexporting entity specifically used as an illustration and layout aid. To move a guideline, simply drag it to a new position. To rotate a guideline, double-click on it and then drag the pop-up rotation handles. Set up guidelines off of the wing tips and other elements to set the stage for drawing the speed blurs (see Figure 18.15).

3. Use the Bezier tool to draw straight-line shapes for the trailing edges from which you want to have vapor trails emitting. The Bezier tool is great for this kind of work because you need only click

SNAP ON, SNAP OFF

Choose the View | Snap To Guidelines option to add a magnetic property to your guidelines. With the Snap To Guidelines option enabled, your objects attract and align themselves to the guidelines on the page like magnets to metal, which aids in page layout. Turn the option on and off as you need it.

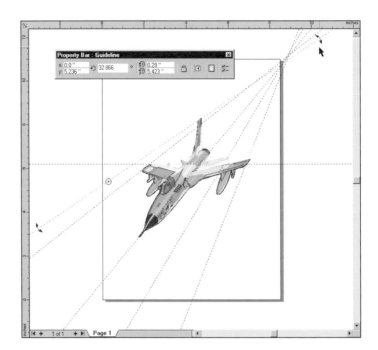

Figure 18.15

Guidelines can help to align objects in a design, set up vanishing points, or block up art before it is drawn.

from point to point to draw a straight-lined object. Try to draw the ending line of the curve in the same angle as the wing edge that it's paired with (see Figure 18.16).

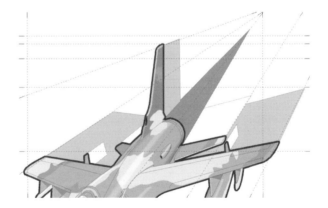

Figure 18.16

Use the Bezier tool to draw objects representing the vapor trails coming off of the wings.

4. Fill all the vapor trail shapes white and then select the Interactive Transparency tool. One by one, drag the tool along each vapor object to give it a white-to-clear fade. Start at the point where the object abuts the wing and then drag out toward the sky. To make the fade look correct for each wing you have to experiment with the placement of the clear point on the Interactive Transparency fountain fill control line. Straight up or straight across sometimes seems to work better than following the flight path. Experiment to find the angle that looks best (see Figure 18.17).

Figure 18.17
The Interactive Transparency tool gives the solid objects the white-to-clear fountain fills that create the vapor trail look.

5. More power, Scotty! For an afterburner flame, use a compound blend element. Use the Bezier or Freehand tool to draw a flame object shooting in the correct flight path. Give this object no outline and a cyan fill. Duplicate and downsize this flame shape for a midpoint and give the duplicate a magenta fill. Duplicate and downsize one more time, for the hot spot, and make this smallest duplicate yellow.

6. Use the Interactive Blend tool to drag between the cyan and magenta shapes to create the pink-to-blue color transition. From the Simple Wireframe view, drag the Interactive Blend tool between the magenta and the small yellow shape to create the yellow-to-magenta color transition (see Figure 18.18).

Figure 18.18
Blend three flame shapes (on left, in Wireframe view) to create the afterburner discharge.

The jet screeches across the sky in the color section and in a file called jetcover.cdr in the \Chapt02\ subdirectory on the companion CD-ROM. (Recall that we started with a boom by using this graphic in Chapter 2.) Open the file to check out the vapor trails or dissect any of the other artwork pieces. For the aircraft nose art, I stole the Slimy Dog tattoo from Chapter 5 and then used the rotation arrows and the sizing and skew handles to put the bitmap in place. It's amazing how much you can get accomplished with just the Pick tool.

The nature of your design will dictate the kind of motion effect that you need. For simple motion, try a fade into the background blend like we did with the first buggy. Or, you may want more steps to indicate motion and position—if you're making a diagram or instruction book, for example. The transparency tricks add the action more subtly, which may also make things look too fast. Sometimes, you may need a few tries to get what you like. The buggy blend along a path had me staring at the screen for quite a while because I kept changing the number of steps from higher to lower numbers. If you can't make up your mind, close the file and work on something else for a while. You start to lose perspective when you work on something too long, but if you come back later things are much clearer.

North Pole Racing

The previous examples dealt with using design techniques to suggest motion. This tutorial looks at a technique that mimics the results that photographers get when they take pictures of speeding objects, such as in Figure 18.19. So, in a sense, this may be the most realistic technique even though it's just an optical illusion.

A speed blur is a great way to make Santa's racing motorcycle look fast. *Santa's* racing team?! Well, every year, I try to come up with an interesting holiday card, and at one time most of our clients were in the motor-sports industry, so this card was a big hit.

This image is typical of photos that you'll see of race vehicles on the move. Photographers, in an attempt to keep the vehicle in focus, move the camera along with the subject as they shoot the photo. The effect is that the subject stays in focus but the surrounding images are fuzzy. Replicating the real or natural world in design is a sure-fire way to make an image more believable, even if it's complete fantasy. This technique has many other uses beyond suggesting speed. For example, this is a good design tool to isolate and emphasize a person from a crowd or other background noise, or to use anywhere else that you want to draw attention to a crisp object surrounded by a sea of fuzziness (see the last tutorial in this section for more details on this technique). Here's how to blur the background to make an object look like it's moving:

1. In typical Shane fashion, again, this image started as an ink drawing. I didn't convert the illustration with the Trace utility, but instead drew objects underneath the bitmap with the Freehand and Bezier tool, to color it, a technique that you learned in Chapter 9 (see Figure 18.20).

2. The next step is to make the rider look like a racer by adding numbers and sponsor logos. Because Santa's race effort is fictitious, I had to invent a bunch of potential companies that would logically stand behind the great bearded one. This wasn't a problem and made for a very amusing afternoon. Using my formula for logos

Figure 18.19
Creating a background in CorelDRAW and then converting the image to a bitmap enables you to add a sense of speed with the motion blur bitmap effect.

START YOUR ENGINES

If you ever want to take an ordinary vehicle and make it look racy, just stick a big number on it and plaster it with sponsor logos. This is a great design trick for nonvehicles as well. To promote a new, fast computer, for example, give it the race-car treatment with a flashy paint color, number plate, and sponsor stickers. You can make a toaster-oven look like it will go 100 mph with this trick.

(serif font over sans-serif, or brush over block type, and so on) and the impressive CorelDRAW font collection, I soon had a collection of appropriate logos.

3. Group the objects in a logo and use the Pick tool to position, size, and rotate the object. To get the upward curve in a logo, use the Interactive Envelope in Single-Arc mode (choose the mode on the Property Bar). Use the Interactive Envelope tool on the logo group before you rotate it. Creating a simple arc with your image horizontally oriented is easier than when it's at an angle. Plaster the rider and the motorcycle with the logos, and you're off (see Figure 18.21).

Figure 18.21
Use CorelDRAW's huge font library to invent racing logos, and then stick them all over the rider and motorcycle to give it a racy look.

4. Draw a box behind your rider at the desired page size (my example is for a 6x4-inch postcard). Then, use a texture fill or a bitmap pattern fill to create an abstract background. Pick something that has strong enough light and some dark areas to make the blur effect interesting (I used the Aerial Clouds texture fill from the Samples Library). You could use a photo or scan of an actual landscape if you wish.

5. Select all the motorcycle-rider objects, group them, and duplicate them. Move the duplicate on top of the bitmap background. Don't forget to make a duplicate of the original CorelDRAW motorcycle objects because you'll again convert them into a bitmap.

6. Select the motorcycle and background object and choose Bitmaps|Convert to Bitmap. (For my project, my goal was a two-color design, black and red.) Two-color projects are cheap to print and look so much nicer than just black alone. For this reason, though, I needed the background to be grayscale. Your project may be different and you may want a full-color background; it's up to

---

PICK YOUR PASSION

If you aren't into motorcycles, you can use my logos to transform any vehicle into one of Santa's racing efforts. My friends have stolen the pieces and theme to create Santa racing everything from dirt-bikes to watercraft for their holiday amusement. Heck, you could stick the red-leather-clad, helmeted rider on a nervous-looking, sticker-clad reindeer!

you. From the Convert to Bitmap dialog box, select the color depth in the Color drop-down list box, enable the Anti-aliasing and Use Color Profile options, and then click on OK (see Figure 18.22).

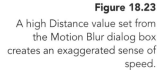

Figure 18.22
The motorcycle and background are merged into one by using the Convert to Bitmap dialog box.

7. Choose Bitmaps|Blur|Motion to open the Motion Blur dialog box. Crank the Distance variable up to around 50 pixels, set the Direction of the blur so that it's coming at the rider (0 degrees), and then click on OK. Increase the Distance value if you want a really exaggerated speed-blur look (see Figure 18.23).

Figure 18.23
A high Distance value set from the Motion Blur dialog box creates an exaggerated sense of speed.

8. Drop the original crisp and colorized version of the motorcyclist back onto the background, and you're finished.

The race is on in the color section and in the santa.cdr file found in the \Chapt18\ subdirectory on the companion CD-ROM. Open the file to see how the motorcycle objects rest on the blurred bitmap. Delete the background bitmap and repeat the steps, to come up with your own fuzzy background image. Try a street scene or other bitmap for a unique look for your racing vehicles. Using the transparent-background technique from the buggies example, you can also place fuzzy objects in front of the motorcyclist to get a really cool look that's full of depth and action (see Figure 18.24).

Adrenaline Rush

Have you ever had one of those adrenaline-induced tunnel-vision moments where everything kind of goes into slow motion and takes on a weird, dream-like look? I've been in several semi-nasty motorcycle accidents where everything took on that surreal appearance, moving in

Figure 18.24
Use the transparent-background technique to place blurry objects in front of the crisp motorcycle to add depth and motion to a scene.

slow motion, with only a small point in focus, very much like the image in Figure 18.25.

This technique is a great way to draw attention to a single area, while the rest of the world around it is lost in speed-blur chaos. Complete the following steps to set the world spinning.

1. In CorelDRAW, import or scan the photo that includes the image you want to emphasize. The focal point does not need to be in the center, but it needs to be pulled away from the edge of the photo.

2. Use the Rectangle tool to draw a perfect square (hold down the Ctrl key while dragging). With the Pick tool, move the square around your photo in Wireframe view to align the center of the square with the area in your photo that you want to be the focal point (see Figure 18.26).

Figure 18.25
The Radial Blur effect draws your attention to the center of an image.

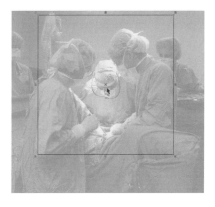

Figure 18.26
Use the midpoint of a square to align the focal point of the radial blur effect.

3. Duplicate your bitmap (+ key), choose Effects|PowerClip|Place Inside Container, and then click on your positioning square. You have to stuff a copy into a square because no other way exists to control the focal point of the radial blur, which defaults to the dead center of a bitmap. The trick of aligning a square dead center over the focal point gives you control of where you want the blur and focus.

Note: *If your PowerClip bitmap isn't aligned with the original, you first need to disable the Auto-center New PowerClip Contents feature, located on the Edit page of the Options dialog box (Ctrl+J).*

4. With your image stuffed inside a square, remove any outline (right-click on the *x* at the top of the on-screen color palette). Then, choose Bitmaps|Convert to Bitmap to convert the PowerClip into a bitmap that will accept an effects filter in Step 5. In the Convert to Bitmap dialog box, set the Color depth to RGB, set Resolution to 300 (or lower for Web applications), enable the Anti-aliasing and Use Color Profile options, and then click on OK.

5. Choose Bitmaps|Blur|Radial Blur to see the dialog box for the filter that adds a nice sense of vertigo to the photo. Drag the Amount slider to a setting that you like, while clicking on the Preview button to test the option. When you are satisfactorily dizzy, click on OK (if you can still focus, see Figure 18.27).

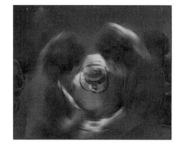

Figure 18.27
Use the Radial Blur bitmap filter to create a blurred, tunnel-vision effect.

6. To soften the transition between your blurred, square, duplicate bitmap and the pristine, original bitmap underneath, use the Interactive Transparency tool; or, if you want to emphasize the blurred square, for an interesting variant I recommend that you use the Interactive Drop Shadow tool instead. You can choose how you want your images to come together. I used the Interactive Transparency tool's fading technique to merge the two images, as outlined in Chapter 14.

7. The round, tunnel-vision feel of the blur begs for the use of curved text. Draw a perfect circle and align its center to the square bitmap. Give this circle no fill or outline, and switch to Wireframe view. To place text along the top of the circle, simply move the Text tool over the circle until the crosshairs cursor changes into a bracket. Click the mouse, and violà! You type text directly on the curve (see Figure 18.28).

8. Drag the Text tool to highlight the text so that you can change the font by using the Property Bar.

9. Select the Pick tool and click on the text to reveal the Text on Curve/Object Property Bar. Change the Vertical Placement value so that the

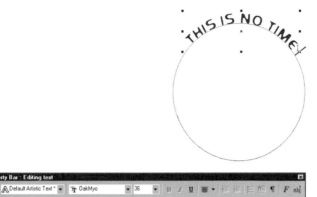

Figure 18.28
Moving the Text tool over a curve enables you to type directly on the curve.

text abuts the top of the curve, instead of being on top of it. Change Text Placement to the bottom option. This moves the text to the bottom, but on the inside of the circle, which is no good. To fix this, click on Place on Other Side in the Property Bar (see Figure 18.29).

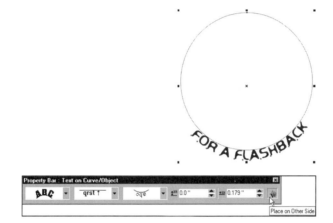

Figure 18.29
Use the Property Bar to change the orientation of a Text on Curve element, for words on the top and along the bottom of a circle.

You can experience the dizziness in this book's color section and in the flashback.cdr file located in the \Chapt18\ subdirectory of the companion CD-ROM.

Beyond f/x

As mentioned throughout the chapter, this design technique has all kinds of uses. In advertising, a catch phrase or call to action can literally be active if you use techniques that suggest movement and make the words jump out at you. Guides or instruction books can use the multiple, subdued images along a path to show how things fit together or come apart. An object can be pulled out of a busy background, for emphasis, or a character can be placed in a blurry landscape with blurry, nightmarish characters in front of and behind the subject.

Of course, the obvious uses in motor-sport logos or images spring to mind. Speed has many connotations that you can exploit in promotional materials or anywhere. Concepts such as "Speeding Into the Future" or "The Company That Is on the Move" can work into appropriately speedy graphics. How many times have you heard the words "fast," "furious," or "high-paced" used in our contemporary world of high-tech business? Now, you too can create graphics that are synonymous with those concepts. Hurry!

Moving On

In this chapter, we looked at many ways to add motion to your static designs. Using blurring, duplicating, and transparency techniques, your objects were given life, depth, and the energy to shoot across the page.

In the next chapter, we take a mildly dizzying look at patterns and Web tiles. CorelDRAW is a great place to design and build all kinds of repeating images, whether they are simple geometric shapes or fluid, seamless tiles. Keep the eye-drops handy, because the retina-punishment continues with the visual bombardment of tessellations, patterns, and tiles.

TESSELLATIONS, PATTERNS, AND TILES

19

This chapter explores repeating images, such as seamless tiles and geometric patterns, for a variety of applications including Web page backgrounds.

Many applications, from the Web to textiles, need interesting designs and patterns. Repeating patterns are a visually interesting addition to a design and can do a lot to set the tone of the artwork. By using a repeating image, you can reinforce a concept or product or even set a mood (for example, a "good" page could have a background with angels, whereas a "bad" one could have little devils). With textures, you can create the look of wood, marble, or other traditional building materials to set the stage for the rest of the design. CorelDRAW ships with many premade patterns and tiles, but it is also the perfect medium to create your own, unique repeating images.

CorelDRAW provides many tools to create patterns:

- The Tools|Create|Pattern command lets you create a bitmap pattern by designating an area on screen which then is available as a tile for use in the Bitmap Pattern Fill dialog box.

- The Tile option on the Symbols and Special Characters docker also makes great patterns, as this section will demonstrate.

- With a little creative program tweaking, you can generate all kinds of patterns in CorelDRAW for many applications.

Once again, if you can imagine it, you can build it one way or another in CorelDRAW.

In this chapter, we look at creating interesting background artwork by using patterns of repeating images. First, we create images that repeat endlessly in one direction, for such uses as Web page dividers. Next, we create an "Escheresque" tessellation pattern of tight-fitting objects, using clones and node-editing. Then, using the Tile option on the Symbols and Special Characters docker, we create a unique background pattern with repeating star shapes. Finally, we create seamless tiles to use as repeating images that extend endlessly in all directions, for Web page backgrounds or other patterned applications.

Never-Ending Designs

Using graphics as page separators for banners and Web pages is very common. The challenge with the Web is to create as small a tile as possible, fooling the viewer with a bitmap that connects to itself to create a never-ending graphic, such as those in Figure 19.1. This way, one tile can be repeated over and over and connected into a row as long as you wish, without increasing the download time.

These same techniques can be applied to any application for which you need a pattern to merge back into itself. Any tubular design project, from embroidered socks to teacups, uses this same kind of never-ending pattern. Several ways exist to create repeating patterns, with the results reflecting the amount of work involved (unfortunately, in this case more *is* better).

Easy

As you may have noticed, you can use a reflection technique to create a seamless row of any image. This is a really easy way to make a bitmap that connects to itself indefinitely. The downside is that hiding the repeat is hard because the images are sometimes very obviously mirrored. The upside is that it's easy. For perfection, you have to buckle up and head into hard territory (which comes later). Here is how to build a never-ending image with the mirroring technique:

1. Start with the image you want to tile. As I said, the upside is that this technique works with anything, including abstract patterns. If you want to use a texture fill (as I have), you first have to convert it to a bitmap using the Bitmaps|Convert to Bitmap command.

2. Duplicate the object and flip it horizontally by dragging the left-center sizing handle to the right while holding down the Ctrl key. Bang. You are done. The two tiles flipped together create a tile that endlessly repeats end to end (see Figure 19.2).

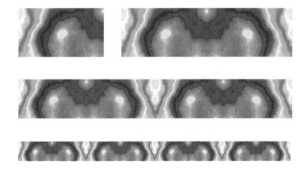

3. You can take this one step further and expand the image into a never-ending tile that goes both ways—perfect for a Web page background. Simply take your horizontal tile (made of two copies of the original), duplicate it, and then flip it vertically. Now, you have a tile that will connect endlessly in both directions for a background image like no other. You can change the proportions in either direction and the tile still meshes into itself (see Figure 19.3).

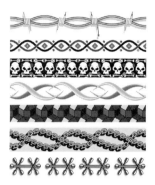

Figure 19.1

It's easy to plan out never-ending designs that repeat forever, for horizontal or tubular applications.

Figure 19.2

Any object will connect seamlessly to its reflection. The top-left tile is duplicated and flip-flopped horizontally to create the never-ending pattern on the top right. This bitmap butts into itself endlessly, as shown in the bottom two rows.

Figure 19.3
Duplicating and flipping the
horizontal tile vertically (on left)
creates an image that repeats
endlessly in all directions (as seen
on the right).

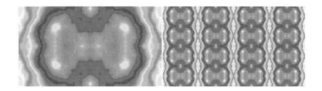

Figure 19.3
Duplicating and flipping the
horizontal tile vertically (on left)
creates an image that repeats
endlessly in all directions (as seen
on the right).

Okay then. So that was *easy*. Now on to *medium*....

Medium

The easy tile is quick and dirty, but not always a solution. Some graphics, such as a string of words, simply can't be mirrored. With just a little more effort you can create a never-ending tile:

1. Start with a graphic that you want to string along, like my chain from the sample Web pages (Chapter 20). The chain (described in Chapter 8) uses perfectly symmetrical curves, so it's a great way to start.

2. Draw a box around the area that looks like the repeat of the rolling chain segment. With the chain, you can easily see where this area is—at the bottom of the swoop. Draw the square at a best-guess, so that each side slices through the center of a flat link (see Figure 19.4).

Figure 19.4
A pattern starts with the target
image, and a rectangle is drawn
around it to define the repeat.

3. Delete all but the pieces necessary for the repeat. Also delete one of the protruding links. It is much easier to start and stop with the same object. Draw two vertical lines and align them with the left and right ends of the rectangle (see Figure 19.5).

Figure 19.5
Vertical lines serve as guides to
align the parts that overlap in the
pattern repeat.

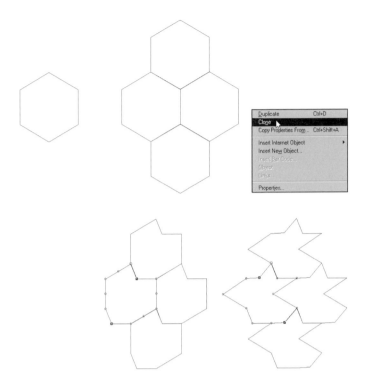

Figure 19.13
An original hexagon (left) is surrounded by three clones (right).

Figure 19.14
Selecting and moving node pairs creates intermeshing geometric objects.

4. When you get a shape that starts to look like something promising (in this case, an animated puppy head), you can stop the node-editing phase and start coloring. You can delete the three clone shapes, because they will not reflect the addition of objects on top of the parent curve. The clones are simply a visual aide to facilitate the creation of the primary shape.

5. Use the Ellipse tool to draw eyes and a mouth, and use the Bezier tool to click in some ear details. The nose is a circle trimmed to the shape of the head using the Arrange|Shaping|Intersection command.

6. Select all the objects in your cyberpuppy and choose Edit|Clone. Move and duplicate the clone groups, as before, to create a pattern of tessellated pooches (see Figure 19.15).

7. You can duplicate and move the clones to create as complicated or as simple a pattern as you wish. You can even use this type of pattern to create the seamless tiles, as outlined in the last section. The beauty of a pattern made from clones is that you simply change the parent object and all the obedient children follow. You can select a single object in the parent group by holding down the Ctrl key when you click on it, and then change the fill or outline. Or, you can drag and drop new fill attributes onto the objects in the parent group and all cloned objects will follow suit (see Figure 19.16).

Figure 19.15
Simple shapes bring the image to life, which is grouped and again cloned to create a pattern.

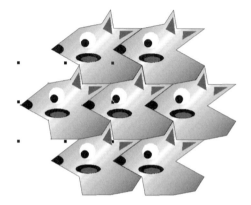

Figure 19.16
Changes to the attributes in the parent group are reflected in any of the corresponding clones.

The tessellation is in this book's middle color section and in the pooches.cdr file in the \Chapt19\ subdirectory on the companion CD-ROM. The clones are still alive in the file. If you drag and drop different colors onto the objects in the parent pooch, you can see how this changes all the duplicates. Not sheep, but cloning nonetheless.

Symbol Patterns

Yes, my Velcro-brain strikes again. While innocently browsing through the CD-ROM bins at the local music store, I saw an album cover that really appealed to me. It was very similar to the graphic in Figure 19.17, with a photo covered in a geometric pattern. Of course, I elaborated on the process, adding a lens effect to the pattern of geometric shapes to get a chaotic and bright effect. Like I said, I never can leave well enough alone.

In addition to being a great source for images and icons, the Symbols and Special Characters docker is set up for patterning. By using the Tile option, any symbol that you choose can be instantly set up as a pattern for any use you can imagine. Unlike the tessellation example, these objects don't interlock, although you can change the density, size, and spacing of

Figure 19.17
Starting with a pattern set up by tiling a symbol, a star object becomes a pattern that is used to recolor a photo by using a lens effect.

the pieces. These patterns, by default, are spaced in an even grid arrangement of horizontal and vertical rows which works well for most applications. In this example, however, I decided to break up the grid pattern into a slightly different variant by offsetting every alternative row of symbols. Either way, the Symbols and Special Characters docker makes for easy patterning, so that you can concentrate on the design as a whole. Here is how to use the Symbols and Special Characters docker to create a pattern:

1. Start a new design (Ctrl+N) and open the Symbols and Special Characters docker (Ctrl+F11). Locate the Stars1 library and choose a star that you like. Change the Symbol Size to .25 inch.

2. Click on the right arrow next to the current library name in the docker, which opens a pop-up menu. Click on Tile Symbol/Special Character. Open the pop-up menu again and click on Tile Options, which opens the Tile Options dialog box in which you can control the size of your pattern grid.

3. In the Tile Options dialog box, change the grid size to .5 inch Horizontal and .5 inch Vertical, and then click on OK. Drag the star onto your page and watch the pattern emerge (see Figure 19.18).

4. A pattern set up in this fashion really has only one original parent shape—the top left one. The rest of the duplicates are clones. Select the top-left star, change the fill to cyan, and give it a .023-inch ice-blue outline (see Figure 19.19).

5. The grid pattern is nice, but too regimented. To create a staggered pattern, shift the stars in every other row one star length to the right. To select all the stars in each alternate row, hold down the Shift key while dragging around them. In this way, you can easily select all the stars in every other row and move them slightly to the

Note: *Getting the density and spacing right with the Tile option in the Symbols and Special Characters docker is a bit of a crapshoot. Experiment with different size numbers and grid sizes until you get what you want. Remember, you can always enlarge or decrease the pattern, so worry about only density and spacing in general. You can also delete pieces to perfect your pattern, as needed.*

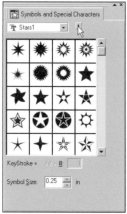

Figure 19.18

With the Tile option enabled, many duplicates of a star symbol create a design.

Figure 19.19

Selecting and changing attributes of the parent shape also changes all the "clone" objects in the pattern grid.

right. Try to align the stars in the rows you are moving so that the top point of each star is midway between the two stars above it (see Figure 19.20).

6. For an even more striking effect, use the Interactive Contour tool to create a second, slightly larger set of stars behind the original. Then, choose Arrange|Separate, and then Arrange|Ungroup All, to break the two curves into separate curves.

7. With the Rectangle tool, draw a box around both sets of stars. Select All (Ctrl+A) and combine the three objects into one (Ctrl+L). This creates a solid rectangle shape, with the fat-star cutouts.

8. Import a bitmap (Ctrl+I), such as my reclining woman, and place it behind the cutout-stars rectangle. Open the Lens docker (Alt+F3) and assign the star cutout shape the Heat Map lens option. Very trippy results (see Figure 19.21).

Figure 19.20

Create a less regimented pattern by moving every other row to the right.

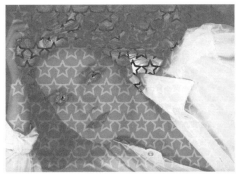

Figure 19.21

Combining both star curves to a rectangle creates a solid shape with star cutouts. If this shape is placed over a bitmap and given a Lens effect, the result is a patterned and recolored image.

The star lens is in this book's middle color section and in the \Chapt19\ directory on the companion CD-ROM, in the stargirl.cdr file. Combining a pattern with other effects can make for some very cool imagery. And it's easy, too.

Tiles: Non-Ceramic

Background patterns are very popular and easy to use to personalize and make a Web page or other art project unique. The challenge with Web pages is to create interesting graphics without using bitmaps that are big and slow to download. This is why background tiles are so popular—you need to download only one small image to fill the screen with a unique pattern. We already saw how using the reflection technique makes anything a tile, and even how to create horizontal, never-ending tiles. Now, we just need to work in both directions simultaneously.

The challenge with creating Web tiles is to create an image that isn't immediately recognizable as a background tile. If your pattern tile has an awkward or stark transition, the duplicate tiles will not merge together smoothly and thus will look choppy or, as we saw with the reflection technique, create an abstract pattern. Bad tiles really do look bad, because bitmaps are unavoidably rectangular by nature and con-

Figure 19.22

A seamless tile can create an interesting background for a Web page, advertisement, or both.

sequently can become a distracting array of boxes in the background if you aren't careful.

Webs For The Web

Remember, you need to work the background into the whole design scheme of the Web page. Web tiles can very easily make a Web page illegible and defeat the purpose of your efforts. The background tile in Figure 19.22, which assembles into a spider web, was a good way to build both the Web site and the printed promotional material.

For the Web, you could decrease the contrast to keep the page legible, and for print, keep it as is. Here is how to design a seamless Web tile:

1. For patterning, starting with a perfect square is a good idea. Draw two lines to criss-cross through the center of the square. Select them both and drag inward on a corner sizing handle while holding down the Shift key to fit them within the square (see Figure 19.23).

Figure 19.23

A perfect square perfectly bisected by two lines is our starting point.

PATTERNS AND UNDERWEAR

All of my pattern and smooth-tiling knowledge actually comes from a stint in the art department of a major underwear manufacturer. Yes, for many months, I was busy arranging flowers and paisleys on sexy negligees and sleepwear. The experience taught me, among other things, how patterns repeat and the need to hide the repeat.

A good pattern dissolves seamlessly into itself to create a never-ending series of images. Most everything that has a pattern, from wallpaper to the aforementioned underwear, is actually just a small pattern area repeating over and over. A relatively small silk-screen press is responsible for repeatedly printing on the fabric, creating the endless roll that eventually becomes the garments. The trick is that the right side of the pattern merges into the left, and the top with the bottom. To get a seamless repeat pattern the old-fashioned way, a designer would tape a piece of paper onto a tube, and then sketch the image so that it would go round and round indefinitely. When the paper is untaped and unrolled, the result is a left-right seamless tile. The process is repeated for the top and bottom, resulting in a square block that fits into duplicates of itself to create a smooth, never-ending design.

"That's great, underwear boy," you think, "but how does this help me?" Well, the concept of a seamless tile works great in creating backgrounds for Web pages. If you design a tile that is seamless (like the previous chain example, but this time in all directions), it will create a smooth, seemingly endless image that flows together in a way that defies its simple, single-bitmap origin. Create a good seamless tile and your viewers will wonder how you defied the rules of physics and got such a huge background image to download so quickly.

2. Duplicate the x-square and flip it horizontally. Select both squares, duplicate, and flip vertically. Now you have a set of squares that already create a seamless tile, with each angled line exiting the square on one side only to reenter on the opposite side. This is the key to this pattern.

3. Use the Shape tool to node-edit the straight lines into the sweeping configuration that is the look of the spider web. You can combine the smaller lines so that they connect at the center to form a larger *x,* as long as you don't change the position where the lines exit the square. As long as you don't change the exit points, you can change the way the lines curve within the square as much as you wish (see Figure 19.24).

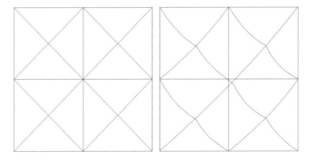

Figure 19.24

The array of squares creates the tile layout, and then the straight lines are curved to suggest spider webbing.

4. Using the small squares as a guide, draw another square the same size and in the exact same location as the four smaller squares. Fill it with black or another subtle dark fill and then delete the smaller squares. Give the lines a thick .033-inch dark-blue outline. Duplicate the web lines, give the duplicates a smaller .008-inch white outline, and offset them a hair up and to the right. This creates the dark, spooky spider web graphics (see Figure 19.25).

5. Select all the lines and choose Effects|PowerClip|Place Inside Container to stuff them inside the dark boundary square. The PowerClip step trims away the parts of the line that stick over the edge when you give them heavier line weights. This finishes up the tile, which is ready to spin into a Web tile (see Figure 19.26).

ANGRY FRUIT SALAD

I hate the see-what-I-can-do design mentality that thrives on the Web, with pages full of gimmicks and gizmos that are put there simply for the sake of showing off the programmer's talent They are disorganized collections of dizzying, random, pointless distractions that fail every traditional design test, and earn the "angry fruit salad" title. If these sites would only come with some sort of virtual aspirin dispenser.

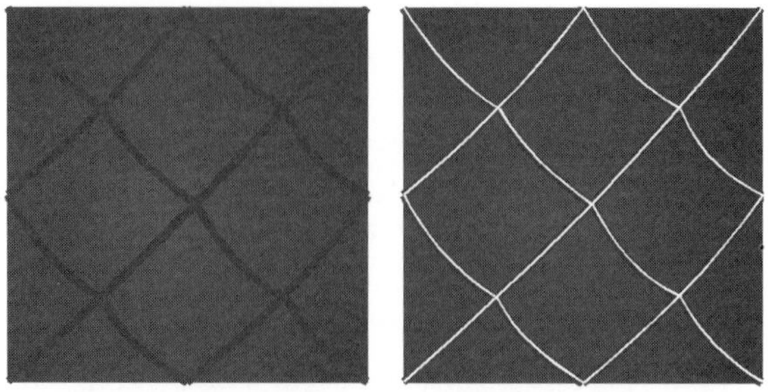

Figure 19.25
Dark coloring in the square and lighter shades on the lines create the web.

Figure 19.26
With everything constrained within a square, the image is tile-ready.

6. Select the PowerClip group and open the Export dialog box (Ctrl+E). To create a bitmap for the Web, set Color to Palette, enable Anti-aliasing and Use Color Profile, and set Resolution to 72 dpi. Click on OK to create a tile that you can use in a Web page as the background.

You can view this and the next example in the middle color section, or you can load it in a Web browser to see the tile in action. With your Web browser running, open the companion CD-ROM's corelmag.htm file, found in the \Chapt19\ subdirectory. The process in Internet Explorer is File|Open, click on Browse, and then locate the CD-ROM's corelmag.htm file. The Web pages in this chapter are still in development, so the graphics are really too big and unruly to download from the Web, but they work great right off the CD-ROM. The native file is called webtiles.cdr and is located in the same \Chapt19\ subdirectory.

Lava Lamp Not Included

Like working with the chain link for the horizontal tile, any graphic made up of smaller units can easily be constructed into a never-ending seamless tile. The freaky background in this psychedelic design is a seamless tile created by using a round, deadhead paisley image that I had lying around (see Figure 19.27). Yes, you read right, a paisley design using skulls.

I created this tile in a flat configuration with the intention of using it as a square tile. When I was using the Pattern Fill feature to create the back-

HTML

To insert a background into your Web page, simply add **background="TILENAME.GIF"** to the **<BODY** tag of your HTML code. Replace **TILENAME.GIF** with the actual name of your own personal web tile.

ground for the title graphic, I remembered that I could change the horizontal and vertical tile size. Reducing the vertical dimension of the tile makes the circles look like they are floating at an angle, so I left it like that. To get the effect for the Web tile, you simply squish the bitmap horizontally or vertically in PhotoPaint. Here is how to make the floating disks seamless tile:

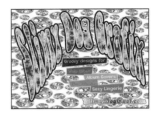

Figure 19.27
A graphic group can be made into a seamless tile; then, using the Pattern Fill option in CorelDRAW, it can be used to fill any object.

1. Start again with a perfect square; then, draw and align guidelines to all four sides of the square. Import the item that you want to make into a tile (in this case, the deadhead paisley). Align the object to the center of the right vertical reference line. Duplicate the object and align the duplicate to the left vertical line. You are ready to start getting seamless (see Figure 19.28).

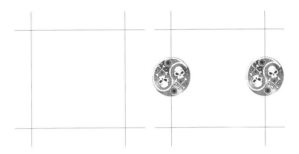

Figure 19.28
A square and reference lines are used to align objects within the tile area.

2. With the square defining the area of the tile, and the art objects aligned horizontally and exactly at the center of each boundary line, your seamless tile is already at work. Where the paisley exits the rectangle on the left is the exact point where it enters on the right. The distance between the two objects, determined by aligning to the reference lines, is critical.

3. Select the paisley pair and move them around to create a unique arrangement for this pattern. Any of the objects can stick out beyond the boundary box, as long as you first start with a pair of objects. Align the object pair to opposing reference lines; then, you can move them freely as a pair and still maintain the seamless tile orientation in the square boundary box (see Figure 19.29).

4. After you place all the object pairs around the square, throw some more objects inside the rectangle. Anything within the image tile needs no special attention. Only the objects that hang over need to be aligned properly, so that they enter and exit the square in exactly the right orientation.

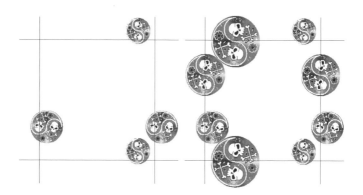

Figure 19.29

By using the reference lines to establish the correct distance between the object pairs, you can move the object pairs around to create the pattern while still maintaining a seamless orientation.

5. When finished, delete all the guidelines. Then, select all the pattern objects, choose Effects|PowerClip|Place Inside Container, and click on the rectangle boundary box to stuff all the objects into a perfect square. Remove any outline, and you have a seamless tile (see Figure 19.30).

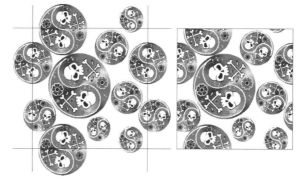

Figure 19.30

Placing more objects inside the tile area finishes off the pattern, creating a seamless tile when the objects are stuffed within a rectangle (shown here on the right, with an outline for clarity) by using the PowerClip function.

6. Select the tile and export it as a bitmap that is appropriate for your current project. For a Web tile, an appropriate bitmap is 72 dpi with an RGB color depth. For printed applications, you'll want a 300-dpi image with a CMYK color scheme. To get a Web tile to appear on your Web page, add the code to your HTML file.

7. In CorelDRAW, you can fill any object with the tile by using the Bitmap Pattern Fill. Open the Pattern Fill from the Fill tool flyout and click on Load to find the freshly made tile. You can use the same height and width values or experiment with different values to make the disks flatter or wider (see Figure 19.31).

This mind trip can be seen in this book's middle color section and in the webtiles.cdr file on the companion CD-ROM (in the \Chapt19\ subdirectory). It is also available as a Web page, called slimy.htm, in the \Chapt19\ subdirectory. You can see how a single seamless tile fills the background with a seemingly solid image. The nice thing is that no mat-

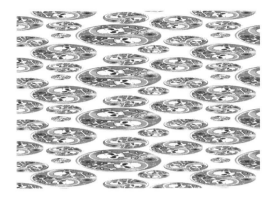

Figure 19.31
The Bitmap Pattern Fill option enables you to fill any object with your new seamless tiles.

ter how big or small you resize your screen or browser, a Web tile will recalculate to fill the whole screen. A clever background tile and a bitmap on top that takes advantage of the transparency options available in the GIF image format can come together to create a pretty cool Web page. Now it's your turn.

Beyond f/x

Patterns are everywhere, and with the Web offering more and more design opportunities, they are no longer a specialized phenomenon. Patterns can be used to set a mood in a design (a fluffy cloud background sets a much different tone than, say, red-hot lava) or to establish the nature of a Web site (a children's Web page with big, fun icons in the background; or, perhaps a business Web site with a subdued, marble background). Patterns can be used in advertising, with phrases like "We have designs on the future" or "Patterned for success" to play off of the concept. Holiday theme backgrounds, with little hearts, candy canes, pumpkins, or whatever icon suggests the current season, are an easy way to add a timely feel to a monthly newsletter or other periodical.

Entire industries are devoted to the creation of patterns for their products. From high-end silk ties to cheap wrapping paper, you'll find patterns everywhere. The textiles industry alone is huge. Think about it. Beyond clothing, patterning skills are needed to create upholstery, bedding, drapery, and even rugs. It's an interesting and rewarding career in itself, if you can handle working with underwear all day, for example. If you are interested, I can even give you a few leads....

Moving On

In this chapter, we looked at many ways to create patterns for use in a variety of applications. From freaky tessellations to simplistic backgrounds made with the Symbols and Special Characters docker, many interesting variants are available with CorelDRAW. After you finish your artwork, you can take it a step further to create seamless tiles for horizontal, vertical, and all-ways applications. These patterns are perfect for both Web and print applications, as either main design elements or as secondary background images.

In the next chapter, we continue to look at ways to use CorelDRAW for on-screen applications. From interface design as a whole, to multistage button elements in particular, we examine the screen as an interactive medium. Press here, click on there, next, back, previous, home, cha cha cha.

BUTTONS AND SCREENS

This chapter explores interface design ideas and dynamic elements for on-screen projects.

If your artwork hasn't evolved to include multimedia and Web page development yet, it's just a matter of time before it will. Whereas the huge multimedia hype of a few years back hasn't quite panned out as anticipated, the influence of the Web has. Everyone and his brother-in-law (in my case, literally—my brother-in-law has a Web development company) is making Web pages these days, with a level of ability that varies from professional to pathetic. I'm no exception, with a handful of obligatory Web sites under my cyberbelt. The nice thing is that you already have the tools and the ability to explore this medium; you just have to take on the challenge.

The advantages to developing on-screen projects with CorelDRAW are many. For starters, you have at your fingertips all the obvious benefits of endless versatility, countless effects, and color options. CorelDRAW objects, as we have seen in many previous examples, are ready for animation; and with Photo-Paint in the graphics bundle, you are ready for the Web development challenge. Basically, you can work all of these resources into your multimedia projects, including all the effects that you've explored in this book.

Using CorelDRAW for multimedia and Web development has incredibly strong advantages beyond the obvious graphics factor. CorelDRAW images are vector-based, which means that graphics designed for a low-resolution, on-screen application, such as a Web site, can migrate directly into other high-res, peripheral support material, such as advertising and printed promotion.

With the never-ending versatility of CorelDRAW artwork, your original efforts in the planning stages (hierarchy charts, dummy pages, site plan, story boards, and so forth) become the groundwork for the actual images. Why make that effort twice? A font change, new fill color, a unique background, and suddenly your composites are fleshed out into the real deal. Recycle, exploit, divide, and conquer.

In this chapter, we look at creating graphics that are useful for on-screen applications, such as Web pages, presentations, and multimedia applications (with the broad variety of Web and multimedia development tools available these days, we depart from the specific, step-by-step format at times to discuss broader-reaching production tips and design principles). The first section deals with creating multiple images for a custom control panel, to animate buttons so that they have at-rest, roll-over, and depressed states, for use in a Web site or multimedia application. After that, we look at planning and developing an on-screen production, using

CorelDRAW as both an organization tool and an asset generator. Then, we look at some of the Web-specific features of CorelDRAW, such as image mapping and actual HTML publishing. It's a wild on-screen ride, with additional support files on the companion CD-ROM, so brace yourself!

Sit, Roll Over, Lie Down

These days, buttons are more prolific on the Web than coffee houses are in Seattle. The graphical user interface (GUI) thrives on buttons, with your entire workday filled with pointing and clicking on those little buggers. What surprises me is that, for the most part, buttons and GUIs look like they were added at the last minute with little or no creativity involved in their layout or construction. I'm far from your super Webmeister, but I at least try to make interesting button shapes and navigation panels, such as the one in Figure 20.1.

Figure 20.1
CorelDRAW objects are perfect for creating multistate buttons. On the left are the buttons at rest; in the center, each button lights up as the mouse travels over it; the buttons flatten out when pressed with a mouse click.

If you plan ahead so that you know what you need before you even start thinking about graphics, you'll be much better off. In this example, I figured out way ahead of time all the buttons that I wanted on the control panel. Then, I created an interface that included all the buttons, with the primary navigation buttons larger than the secondary options. In CorelDRAW, creating custom button designs that are based on your exact needs is easy, and the result is a unique interface that is much more interesting than those rectangles everyone else is using.

After your basic interface is in place, creating graphics for multiple button states is easy. Instead of just lying there, your buttons can be very animated. They can change colors when the pointer is moved on top of them (called a *rollover*), when they are clicked on (*mouseDown*), and when they are released (*mouseUp*). Even if you aren't creating images for on-screen applications, faux interfaces and buttons make interesting design elements for print applications.

Before you begin in CorelDRAW, you need to establish the number and type of buttons that you want in your control panel. I needed a total of six buttons, with two of them as large arrows for Next and Back navigation. I chose an up/down configuration of the buttons to facilitate a round center area that could later be filled with an animation or logo design. The oval center mapped out the look of the control panel, although the same basic scheme would work for a left/right orientation of the buttons.

After you establish the number and type of your buttons, follow these steps to design and build your custom GUI by creating graphics for all the button states:

1. Use the Ellipse tool to draw an oval and then use the Rectangle tool to draw a perfect square, centered on the oval (hold down the Ctrl key as you drag). Duplicate the square and enlarge it slightly. Move the pointer over a corner of the selected square, to round out the corners on the larger rectangle by dragging the node down (CorelDRAW automatically switches the Pick or Rectangle tool to the Shape tool when you hover over a node). Select the smaller rectangle and rotate it –45 degrees, like a diamond. These three shapes will generate all the buttons for your custom interface (see Figure 20.2).

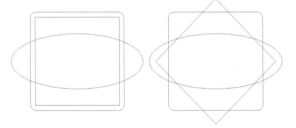

Figure 20.2
Two simple squares and an oval are all that you need to create a custom button interface.

2. Select the oval shape and choose Arrange|Shaping|Trim. Enable only the Leave Original Other Objects option, click on Trim, and then click on the round-cornered square. This cuts the oval away from the center of that shape.

3. Select the diamond, click on Trim, and click on the round-cornered curve again. Select the round-cornered curve and create four individual buttons with the Break Apart command (Ctrl+K).

4. Select the oval again, click on Trim, and then click on the diamond. This creates the up and down arrows after you use the Break Apart command (Ctrl+K) to separate the shape into two curves. Fill all of these buttons with a neutral gray color (see Figure 20.3).

5. Drag the Interactive Extrude tool onto your shapes, using the Bevel and Lighting options on the Property Bar to add depth and dimen-

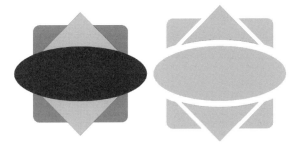

Figure 20.3
Use the Trim command on the shapes to create three separate curves (on left). Use the Break Apart command on each curve to create the individual buttons (on right).

sion. Use the Effects|Copy Effect|Extrude From command, and the Copy VP From option (on the Property Bar), to give all the elements the same Extrude values.

6. Add text elements to label each button. I used a font called BankGothic. When finished, duplicate the entire button group and set it aside.

7. To freeze the bevel groups, choose Arrange|Separate, followed by Arrange|Ungroup All, so that all the pieces can be individually manipulated. You do this so that you can give the top pieces of the beveled buttons an interesting custom color blend, so that they look more like shiny metal.

8. The oval object was exported as an Adobe Illustrator file for use in CorelDream. I used the 3D program to create the cells for an animation that plays continuously inside the navigation panel. (See Chapter 22 for more details on working with CorelDream.) The center panel oval could also be a great place for a message board that changes to tell you what each button does as you roll over it. I also included a Help button, to access an instruction page, which is a feature you might wish to add to your interface design as well (see Figure 20.4).

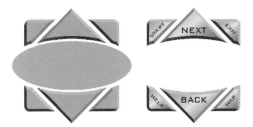

Figure 20.4
The button shapes are given depth with an extrude bevel; the faces are filled with a custom color blend to look shiny.

9. Each of the black-text buttons in this first group was selected and exported for the button-at-rest graphics.

10. Select and change the black-text elements to red-filled, yellow-out-lined text elements. These, again, were individually selected and exported for the roll-over button graphics.

11. Select the duplicate button group with the live bevels from Step 6. Change the bevel depth from deep to very shallow on each button shape, using the Property Bar. Also, change the text to some other color, such as blue. These buttons, when individually selected and exported, will become the button-depressed graphics (see Figure 20.5).

Each button graphic was imported into Macromedia Director as its own cast member. The button-at-rest group was laid out on the page, with the animation oval in the center, thus completing the console. The Lingo script (Director's scripting language) swaps out each button graphic, de-

Figure 20.5

The buttons are given bright-colored text for the roll-over group; a duplicate set is given shallow bevels for the button-depressed group.

Figure 20.6

Simple geometric shapes generated in CorelDRAW (left) are quickly transformed into multistage button graphics in Photo-Paint (right), using plug-in filters from Alien Skin.

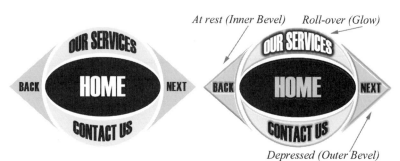

INSTANT ANIMATED BUTTONS

Instead of creating all the elements for your buttons in CorelDRAW, you can take advantage of a third-party plug-in to speed up the process in Photo-Paint. For example, the same simple steps used to create the beveled effects for the puzzle pieces in Chapter 7 can be used to create multistage buttons. Simply create flat geometric art in CorelDRAW and export it as a bitmap to manipulate in Photo-Paint (see Figure 20.6, on left). Then, use the Magic Wand tool to select the color areas of your button art, and use filters (such as Alien Skin's Eye Candy collection) to transform it instantly into a 3D-looking button (see Figure 20.6, on right). Use the Inner Bevel filter to create the button look. Use the Glow filter for the roll-over effect. Finally, the Outer Bevel filter makes an object look depressed. It's the quickest and easiest way to create very cool multistage button graphics.

pending on the state and location of the mouse. If the mouse rolls over a button, the program swaps the existing graphic with the roll-over art. If the button is depressed, the art is again swapped out, this time with the button-depressed art. You can also get the same action on a Web site by using a little creative coding or by using after-market Java programming tools. Getting multistage buttons to work in your on-screen events is very easy. You simply need a unique graphic for each of the button states, and then computer programming takes over and makes the magic happen.

You can watch the button action work firsthand by starting the doggone.exe program, nestled in the \Chapt20\ subdirectory of the companion CD-ROM. With the program running, click on the spinning globe to initiate the introduction sequence. After the introduction (which you can skip by clicking on the slow-scrolling text), the control panel appears with the buttons made in this exercise. They just sit there until you move the mouse over them, at which point they spring to life. Click on the Next button to move to the next screen, and notice how the button changes to the button-depressed graphic when you do. This is a pretty common example of a button action, which you can expand on to create your own cool interface.

All kinds of ways exist to get animated buttons (see the sidebar "Instant Animated Buttons" for more ideas). The potential is really unlimited. The native button pieces are in a file called buttons.cdr, also located in the \Chapt20\ directory. This file also contains the custom interface from another example. These custom button shapes were made in exactly the same way: start with simple shapes, create custom shapes by using the Trim function, and then add depth and shading with the Interactive Extrude tool. Much more interesting than a row of rectangles.

Animated Interface

Whereas my workload at one time was predominantly for projects destined for paper, that has long since changed. Now, on-screen projects make up the bulk of my responsibilities. Web page graphics, interface design, multimedia kiosks, and speaker-support presentation material are the kinds of projects that now constitute most of my workload. The image in Figure 20.7 is the main navigation screen for an information kiosk that sits in a cybercafé.

For this project, I first mapped out all the graphics in CorelDRAW for final assembly in Macromedia Director (Director has long been the de facto program to create multimedia applications, on both the PC and Mac

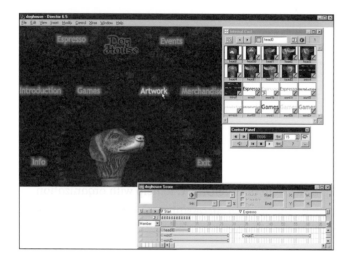

Figure 20.7

CorelDRAW is a great program to design an interface; use Macromedia Director to produce the graphics that you need to bring the interface to life.

platforms). This process of designing the project in CorelDRAW first and then producing the pieces for use in another program has many uses. In addition to multimedia development, you can design Web pages in the same way. Although you *can* publish Web pages directly from CorelDRAW by using the Publish to Internet feature (as discussed later in this chapter), anyone serious about Web development/management uses other, purpose-specific programs. Here is how to design an interface in CorelDRAW and bring it to life in Macromedia Director:

What Is Director?

If you are new to multimedia creation, think of Director as the assembly tool to piece together all the elements, such as graphics and sound, into a new and unique on-screen experience. Director is a much better tool for combining all the assets than it is for creating the necessary assets. Director isn't an illustration package, bitmap editor, or 3D modeling program, but, as the name implies, the overseer of a Hollywood-like production. Director doesn't create cast members, it tells them where to be and what to do. You need an outside source for your digital actors. CorelDRAW and Photo-Paint are great places to design and generate the graphics that become actors within Director. For this reason, the Corel graphics suite is a perfect companion to Director, making a powerful alliance with amazing potential.

The way in which I use CorelDRAW with Director is essentially the same way that I use it to produce a Web site. Because CorelDRAW is object-oriented, anything that I create in the CorelDRAW workspace is infinitely malleable and recyclable. This is a key feature, because I can begin by storyboarding in CorelDRAW, gathering pieces and text to help visualize the screens, and then use those pieces later to generate the actual graphics. Images generated within Director, on the other hand, using its simplistic bitmap editor, are just that: bitmaps. This means that you can't enlarge or distort the images without losing resolution. CorelDRAW objects are more flexible, and although you eventually need bitmaps for all images for use in Director (or the graphic elements on a Web page), during the planning/layout stages it's nice to be able to design freely without any limitations.

1. Start building a site map in CorelDRAW, to help with organization and visualization. The key to a successful project is organization, so a simple flowchart (see Figure 20.8) is the first place to start. After you know exactly what you need, the design task is much simpler. For a main navigation screen (such as a home-page graphic), if you can boil down your project to a finite number of pages, you can work that into your design.

Figure 20.8
Outlining the project in CorelDRAW with a flowchart not only helps in the organization process, but also begins to create assets (such as the text objects) that you can use later.

From my flowchart, I narrowed down the project to eight possible destinations, with strong symmetry resulting from the four destinations on the left mirroring the four destinations on the right. Planning the project in advance not only influences the design as a whole, but also gives you a better sense of scope. With every area/ page mapped out, dividing the workload is much easier, too, if you are working in a group. Simply assign certain pages to certain people, or specific elements on each page. Proper planning is just not emphasized enough in design books, and it's really one of the greatest design challenges. After you know what to do, doing it really isn't that hard.

2. For the easiest transition from CorelDRAW to Director, set up your page at the same size as your Director movie (to find out how big your movie is, in Director, right-click on the movie and open the

Movie Properties dialog box). In CorelDRAW, change your page size
to match your Director movie. Double-click on the page (or choose
Layout|Page Setup) to open the Options dialog box. Change to Land-
scape (horizontal) format, change the Paper to Custom, adjust the
Resolution to 72 dpi, adjust your movie size (typically, 640 pixels
wide by 480 pixels high), and then click on OK to resize your page
(see Figure 20.9).

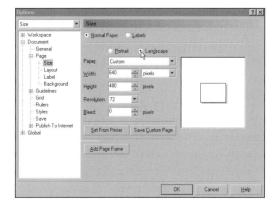

Figure 20.9

For the easiest cross-application
compatibility, set the page's
physical dimensions in
CorelDRAW to match those of
your target destination.

For the Dog House Project, each destination is given a text description
and a unique location on screen. The concept was to have the 3D dog
head rotate and look at whatever button was selected. Use CorelDRAW to
begin to visualize the home page. Copy the flowchart file and use the text
elements as pieces for the main home page navigation graphics. Use the
gear shapes from Chapter 16 to use as design elements here.

To get the images that I wanted for the dog's head looking around, I sim-
ply scanned a real-world object. Choose File|Acquire Image|Acquire to use
photos from your digital camera, or scan a toy or other real-world object
by using your flat-bed scanner (that's how I got the dog head images!).

UNDERSTAND BANDWIDTH

The complexity of your on-screen design is limited to the available *bandwidth*, or data-transfer rate. If you are
designing a Web page, you don't want it to take so long to download that your audience loses patience and
moves on. For a multimedia kiosk, which accesses a local hard disk or CD-ROM rather than downloading off the
Internet, your design isn't limited by bandwidth issues. This kiosk design, for example, is far too complex, with
large image files and complicated programming, to make it practical for a Web site, but it runs great on a single
computer. So, although you can port a Director movie directly to the Web by using Macromedia's Shockwave
technology, this typically isn't a good idea unless you can design the program to download quickly and efficiently
from the beginning.

Use the scanned image as a design element in your page layout. Experiment with different layouts of the elements on the page to achieve a sense of balance and functionality. My first layout idea (see Figure 20.10) had the text elements imbedded in the gear pieces, which I later abandoned in favor of a simpler design. With CorelDRAW's flexibility, you don't have to worry about wasting time during this initial layout process because you can always reuse and recycle your pieces.

Working in CorelDRAW also helps you to expand your potential without adding too much work. While laying out the pieces for my home-page design, I decided that animating my gear shapes, to create a dynamic live interface, wouldn't require much more effort. Thus, I positioned the gear shapes in two symmetrical halves, with the right half mirroring the left, but with each gear advanced in the mirror copy by one tooth. This meant that I could use the image for one animation cell, and then simply flip it horizontally to create the second animation cell. When these two copies are looped, it looks like the gears are animated. (This process sounds complicated, but it really isn't; it's outlined, step-by-step, in the next chapter.)

Lay out all the gear shapes on the page, layering duplicate copies to create a sense of depth. For a background, draw a rectangle and fill it with the Blue Lava Texture Fill, changing the default colors from blue and white to blue and black for an eerie color scheme. Give the closest set of gears a purple outline and a blue fill. To make them look strangely translucent, I used the Custom Color Map Lens effect, again changing the default colors to black and blue. This gave the home page a unique, layered look.

To make the text glow, use the Interactive Drop Shadow tool, as outlined in Chapter 4.

> **CLEAR TRANSFORMATIONS**
>
> If you change your mind about an effect or modification you have made to text, you can usually restore the original version without having to retype it. Choose Arrange | Clear Transformations, and that should return your text to its previous state, before you tweaked it. If you want to unwrap text that is on a path, choose Text | Straighten Text.

Figure 20.10

By using the flexible and object-oriented design tools of CorelDRAW, you can easily begin to organize and visualize your multimedia or Web project.

Keep working on your graphic in CorelDRAW until you are satisfied with your interface design. Now, you need to export the image into Director (or another multimedia development tool). Essentially, the following four ways exist to do this:

- *Use the Copy/Paste shortcuts.* This option is available because you set up the page at actual size. Select the element in CorelDRAW and choose Copy (Ctrl+C). Switch to Director, find an empty spot in your Cast, and Paste (Ctrl+V). Set your preferences in the Image Options dialog box and click on OK. This produces acceptable results, but the images can get grainy in the process. For better results, read on....

- *Select your single element in CorelDRAW and Export it (Ctrl+E).* With your object selected, open the Export dialog box (Ctrl+E). Change the Files of Type option to JPG-JPEG, enable the Selected Only option, and click on OK. In the Bitmap Export dialog box, enable Anti-aliasing and Use Color Profile, set Size Equals to 1 to 1, and set Resolution to 72 dpi. Click on OK to generate the bitmap. In Director, locate another free spot in your Cast, choose File|Import, and then locate the bitmap you generated in CorelDRAW. This gives you the best possible results, with a smooth-looking graphic in Director.

- *Export the entire page as a single JPG bitmap and then import it into Director.* This is useful for whole-screen graphics, such as a background or even the entire layout. You can then use the Paint option in Director to cut out individual elements of the page to create different Cast members (double-click on the cast member to open the Paint dialog box in Director).

- *Use the screen-capture shortcut.* In CorelDRAW, click on the Zoom tool and then click on the Zoom Actual Size button on the Property Bar. Choose View|Enhanced to get the best possible on-screen rendering of your art, and then press the Ctrl and Print Screen keys. This copies the current screen to the Windows Clipboard. Find a spot in your Director Cast and Paste (Ctrl+V) the screen into place. The screen-capture shortcut is one of the great advantages of designing on-screen artwork.

To facilitate button animation in Director, you need an image for each effect or motion that you are after (as in the first example in this chapter). For example, I wanted my buttons to change color both when the mouse rolls over them and when clicked. In Director, you have an amazing amount of control to manage all kinds of events by using its scripting language, Lingo. If you have the time, you can program a single button event to do almost anything. But, you must plan for each event beforehand, such as in this project, in which I needed four graphics for each button: button-at-rest, roll-over, button-depressed, and a graphic to change the position of the dog's head.

With eight buttons in my example, the dog head, and the background images, the home page alone requires 34 unique graphics. To make things even more tricky, for the roll-over programming to work seamlessly each related graphic must have the same physical dimensions as the one it is replacing. Again, this sounds intimidating, but it isn't that hard.

Creating all the unique pieces is a bit of busy work, but when you see them come alive in Director you'll get a big smile on your face.

After you have all the pieces in Director you can drag them onto the Stage or the Score to begin programming your movie. If the pieces aren't exactly the same size (they should be, but sometimes they can be a pixel or two off), you can resize and tweak them after they are sprites on the Director stage; drag on the sizing handles, just like you do in CorelDRAW.

Building a movie in Director becomes a simple function of arranging on stage the assets created in other applications, such as CorelDRAW, CorelDream, or Photo-Paint, in the order that you want them to appear. This is an over-generalization, and Director does have a pretty steep learning curve, but much of the work is in the planning stages and image preparation, which is similar to any other complex project that you may have accomplished. A print catalog has no fewer steps preparing images and text, and the disadvantage is that you must also consider traditional printing-on-paper problems. On-screen development means you just have to be able to see the image somehow, and as we saw, you can then screen-capture and paste it into your project. So, ultimately, multimedia programming could be easier and more profitable than what you are currently doing. Maybe.

Web Site From Hell

Designing for the Web is the new challenge for the contemporary artist. CorelDRAW offers many features to help you create a powerful Web experience, and it offers the flexibility to deal with some of the limitations and challenges unique to the medium. No other design forum has issues such as "download speed" or "target audience screen resolution" dictate project parameters, which can make designing for the Web very frustrating. Suddenly, demographics also include modem speed, monitor size, and display capacities. It's a barrage of technical concerns that is enough to make a right-brainer cry.

This section deviates from the step-by-step formula to focus on Web-specific tips and tricks. I used these techniques to create the Web page design in Figure 20.11, which is the "old" CorelDRAW f/x site (see the sidebar "Publishing Chaos").

Figure 20.11
CorelDRAW makes planning the whole look of a Web page easy; you can generate directly from the file the Web-friendly graphics and any other support graphics you may need.

Web design is a huge topic in itself, with volumes already written on the subject. So, I'll just hit you with a few of my own favorite insights and some CorelDRAW-specific tips and tricks.

PUBLISHING CHAOS

Much like the Web, the universe of traditional publishing is also always changing. Mergers, acquisitions, news and current events, and last-minute editorial changes can all impact your Web publishing projects. For this reason, designing your Web projects in CorelDRAW is a great idea because you can easily make changes to the object-oriented graphics to keep things up to date. To reflect the changes in title and publisher of this book between version 8 and version 9, I updated the graphics in the CorelDRAW 8 f/x Web site home page design to reflect the new title and publisher. However, after I updated the graphics, I decided to create a brand-spankin' new CorelDRAW 9 f/x and design Web site, with less scary graphics, for broader consumer appeal. I also didn't want to discard the techniques for creating the old graphics, outlined in this section, for those of you not familiar with the version 8 book.

To satisfy all comers, both the old and new Web sites can be viewed on the companion CD-ROM. The old site is in the \Chapt20\fx8web folder (double-click on the index.html file to launch), and the makings of the new site are in the \Chapt20\fx9web\ folder. The old site is pretty much history, but the new site will receive online updates throughout the coming year. Access the CorelDRAW 9 f/x and design Web site at http://www.slimydog.com/corelfx9. I will update the new Web site periodically, to offer book news, cool techniques, links, and other information related to this project, so check there from time to time. You can also email any questions to me directly from that site.

Webbing In CorelDRAW

Designing a Web page layout in CorelDRAW has many advantages. The flexibility and techniques available to you for printed projects are just as available (if not more so) for projects that will end up on the Web. The Web even allows you to take your graphics further, by adding animation, sound, and interaction. You can migrate your CorelDRAW Web page design effortlessly to printed materials at the correct resolution, for cross-promotion projects. Additionally, as you'll see with the upcoming example, CorelDRAW enables you to publish HTML pages directly from the program. The Publish to Internet features in CorelDRAW 9 offer powerful HTML translation (including tables) to achieve WYSIWYG (What You See Is What You Get) porting direct from your CorelDRAW files to the Internet.

CorelDRAW's nice Web-publishing features are handy as support tools; however, I highly recommend that you use a specifically Web-oriented package to build and maintain your Web sites. CorelDRAW should be your primary source for graphics but not your primary Web building and maintenance tool because it simply doesn't have the power needed. The HTML publishing features in CorelDRAW, with their tables, layers, and styles support, are very impressive but not enough to produce a Web site.

A Web site typically needs more than just pretty text and pictures; it also needs animations, forms for viewer input, email support, and maybe even online shopping opportunities and the like, all of which CorelDRAW doesn't support. In addition, a single change on one page can have an impact on many pages on a site; purpose-built, Web-site-specific software packages are designed to manage link changes, and CorelDRAW simply isn't. With all the links, graphics, and other issues, using CorelDRAW to build a Web site simply isn't the best solution any more. Rather, you should compose a site as a whole by using Web-specific software. Microsoft FrontPage, Adobe PageMill, NetObjects Fusion, and Netscape Communicator Gold are all much better products for real-world Web building. These programs not only allow for painless Web page creation, they also offer flexibility and power (such as data entry forms, Java applets, email options, and so forth) that you won't find in the focused CorelDRAW graphics suite. CorelDRAW is for graphics creation, and it excels as an asset-builder, but as a Web site builder, it lags. Use CorelDRAW's powerful graphics tools to enhance your Web site, but exploit true Web-building power elsewhere.

That's just my two bits on the topic, and anything is possible. Building a nice site with nothing more than CorelDRAW is perfectly feasible. Heck, most of my first Web site was built by using CorelDRAW for the graphics, and nothing more than Notepad to do the HTML coding. If you are looking to throw together a few pages for a personal site, then CorelDRAW is all you need. However, if you find that your business now includes building and managing complex Web sites, then get an additional Web management program.

Making Pages

Although you may want to build and manage a site with other software, CorelDRAW is still an invaluable addition to the Web designing experience. As you saw in the last tutorial, the advantage of an object-based design application such as CorelDRAW is that you can use the same pieces through all stages of the Web building process.

After creating a flowchart, I suggest mocking up the entire Web site, page by page, in CorelDRAW. This helps you to work out design problems and other Web-specific issues. Remember that Web design is both horizontally biased (screens are wider than tall, unlike printed pages) and vertically enhanced (you can scroll down indefinitely).

Working with the screen set at the actual resolution and color depth of your target audience also helps you to create a more appropriate design (see the sidebar, "Stay On Target," later in this chapter).

The advantage to creating the pages in CorelDRAW first rather than in a Web-builder program is that you can design whole-page artwork instead of slapping in buttons and graphics haphazardly as you go along. The whole-page design can then be broken into smaller pieces and reassembled into one solid graphic by using an HTML table. Breaking up an otherwise solid graphic like this enables you to create animations for specific sections of the page and take advantage of speedy-download tricks. If you use common graphics in more than one page, they need to be downloaded only once, thus speeding things along.

Figure 20.12 shows how the top of my full-page graphic is broken up into four sections. The right sections change with each page, while the left two pieces are common to all pages. These left two pieces were also made into animated GIFs, to add motion to the site; they need to be downloaded only once and are common elements on every page.

Another bandwidth-saving trick is to use a horizontally repeating graphic for page breaks. The chain page-break graphic on my test site is actually just one small bitmap that is tiled four times across the page (see Figure 20.13). Once loaded, the graphic can be used as many times as you like without increasing future download time. (Creating these kinds of repeating graphics is explained at length in the next chapter.)

Figure 20.16
The Internet Objects toolbar lets you assign a URL to each object in your CorelDRAW file.

6. In the next window, pick either JPEG or GIF. GIF used to be more universally acceptable and is still the only format that supports multiple frame animations, but it's your choice. GIF images enable you to assign a transparent background, whereas JPEG images can compress to smaller sizes and support more colors (I use JPEG whenever I can). After you make your choice of image format, enable all the other options in this Publish To Internet dialog box and then click on Next.

7. On the next screen, choose the file name of the HTML file that you are creating and then click Finish. After CorelDRAW generates the HTML code and the graphic, it launches your primary browser and opens the page so that you can see the results (Figure 20.17).

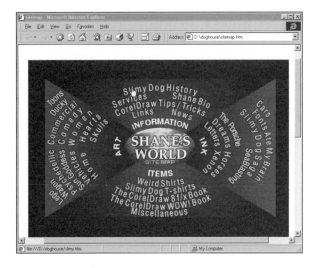

Figure 20.17
After CorelDRAW generates the HTML and Web-friendly image, it launches your browser and opens the page so that you can see the results immediately.

With the CorelDRAW-generated page open in the browser, you can check that the links are working correctly. Move the cursor over a *hotspot,* a linked object, to see whether the link information in the browser's status

GIFS OR JPEGS

Creating images for the Web also means choosing between these two file formats for your bitmap images. GIF images are limited to 256 colors (although dithering can simulate colors beyond the 256-color palette), whereas JPEG files can be in the millions of colors. You used to have to address the least common denominator when building a Web site, which was a screen size of 640x480 and a color depth of 256 colors, but with technology changing so fast the bar has been raised a bit to larger screen sizes and bigger palettes. But, the old rule remains if you want to guarantee that your site can be viewed by all.

The GIF format, although limited in color depth, also supports multicell animation, whereas JPEG images do not. Because I use so many animations and don't find the 256-color palette an insurmountable restriction, I use the GIF format almost exclusively. For nicer images (it really makes a difference with photos, for example), the JPEG format is better and it also takes advantage of file-compression technology. When you save a JPEG, you have the option to change the quality factor. Choosing lower quality means smaller files, but it also degrades the image (save a copy of the high-quality original before you start experimenting with the quality-factor option, in case you need to start over). If you use the JPEG format, find a happy medium between small file size and high quality. (The CorelDRAW 9 JPEG Export dialog box lets you preview the results of the compression before you execute the export.)

If you use the CorelDRAW 9 Publish To Internet Wizard, the default action is to export bitmaps greater than 256 colors in the JPEG format rather than the GIF format. Remember, you can mix and match both formats within one Web page, although, as in my example, if you build a big graphic in pieces and then assemble it with a table you will want to stick to the same file format within that connecting graphic.

bar is correct. If not, simply toggle back to CorelDRAW from the browser window (Alt+Tab), make any changes, and repeat the Publish to Internet process until everything is perfect.

Enabling the Publish to Internet feature's Single Image with Image Map option creates two files: the bitmap, and an HTML file that contains the image map information. You can open the file directly with your browser or use a text editor to drop the image map text section into your own HTML file. Text elements require some very complex coding to define the hotspots, but regardless, it's all automated (see Figure 20.18).

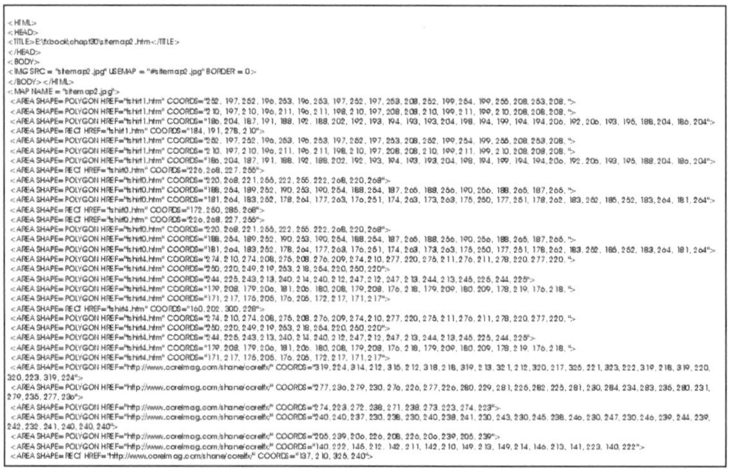

Figure 20.18

CorelDRAW creates both the bitmap and the HTML coding that defines the image-mapped hotspots. You can use the file as a standalone page on your Web site, or copy and paste the text into your own HTML code to take advantage of the complex image-mapping programming.

screen designs work the best for Web applications or multimedia events, where CorelDRAW's design flexibility turns into dynamic interaction. Multiple-graphic objects, such as buttons that change or animations that move, make on-screen experiences much more interesting. Just don't get too crazy and make everything sing and dance, or your interactive audience may just sit there, too dazzled to move.

Moving On

In this chapter, we looked at how CorelDRAW can help you create on-screen applications. CorelDRAW is a natural for creating images for Web sites and multimedia applications. With the handy, bountiful Corel clip-art and font libraries at your disposal, your Web sites should be bursting with creative imagery. The versatile nature of CorelDRAW artwork makes Web site management a snap and also facilitates easy Web promotion with the artwork migrating painlessly to print applications. Without question, CorelDRAW is an indispensable weapon in the sticky World Wide Web war.

In the next chapter, we continue to look at ways to use CorelDRAW for Web enhancement, by using the program to create interesting animations. The flexibility that CorelDRAW affords is perfect for designing the multiple images necessary for on-screen animations or movies. With the ability of Photo-Paint to assemble and manipulate movie files, you have powerful animation capabilities right on your desktop. Get ready to make your Web sites sing and dance because we're off to explore the possibilities of computer-aided animation.

21

ANIMATION
ACTION

Using CorelDRAW to create unique cells, and Photo-Paint to assemble them, you can create animated movies for on-screen applications such as Web pages.

Images that create the illusion of movement are becoming very commonplace. With everyone clamoring to get on the Web, many designers are being pulled into the electronic design forum by their clients. Multimedia and Web applications are both a blessing and a nightmare because the promising new opportunities also bring along a host of technical difficulties. Suddenly, designers are supposed to be programmers, 3D artists, audio-engineers, and, of course, animators.

It does make sense that electronic print designers would take on the tasks of electronic formats. If you have the artwork for other projects in the computer, you are prepared to handle Web or multimedia projects. The art is in place, so you just need to find some ways to make it more alive. Luckily, with a few tricks, even the most animation-challenged artists can bring artwork to life in CorelDRAW.

Animation goes beyond the traditional sense of creating happy, dancing cartoon characters. With contemporary media, such things as advertising banners, buttons, pointers, and even text can be image stacks that refresh in sequence to create live images.

In many examples in this book and on the companion CD-ROM, we have already touched on the theory of adding motion and other effects to bring artwork alive. In this chapter, we walk through the complete process of transforming artwork into a set of *cells*, which can be assembled into an interesting, animated entity for your Web site or other on-screen application.

First, we use animated text effects with multiple images, as well as Lens effects, to attract attention to the headlines on your Web site. After that, we create a word out of jiggling gelatin, altering the background colors to electrify and bring an advertisement to life. Finally, we create perpetual motion by using frames for the intermeshing-gears animation located in Chapter 20's on-CD Web examples. You may think cartoons are for kids, but I guarantee that animations will be a part of your very adult design world if you continue to function as an electronic artist.

Biking Madness

The problem with animation for many commercial applications is that it's way out of the budget of most projects. I already charge an exorbitant amount for a single illustration; imagine the cost of, say, 10 illustrations for a complex animation. Also consider the insane amount of work to organize and orchestrate such an undertaking. To make our hero in Figure 21.1 ride and leap would require a lengthy photography session to get the necessary reference material, weeks to ink up the illustrations, and then hours of colorizing and assembling the images in the computer. It's the kind of project that's just not going to happen with your average client.

However, with a few simple tricks, you can add a dynamic sense of motion without actually moving anything. Your goal is simply to create an interesting, animated graphic out of a static image, to make your Web pages dance and sing like everyone else's. Little tricks like this bridge the gap between expensive animation and low-budget images that bring a Web page to life.

This project started as one of my many ink illustrations. It was scanned as a 1-bit bitmap, imported into CorelDRAW, and then colorized in the now-all-too-familiar process. I won't bore you with redundant details, but the process is detailed in Chapter 5. The ink illustration turned out to be the limiting factor in this project. I had no intention of using this illustration for anything but its original purpose (a bold T-shirt design), so the image of the cyclist is connected to the black background. Not the kind of graphic that lends itself easily to animation, but I really wanted it on the Web site.

Left with few options, I came up with the flashing color scheme similar to the angels double-vision technique from Chapter 9, only I didn't have the luxury of foreground/background flexibility. Here's how to attract attention and add interest to an existing graphic by adding a flashing background color effect:

1. To create a different color scheme for the background in each animation, you can either recolor the background by hand or use another object on top of the background, which changes how it looks with a Lens or Transparency effect. Creating a new effects object to modify the look of your image offers more flexibility with less work, so that's what I recommend.

    Draw a yellow rectangle and place it in front of the background coloring elements, but behind the rest of the design. The easiest way to do this is to work in Wireframe view, send the rectangle to the back, choose Arrange|Order|In Front Of, and then click on the background coloring object. Now, it should be in place within the image stack.

2. Select the Interactive Transparency tool, change the Type setting on the Property Bar to Fountain, and then click the Radial button. The transparent yellow mixes with the existing background colors to

Figure 21.1

Use a Lens effect to alter the background of an illustration, adding a dynamic sense of motion to animate a static image.

create new colors, just like on an artist's palette. In this illustration, the yellows mix with the colors underneath to create oranges and yellowish browns.

3. Open the Export dialog box (Ctrl+E) to create a Web-friendly, 72-dpi, RGB bitmap in TIFF format. Don't be too concerned about actual size or color depth at this point; just export at 72 dpi and RGB (16 Million Colors), and we can tweak the images specifically for the Web later (see Figure 21.2). When we assemble these images in Photo-Paint as a movie, we also tweak the size and color palette to exactly what we need.

   Remember to number the cell, such as foes1.tif, so that each file is unique for each individual cell. This also keeps track of the creation order. Be sure to use the same settings for each export, because even a slight variation will be noticeable. (For example, I didn't enable anti-aliasing for one of the cells in my splash page graphic animation, resulting in an unacceptable fuzzy-flash effect.)

4. With the transparency rectangle selected, change the fill value from yellow to cyan and repeat the Export process to produce cell number two (foes2.tif). Then, fill the transparency rectangle with magenta and Export, producing cell number three (foes3.tif). Finally, fill it with black and Export once more to produce cell number four (foes4.tif). Save your CorelDRAW file and exit the application.

5. Start Photo-Paint and open the first of the cells that you just created (foes1.tif). Choose Movie|Create From Document to convert from a single image to a multiframe AVI (movie) format. Don't worry about cropping anything yet if your cell has image information that you don't want included (such as the white space on the right of the image, created during the Export process from CorelDRAW).

Figure 21.2
A yellow rectangle with a radial fountain transparency (right) mixes with the original background colors (left) to create a cell in the color flash animation (see the middle color section).

6. Time to add some frames. Choose Movie|Insert From File and then click on file number two that you exported out of CorelDRAW. In the Insert File dialog box that pops up, choose either Before or After (I usually work sequentially from beginning to end, so I choose After) and then click on OK. Now, you have a two-frame movie. Because the images are the exact same size, with the pieces in the same place, only the background changes.

7. Repeat the process until you have a movie file that contains all of your image cells (see Figure 21.3). Save the AVI to disk.

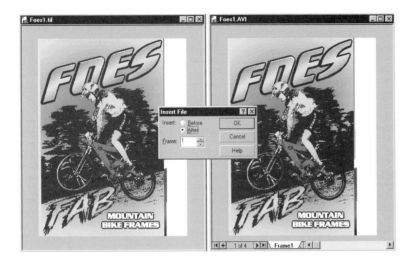

Figure 21.3
A single-frame bitmap can be made into a multicell animation in Photo-Paint.

REPETITIVE-MOTION INJURIES

Public service announcement time. Because I used to be in charge of office automation for Southern California's top grocery chain, I'm also an expert on proper workstation habits. Make sure you're in a natural work environment in which you're comfortable, and use proper posture. Get a good chair with solid lumbar support, and a computer desk that has an adjustable keyboard rest, so that your keyboard is in a position that's comfortable for you. The new ergonomic mice and keyboards are nice. Position your monitor so that you can look either directly at it or slightly down at it (as if you were talking to someone your height or slightly shorter or reading a book). Make sure that no surrounding lights are reflecting back at you on-screen. Finally, on a regular basis, get up and stretch your back and neck, touch your toes, and exercise your eye muscles.

Many problems, such as headaches and the inability to focus after working for long periods, are the result of not stretching your eye muscles. When you stare at your computer monitor all day you end up using a very narrow range of your eye muscles. Take an occasional break and focus on something really far away, like mountains, planes, or the person walking past your window (or cubicle). Then, focus on something really close, like your finger near your nose, your elbow, your next deadline, and so forth. This will stretch your eye muscles. Repeat this exercise a few times a day, especially before you get into the car and try to drive. Nothing is more frightening than trying to drive after a day at the computer, when everything past the windshield is just a big fuzzy blur! Stretch everything before and after the commute and you will be in much better shape. Oh, and don't forget to drink plenty of liquids, defrag your hard drive, and remember to write timely thank-you notes.

Note: *To test your movie, choose Movie|Control|Play Movie, which loops the current frames. To stop the movie so that you can continue editing, choose Movie|Control|Stop Movie.*

Figure 21.4

The Paper Size dialog box enables you to change the size of the image area and trim away unwanted material from all cells in a movie.

8. With the movie working and all the frames in place for smooth animation, you can start to fine-tune the image. For starters, you need to get rid of all that dead space to the right. Choose Image|Paper Size to open the Paper Size dialog box, in which you can trim down your frames.

First, disable the Maintain Aspect Ratio option; otherwise, any changes that you make to the width also affect the height. Change the Placement to Centered Left, so that your changes are to the right side only. Decrease the Width value, using the preview window as a guide. Keep downsizing until all the white space is trimmed away from the right, and then click OK. Even though you can view only one cell in the Paper Size preview window, the changes affect all cells (see Figure 21.4).

9. You can repeat the trimming process as many times as necessary to reduce the image down to just the desired material. With the movie working and appearing perfectly, it's time to manipulate it further for your application.

10. Select Image|Resample to open the Resample dialog box, in which you can control the movie's physical size and resolution. First, change the Resolution value to 72 dpi, which is what on-screen applications call for. Change the Image Size setting to the exact size that you need, and then click OK. All cells in the movie will resize in unison.

11. If you want to use the animation as an AVI for multimedia applications (or something similar), the RGB format is fine. For an image stack to use in a Web page, you need to convert the graphic to a 256-color palette. No sweat, Photo-Paint is here to serve you. Choose Image|Mode|Paletted (8-bit), which opens the Convert to Paletted Image dialog box. Change Palette to Adaptive, and Dithering to Ordered. Click on OK to convert your movie.

12. To use the movie on a Web site, save the animation in GIF format. Choose File|Save As, change the Files of Type to GIF-GIF Animation, and click on Save. In the GIF89 Animation Options dialog box, you can control things further.

13. On the File Settings page, modify such things as Repetition to your taste. (I tend to always choose the Loop Frames and Forever options for nonstop animations. However, sometimes, you'll want an animation to play only once or a few times.)

14. On the Frame Settings page, you can assign a Transparency color (in this case, the None option is used because we aren't using a transparent background in this example). This page has the Frame Delay option, which is how short or long you want a frame to display on screen. If you prefer, you can control each frame individually so that one frame can display longer than another. Change to one frame (or hold down the Shift key to select multiple frames) by clicking on it in the left preview window. Click on Apply All to make your changes stick, and then click on OK to save to disk.

Hanna-Barbera should be shaking in its shoes, because you just learned how easy creating animations is. To view the animation, you can either stick the GIF file in a Web page and view it with a browser, or just view the file itself using a browser (File|Open), or use the Windows Media Player to view the AVI or MOV format movies (double-click on the files and they should automatically play). This movie is called foes.avi and is located in the \Chapt21\ subdirectory of the companion CD-ROM. This subdirectory also includes foes2.avi, for which I took a cell from the first animation and created a new one. I used Photo-Paint's tools to copy the rider, change the background, and then paste him back into place. This created two frames of moving background, which assemble into another movie.

You can animate any stack of bitmaps into a movie or GIF file by using Photo-Paint; you can also take advantage of the program's built-in bitmap-editing features. Not only can you assemble a stack of images, you can also trim down the animation to size and change the color depth to customize the animation for its specific assignment. No better or easier way exists to make an AVI into a GIF for the Web. It's the kind of power that's easy to abuse, as can be seen in the silly dance.avi file, also found in the \Chapt21\ subdirectory of the companion CD. I created this movie from a brochure that I made many years ago and just recently happened to stumble across; the movie is a series of still images of me dancing around like an idiot.

If you want to work through the tutorial step by step, the original bicycle file, foes.cdr, as well as each of the exported, numbered bitmaps (foes1.tif, foes2.tif, and so forth), are in the \Chapt21\ subdirectory. It's an easy enough concept to grasp, so I won't bore you with the step-by-step details of assembling the frames in Photo-Paint for the following examples. After you know how to do it, you can create an animation out of nearly anything.

Note: *If you want to target your results to a specific audience using a known browser, you can specify this preference in the Palette option. Change Palette to Netscape Navigator or Microsoft Explorer to use a color palette that is optimized for either of those products.*

TRAP

A very common mistake is to build a Web site using a color table that is specific to your machine and not your audience's machines. A buddy of mine built an entire Web site on his PC to show his client, and it looked awesome. When he went to his client's office, his client was using a Mac, which has a different system palette. They loaded up the site and it looked awful. Not a good way to make an impression! In such a situation, find out the exact color table that the big decision maker is using, so that your presentation will go better. If you have no idea and thus want to make your Web site as universally viewable as possible, select the Adaptive color palette from the Convert to Paletted Image dialog box.

Jay-Eee-Ell-Ell-Oh, You Know?

This animation (jello.avi in the \Chapt21\ directory on the companion CD-ROM) came from a conversation with the marketing staff at The Coriolis Group. For those of you unfamiliar with the world of publishing, the marketing people start promoting the title long before it's even finished. They were picking my brain at the beginning of the project for features they could promote, and in the course of the conversation jiggling Jell-O somehow got thrown into the mix. They loved the idea, and I hung up the phone thinking, "Well, now I have to figure out how the heck to do that!"

The solution to creating cells for jiggling text came from the Brian the BrainBot example (from Chapter 16). If a blend could build and rebuild the robot arms automatically, then why not the jiggling gelatin? The attraction of using a blend like the robot arm example is that you can select and move one of the control curves and the image will rebuild automatically. The same kind of trick works here to rebuild the gelatin text after each move. Here's how to make text with a rigid base jiggle on top:

1. Start with text that's at an angle, and use the Perspective function to alter it. Fill it with dark red and duplicate it. Move the duplicate above the original and fill it with pink. Drag the Interactive Blend tool between both objects and create a 200-step blend, using the Property Bar to increase the number of steps (see Figure 21.5).

2. Select the top control object and duplicate it. From the Fountain Fill dialog box (F11), use the Cylinder 22 preset to give the top of the

Figure 21.5

Create a solid-gelatin text object by blending two objects together.

PROGRESS, PROGRESS, PROGRESS

As technology has so rapidly changed in recent years, so has the nature of a commercial art studio, such as ours. At first, our office was essentially a big warehouse filled with tables for paste-up, mechanical-drawing machines, a giant stat-camera, rollers and waxers, and a pukey little computer for bookkeeping. Over the years, those pasteup tools were all tossed, the pricey mechanical-illustration machines were declared worthless, and even the trusty camera was chucked in favor of a scanner. Soon, everything was electronic, and even such things as ink illustrations began to fade away in favor of high-tech, computer-generated images. Just when we got really good at making pretty pictures for print, our clients started asking about multimedia and Web projects. The challenges just never stop!

gelatin a nice set of reflections. (You don't want the whole blend to have this fill, just the top, which is why you duplicate the control object first.)

3. Now you have the live Jell-O (or Slime-O) word, ready to get a jigglin'. Select the top copy with the custom color blend and press the Tab key. This will toggle and select the control curve right below the top text element. Hold down the Shift key and select the very top piece again. You now have both top pieces (which you can't group together, because of the live blend, so you have to do this little Tab-Shift-select move each time).

4. With both the top coloring object and the control object beneath it selected, you can move them around anywhere, and the blend will rebuild to create a new jiggle. You can move, resize, twist, slant, or whatever you prefer for mild-to-wild gelatin activity (see Figure 21.6).

Figure 21.6

Moving the top coloring and blend control objects creates cells for a jiggling animation.

5. Set your gelatin text in any stage setting that you prefer. My set is a campy, '50s-looking ad, with the text centered in a white burst made with the Polygon tool. The text is arched along a circular path at the top, and the font is called Beatsville, which looked sufficiently corny for this application.

6. With the stage set, you can set out to generate each animation cell. I wanted to use this as a Web animation, which usually means trying to milk the most animation out of the fewest cells. Four is the minimal number of cells to get the gelatin word to jiggle back and forth, with cell two repeated twice to create an endless loop. The animation goes like this: left-center-right-center, so you need to generate three cells. This animation will repeat endlessly as left-center-right-center-left-center-right-center-left-center-right-center, and so on. Basically, you need to generate three cells: left, center, and right.

7. Working out the logic for this animation also revealed an interesting possibility for a flashing background effect. Notice that every other cell is in the center. Changing the background on that cell to an-

other color causes the graphic to flash, which is what I did to my animation.

Export each cell, moving the top pieces as shown to create a stack of images that assembles into a jiggling-gelatin text object. Change the background color for every other image for a flashing effect. The movie is called jello.avi and is found in the \Chapt21\ subdirectory on the companion CD-ROM. The parent file, jello2.cdr, is also located there. If you load the CorelDRAW file, you can see how selecting and moving the top two pieces of the Slime-O causes the blend to rebuild the rest of the object in the new orientation. Blends make for quick and easy animations, and the color-flash technique produces eye-catching icons on a Web site.

While you are perusing the CD-ROM, take a look at the splasha.avi animation, also located in the \Chapt21\ subdirectory. This animation also uses a live blend to aid in creating the cells in an animation. In this example, a white circle is blended to a black one, but for each cell of the animation I changed the colors of these control circles. I lightened the dark circle by 10 percent each time and darkened the white by 10 percent. So, in the span of 10 frames, the blend logic is reversed; what was once black becomes white, and vice versa. The live blend automatically generates the in-between shapes each time, making the process simple.

Text That Lives!

Many ways exist to animate text to grab attention on a Web site:

- Create multiple copies of a headline (as in the world.cdr file from Chapter 9, located in the CD-ROM's \Chapt09\ subdirectory).

- Create cells in which each duplicate is moved slightly (such as jitters.avi in the \Chapt21\ subdirectory on the CD-ROM).

- Create spinning logos with the Interactive Extrude tool (as outlined in Chapter 3 and demonstrated in fxspin.avi, in the \Chapt03\ subdirectory on the CD-ROM).

- Export two complex still images with slightly different backgrounds and use different anti-aliasing settings for each cell (check out weenie.avi in the \Chapt21\ subdirectory on the CD-ROM).

In short, if you can think of it, you can animate it. However, some effects are so cool that they defy their easy CorelDRAW origins. The text-through-a-keyhole effect (fisheye.avi in the \Chapt21\ subdirectory on the companion CD-ROM) is a perfect addition to a Web site; it's the result of simply moving a lens over some type. Another great payoff with just a little investment. Here is how to create the fisheye text:

1. Start by using the Artistic Text tool to type the phrase that you want to appear in the keyhole. I used a font called AmerType, which looks like it was typed on an old-fashioned typewriter. Color this text white (or any color you prefer).

2. Rest your text on a black (or any color you prefer) background object. Draw another box on top of the text, and then open the Lens docker (Alt+F3). Give this object the Fish Eye lens, at a rate of 150%. This distorts the text beneath it (see Figure 21.7).

Figure 21.7

A text object (in Wireframe view, top) is distorted by a rectangle with the Fish Eye lens (bottom).

3. Start with the Fish Eye lens over the left side of the text and, with the lens object selected, open the Export dialog box (Ctrl+E). If you use the Selected Only option, only the rectangle will export, but because it is also a lens the rectangle will export the distorted text below. This makes lens effects ideal for creating animation cells; each cell is the exact same size as the lens object, so you don't have to trim down the image with other tricks (such as using the PowerClip feature) before each export.

4. Repeat the Export process many times, each time moving the lens object a little to the right before the export. The bigger the move, the fewer the cells in the animation. You can get away with just a few connecting images for a Web graphic, but if you use too few images, the text will be hard to read. I created 23 cells for a smoother, easier-to-read animation.

Lens effects lend themselves to all kinds of animations. If you place a Heat Map lens over an object, for example, and then change the Palette rotation value for a stack of animation cells, you can get a very freaky effect. Or, use a Transparency lens over an object, varying the opacity in each cell to fade to or from black. Or keep things simple, and just change the fill value of the object. Check out the dogban1.avi in the \Chapt21\ subdirectory on the companion CD-ROM, for which I just changed the

DON'T GO GRAY

Colors: 256=256. Interestingly, a file created with a 256-color palette often is the same file size as one created with 256 shades of gray. You may not save any file size by creating black-and-white images for animated Web GIFs. Because you can't save a GIF in the 1-bit black-and-white color depth to take advantage of a smaller file size, you have to use the 256 shades of gray option, which could create a file that's the same size as one that uses 256 colors. So, go for the color option and see whether it's much bigger than black and white.

Fountain Fill in the Web banner a little for each animation cell. The variety of animations that you can generate in CorelDRAW is limited only by your energy and imagination.

Perpetual Gears

As demonstrated in the last chapter, you can use animated gears as navigation buttons. Although these look complicated, they are a great example of something that looks hard to create but isn't. They also serve as a perfect example of *closure* (see the sidebar, "Closure"). The animation is only two frames, but it repeats endlessly to look like turning gears. Here is how to get the machine moving:

1. Start with a set of gears, as outlined in Chapter 16. Arrange them inside of a boundary box, which guarantees that both bitmap cells have the same physical dimensions.

2. Position the gears as you desire and combine them into one group. Duplicate this gear shape and boundary box and move it off to the side. Select and duplicate the gear shape in the first group one more time.

3. Break apart this duplicate into the individual gears again so that you can manipulate each one individually. Select each free gear and rotate until the gear teeth are exactly in between those below it. Repeat this for all the gears.

CLOSURE

Closure is more than ending an experience in your life; it's also your eyes' natural tendency to fill in the blanks to make things whole even when they aren't. A movie or cartoon is actually a series of static images, but you see it as a solid stream of motion. Another example is water flowing out of a faucet or hose. It looks to be a solid stream, but is really round bursts of water, one after another. (If you blink your eyes really fast, sometimes you can catch the droplets in the stream. If not, high-speed cameras will convince you.)

Your "stupid" eyes that don't see what's really there are what make things like movies, television, laser light shows, and even your computer monitor possible. Your monitor is actually a single row of pixels refreshing from top to bottom. This row refreshes so fast that you think it's a solid image.

To prove to yourself that this is happening, stand in front of your monitor, stick your tongue out, and make an obscene raspberry noise. This vibrates your head and eyes and breaks up the closure phenomenon enough to see the scan lines in the screen. Vary the pitch and frequency of your tongue vibration and you can see the screen begin to flash, wiggle, and wave (works best on monitors with a slow refresh rate). For more proof (or to avoid spitting on your expensive computer equipment), take a picture of your television screen with a high shutter speed, and you'll see the scan lines.

4. With the top gears in the rotated orientation, select them all and combine them back into one curve. Delete the reference curve for this set, and you should have two gear groups (see Figure 21.8).

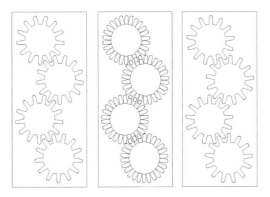

Figure 21.8

An original set of gears is duplicated and each object is rotated to create the in-between gear orientation.

5. Shift-select both of the gear curves and fill them with an appropriate color. I used the Gold Plated fountain fill preset to give the objects a metallic look.

6. Use the Interactive Extrude tool to drag on your objects and create an active extrude group. Use the Property Bar to modify the extrude group, to create the beveled, dimensional look, just like we did with the gear shapes in Chapter 16. Be sure that the vanishing point for the extrude group is set to VP Locked to Object and not To Page. This feature makes the gears look amazing.

7. Select the nonextruded gears, choose Effects|Copy Effect|Extrude, and then click on the other completed gear extrude group. Sometimes the vanishing point goes awry during this process, making the duplicate look wrong. If this occurs, use the Copy VP From option from the Vanishing Point Properties pull-down on the Property Bar to copy the identical vanishing point values to both extrude groups (see Figure 21.9).

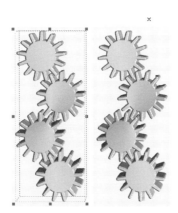

Figure 21.9

Add depth and shading with the Interactive Extrude tool on a gear curve; then, copy the values to the second gear group.

Figure 21.10
Animation techniques can add a sense of motion to a static image, such as this flyer, where animation cells are placed in a movie-like film-strip border element.

You now have the two frames needed to create the perpetual motion gear animation. You can watch the gears twirl in the Web example in Chapter 20. Even though only two frames are used, the gears appear to be counter-rotating, like a fancy piece of machinery.

Beyond f/x

With increasingly more traditional designers being pulled into new media markets, animation is becoming a more common task. You can use animations to add interest and gain attention in many applications, the most obvious being Web pages. Things like information kiosks to automatic teller machines use the kind of animation that you can produce right this minute with the hardware and software sitting in front of you! Even print media can benefit from animation; for example, you can use a set of cells as a border element to suggest motion (see Figure 21.10). Animated buttons and those annoying ad banners that show up everywhere on the Web are just a few of the things that you can create with multiframe images in CorelDRAW.

Moving On

In this chapter, we looked at many examples of how to assemble images created in CorelDRAW into animations. You can use these animations in many applications, including Web pages and multimedia programs. Virtually any stack of images can be made into a playable movie by using the animation power of Photo-Paint. It's a simple process, with only your time and patience limiting the complexities of your animations.

In the next and final chapter, we look at another high-tech trend in the world of design: 3D modeling. Now that CorelDRAW ships with CorelDream as a companion product, your designs can benefit from the magic of virtual reality. Relax, no special goggles are needed to enter this cyberspace, just your mouse, keyboard, and a little creativity!

BEYOND TWO DIMENSIONS

22

This chapter explores using CorelDRAW with 3D modeling applications such as CorelDream and RayDream designer.

In desktop publishing, there are many ways to achieve a look that is much more than just flat images lying on the page. Throughout this book, we have added depth with highlights and shadows, created the illusion of dimension with the Perspective and Extrude tools, and even spun objects in virtual space.

To communicate with others involved in a project (as in the box art example in this chapter), you'll want to take flat artwork and arrange it in a 3D-like orientation. By using the Skew features within CorelDRAW you can produce a convincing look from your existing working illustrations.

Sometimes, though, the 3D capabilities of CorelDRAW simply aren't enough. Getting the kind of subtle depth, shadow, and reflection in CorelDRAW that some projects demand just has too many challenges (imagine trying to render an image of a poster stuck to a corrugated aluminum wall). These kinds of tasks are achieved with relatively little effort in the new, virtual-3D applications such as CorelDream, TrueSpace, 3DStudio, and RayDream Designer. Although CorelDream is not bundled with CorelDRAW 9 (it was included in the CorelDRAW 8 Graphics Suite), the tutorials in this section work pretty much the same in RayDream designer (CorelDream is really just a private-label version of RayDream). If you don't have RayDream, the techniques apply to any 3D-modeling package.

In this chapter, we start with 2D art files and examine ways to add depth to your designs, both in CorelDRAW and in CorelDream. In the first example, we create pieces in CorelDRAW to build bitmap stickers to stick on a box in the true 3D environment of CorelDream. Then, we examine other ways to mix and match the powers of CorelDRAW and CorelDream to create objects that would be impossible or very difficult to create in either of the programs alone. We use CorelDRAW to create the specialized shapes that, when manipulated in CorelDream, turn into true 3D objects. We then walk through the process of creating basic CorelDRAW shapes that we transform into pulleys, gears, bottles, and vases in CorelDream. All of these examples are fairly simple; my goal here isn't to impress you with art but to reveal some techniques that I use to create cool, 3D objects with relatively little effort. We are in for a lot of 3D fun, and you don't even have to wear those goofy glasses!

The Camel Box

When you use CorelDRAW to create 3D mock-ups, they occasionally fall together easily with acceptable results. However, the more you use

CorelDRAW for such projects, the more attractive the power and versatility of virtual 3D packages will become. The virtual workspace of CorelDream and other 3D applications enables you to build all kinds of amazing dimensional objects, such as the box in Figure 22.1.

CorelDream enables you to construct any object, no matter what the shape or the level of complexity. This power is enhanced even more when you add the simplicity and familiarity of working within CorelDRAW to create pieces for assembly in the virtual world of CorelDream. In this example, the top, sides, and bottom of the box started as CorelDRAW objects, as did the interesting inlaid-marble pattern.

Even the amazing power of CorelDream is essentially limited to sculpting objects. To go that extra mile and custom-tailor a unique coloring scheme or pattern, you need to use our old pal, CorelDRAW. Because CorelDRAW has all the power to create flat artwork, marrying the two technologies just makes sense.

In this example, we create artwork in CorelDRAW that will be exported as a bitmap and pasted, like a virtual sticker, onto a CorelDream object. CorelDream objects can be painted with an almost endless variety of textures and colors, including bitmaps from external sources. Take advantage of that power to design specialized artwork in CorelDRAW that you can use in CorelDream for patterns, signs—you name it. Here is how to prepare 2D artwork in CorelDRAW for coloring in CorelDream:

Figure 22.1
Use CorelDRAW to create both the dimensional box sides and the inlaid-marble bitmap image for an ornate jewelry box, and then assemble it within CorelDream.

1. Prepare artwork in CorelDRAW to use as a sticker in CorelDream. I created shapes and filled them with the Alabaster texture fill, found in the Samples Library. It has a marbled look, and by changing the color scheme you can get different colors for different shapes. I used symbols for the camel and palm trees and used other basic shapes to create an ornate design that looks like inlaid marble. To save time, you can copy and paste the pieces for use on the other two sides. Figure 22.2 shows the Wireframe view of the shapes used to create the flat graphics. Check out the color section in the center of the book to see them filled in.

2. Drag-select the objects in each section and group them. Then, select the group and use the Export dialog box (Ctrl+E) to create a bitmap for use in CorelDream. Be sure to export each image in the Windows bitmap (BMP) format, which is suitable for CorelDream, and enable the Selected Only option to create a unique graphic for each side. Export the bitmap at 16 million (RGB) colors and at a resolution that is suitable for your application. Repeat the process to produce a separate bitmap for each side, and then exit CorelDRAW.

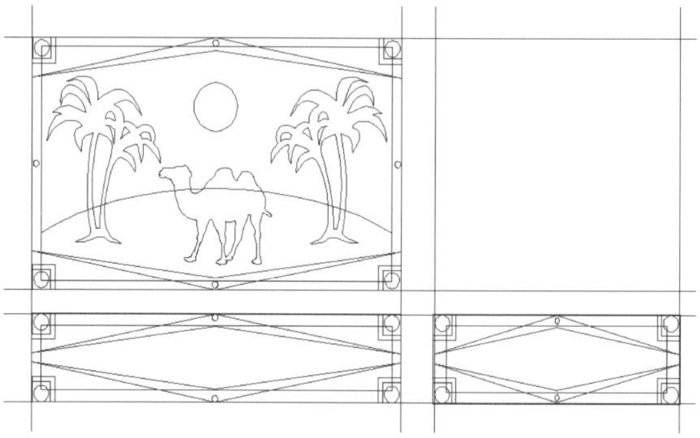

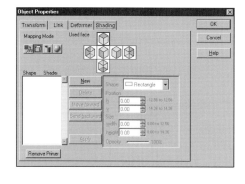

Figure 22.2
Build graphics in CorelDRAW by using simple shapes and symbols for an inlaid-marble look.

3. Start CorelDream and construct the basic box by using the cube primitive. This technique enables you to apply a decal on one side of an object, so you should build the box out of thin rectangles, to look like boards.

4. From the Shaders browser, choose Shader|New, title the shader Top, and click on OK. This creates a new default shader sphere (in red). Double-click on it to open the Shader Editor. Change the view to Flat Preview and choose Type|Texture Map. Locate and click on the bitmap that you created for the top of the box, and then click on Open. Now you have the sticker inside of CorelDream (see Figure 22.3).

Figure 22.3
Use the Shader Editor to load a bitmap for use in CorelDream.

5. The new image should appear in the Shaders browser. Under the Objects tab in the hierarchy window, locate the object that you want to stick this image to. Right-click on the object name and choose Properties. Under the Object Properties dialog box, click on the Shading tab to reveal its options. Under Mapping Mode, click on the Box Mapping button, and then click on the side of the box you want the sticker to appear on. Click on OK when finished (see Figure 22.4).

Figure 22.4
Use the Object Properties dialog box to choose where the sticker will appear on the cube.

6. Now, when you drag the sticker image from the Shaders browser onto your cube, it will color the selected side. If nothing seems to happen, change the options under the View menu to Default

Quality|Better Preview and Object Quality|Better Preview. Repeat this process to add the CorelDRAW image to each side of a CorelDream object (see Figure 22.5).

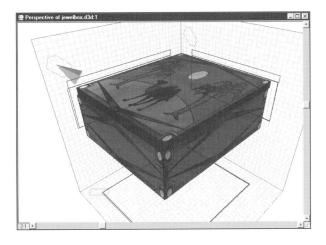

Figure 22.5
Any graphic can be stuck to a CorelDream object.

The box reveals its treasures in this book's middle color section and in the camelbox.cdr file in the \Chapt22\ subdirectory on the companion CD-ROM. The CorelDream file, jewelbox.d3d, is a demo file with the stickers attached to cubes. If you load it you can see how each of the object properties has been adjusted to make the sticker appear on the correct side.

2D To 3D

As I said before, I'm far from a 3D modeling expert. It has been a slow, arduous task for me to evolve into the world of virtual space. I just don't have a brain that works well with objects in three dimensions, like some sort of digital depth perception. (Is it a cone or a tunnel? A tunnel or a cone? I can't tell! AAGH!)

The wagon in Figure 22.6 is my coffee table. It has a long and interesting history, but I'll leave that story for those curious enough to browse my

Figure 22.6
Objects created in CorelDRAW get depth and dimension in CorelDream to populate a littered digital landscape.

personal Web site (www.slimydog.com/shane). The significance here is that I used a measuring tape to figure out the actual dimensions, and then created those pieces in CorelDRAW, where dimensioning is easy. I created a flat rectangle for the base, more rectangles for the sides, and circles at the right size for the tires. Then, I exported the pieces as an AutoCAD (DXF) file and imported them into a 3D application. (Caligari TrueSpace, actually. This was before CorelDream existed.) With all the pieces at the correct size in proportion to one another, extruding the rectangles into boards and building the wagon was easy. When you use each application for its strong points, the process is smoother.

In many instances, CorelDRAW is just easier to work with than these 3D virtual work spaces, especially when creating flat objects. Save yourself a lot of hassle and start by creating basic objects in CorelDRAW; use CorelDream (or your program of choice) to give them depth and substance. I could write volumes on the topic of using CorelDRAW with CorelDream, but here I'm just going to show you a couple of my favorite, and perhaps not so obvious, tricks. I recommend that you get a copy of *Ray Dream 5 f/x*, by Shamms Mortier (Ventana 1997), if you are serious about 3D modeling. I'm just a CorelDream-dabbler.

Gears

As we have seen in other chapters, gears can very easily be created in all sizes and shapes within CorelDRAW (see Chapter 16). Instead of using the Interactive Extrude tool in CorelDRAW, you can give curves depth in CorelDream. It's a very simple process, with most of the work happening in CorelDRAW. Here's how to create 3D gears:

1. Create a gear shape, as you have many times before, based on the lessons in Chapter 16. This time, add an interesting spoke pattern in the center.

2. Select the gear shape and give it no fill and just a black hairline outline (see Figure 22.7). Select and Export (Ctrl+E) the shape as an Adobe Illustrator (AI) file. This is a vector format that CorelDream can use. Save the CDR file of the gears and exit CorelDRAW.

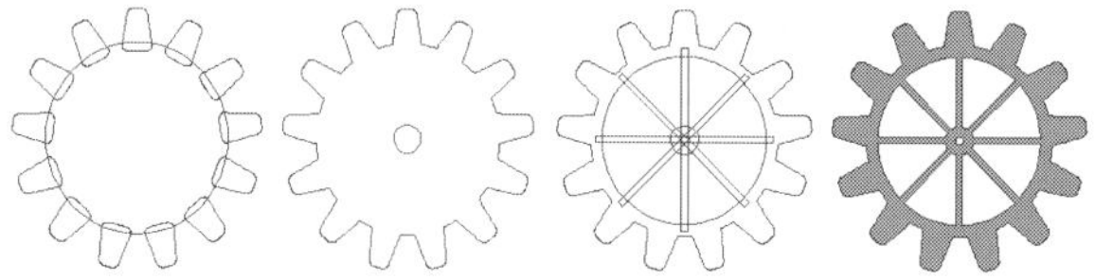

Figure 22.7
Use the CorelDRAW tools to create a gear shape with cut-out spokes.

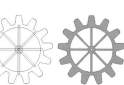

3. Start CorelDream and create an empty scene. Grab the Free Form Modeler icon and drag it into the Perspective window. Name the object Gear and click on OK. Choose File|Import to import the Adobe Illustrator gear file that you just created in CorelDRAW. Dream may warn you that the image is complex, but just click on Proceed to continue. This imports the wireframe and also extrudes it, but at very strange proportions (see Figure 22.8).

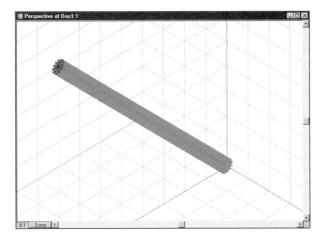

Figure 22.8
Importing the AI outline as a free-form object automatically extrudes it into a 3D object.

4. To bring the extrusion back into the desired proportions, use the selection tool to click on the pink line (sweep path) on the right wall. Grab the right point of the sweep path and drag it left, while holding down the Shift key, until the gear has the dimensions you desire (see Figure 22.9). Now, you can manipulate the object within CorelDream just like any other object, to create your own mechanical illustrations.

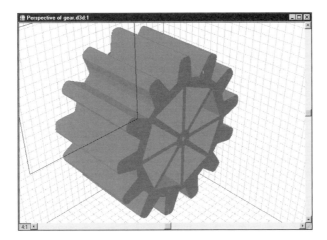

Figure 22.9
Reducing the sweep path brings the dimensions of the gear back to normal.

That's it. This file is called gear.d3d and is found in the \Chapt22\ subdirectory on the companion CD-ROM (all of these examples are in this subdirectory in CorelDream format if you want to steal them for your own dimensional designs). You can use this sweep function to add depth to any wireframe generated in CorelDRAW; for example, you can launch your company logo into the world of 3D. The sky is the limit here, and adding depth with the sweep feature is probably the most common use of the DRAW/Dream duo.

Pulleys

An obvious way to get your objects into the 3D world is to add depth with sweeping (the CorelDream equivalent to Extruding in CorelDRAW), as in the last example. The next several examples use a technique that I love to use to produce shapes and figures that look far from common. The basic premise is to design a shape in CorelDRAW that is a cross-section of the shape that you want, and then cut it in half. With this one-half cross-section prepared in CorelDRAW, you are ready to bring it to life in CorelDream, where you spin it into existence.

The trick here is to use the Torus preset in CorelDream to create the 3D object from the cross-section. Again, the work in CorelDRAW for this shape is critical. The first example is pretty easy and will unlock the mystery of this technique for the more difficult examples to follow. Here is how to spin your objects into the third dimension:

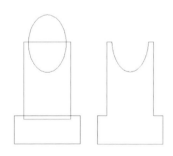

Figure 22.10

Weld together two rectangles and add a circular notch to create the shape for a pulley object.

1. Draw an oval and two rectangles. Weld together the two rectangles and use the Trim function to cut out the round end of one rectangle, as shown in Figure 22.10. This creates half of a cross-section of a pulley. Select the shape and, as before, Export (Ctrl+E) it as an Adobe Illustrator file.

2. Create an empty scene in CorelDream and, once again, drag the Free Form icon into the Perspective view. Name this object Pulley and click on OK. Choose File|Import to import the pulley shape from CorelDRAW. This automatically sweeps it as before, which isn't what you want; but don't worry about that at this point.

3. Choose Geometry|Extrusion Preset|Torus, which spins the wireframe object into a 3D object. In the Torus dialog box, change the Distance to Axis value to 1 inch (this is a guessing game at this point, but for the pulley example, it isn't critical). Click on OK and watch the fun! The Torus preset spins the outline around 360 degrees on the axis that you set in the Torus dialog box, creating a 3D object (see Figure 22.11).

4. After you spin the object into a CorelDream object, you can manipulate it in any way imaginable by using any of the program's fill or texture effects.

This is another simple shape made into something pretty cool in CorelDream. This file, pulley.d3d, is also in the \Chapt22\ subdirectory on the companion CD-ROM.

Figure 22.11
The Torus command spins an outline 360 degrees on an axis to create a solid object.

Bottle

In this example, we use the same Torus technique used to create the pulley, but we use it on a much more complex shape created in CorelDRAW. Here's how to make a glass bottle:

1. Starting in CorelDRAW, use rectangles and ovals to map out a simple bottle shape. Use the Shape tool to round out the corners of the rectangles. Combine all the shapes into one object by using the Weld function.

2. Round out any harsh corners and perform some fine-tuning with the Shape tool. Draw a vertical line and center it to the bottle shape. Using the centered line as a reference, draw a rectangle that covers half of the shape, and then use the Trim command to cut away half of the bottle (see Figure 22.12).

Figure 22.12
Use simple shapes to build a bottle outline, and then draw a rectangle to cut the bottle in half with the Trim function.

3. Just as you did with the pulley shape, you can spin this bottle outline into a solid bottle shape in CorelDream. This would work in most cases, but with a few more steps, you can create the outline that will become a true 3D bottle—including a solid bottom, hollow interior, and open end. Select the bottle outline and use the Interactive Contour tool to create another shape inside the curve, at the width that you want your glass to be. Separate and freeze the contour shape so that you can combine it with the original bottle outline.

4. Draw another shape with the Freehand tool, as shown in Figure 22.13, to use as a template, so that you can cut away the right side of the

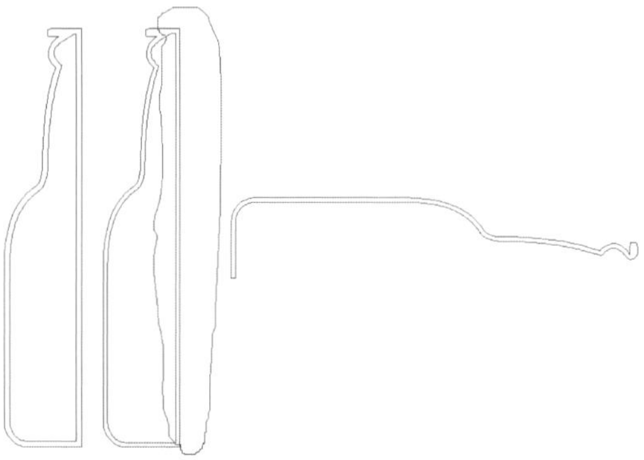

Figure 22.13

Use the Interactive Contour tool to create a second, inside shape, which will become the glass outline when the excess is trimmed away.

Figure 22.14

The outline is made into a perfect 3D bottle by using the Torus feature.

bottle curve with the Trim function. This leaves you with your glass shape. Rotate the outline –90 degrees and Export (Ctrl+E) it as an AI file. Exit CorelDRAW.

5. Start CorelDream. Follow the same steps that you used with the pulley, but enter a smaller value, such as .55 inch, in the Torus dialog box. This should spin into a nice bottle shape that looks just like a real bottle, complete with open neck and hollow interior. Use a semi-opaque glass fill for some cool effects in CorelDream (see Figure 22.14).

This image can be swiped out of the bottle.d3d file in the \Chapt22\ subdirectory on the companion CD-ROM.

Vases

This is a variant of the bottle technique in which the shape is designed to exaggerate the hollow interior of the object; in this case, a flower vase. Here's how to make a vase:

1. Again, the magic happens in CorelDRAW with simple shapes. This time, I wanted a definitive lip at the edge of the vase, so I used half-circle shapes as primitives to get the angle. This isn't a difficult process; it's exactly the same technique used with the bottle, but we end up with a shape that will spin into a vase. Don't worry about bisecting the artwork exactly. Concentrate on the left side only, knowing the rest will be trimmed away (see Figure 22.15).

Figure 22.15

Strange shapes merge together to create a cross-section of the vase.

2. With the basic vase outline in place, again use the Interactive Contour tool to create the inside line (see Figure 22.16). It can be as thick or thin as you like (but, if it's too thick, your vase will look like it's made of concrete). Trim away the excess, rotate –90 degrees, and again Export as an AI file. Close CorelDRAW and ready the virtual bouquet....

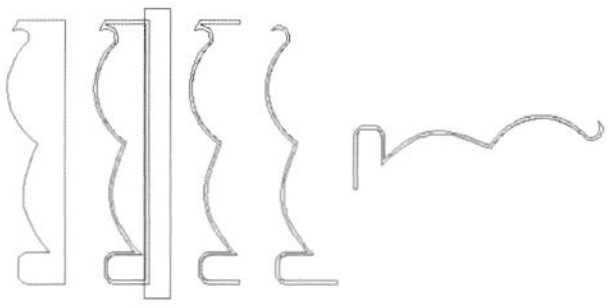

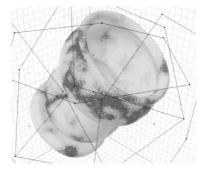

Figure 22.16
Take the vase outline and create the hollow insides with the Contour and trimming steps.

3. In CorelDream again, you can spin the object into a lovely addition to any virtual living room. (If only decorating my real living room was this easy.) The value that you use in the Torus dialog box is, again, just a good guess (try 1 inch). Use a marble or other shader to make the vase look good in CorelDream (see Figure 22.17).

Figure 22.17
The strange shape from CorelDRAW results in a nice vase in CorelDream.

This file is called vase.d3d in the \Chapt22\ subdirectory on the companion CD-ROM. You can export all of these pieces in the 3D Metafile (3DMF) format from CorelDream for manipulation back in CorelDRAW (see Chapter 13). Take advantage of all the applications in your CorelDRAW design suite to produce the results that you want.

Caught In The Web

I love the image of a robotic spider on a wiry web, as in Figure 22.18. It captures the high-tech feel of the Inter*net* and enforces my personal surfing

Figure 22.18
Using artwork from CorelDRAW, a 3D image created in CorelDream comes to life.

experiences—I think the Web is so very much like a sticky spider's web because you innocently wander in and get stuck there forever.

To start the project that I wanted to build in CorelDream, I began by brain-storming/doodling in CorelDRAW. I like to start in CorelDRAW whenever I can because I find that building complex shapes is difficult in the 3D modeling environment but is an easy task in the comfortable, flat world of CorelDRAW. I wanted to build a complex-looking mechanical leg system for my virtual spider to walk around on, by converting flat pieces in CorelDRAW into 3D bits in CorelDream. Here's how to build the spider bits in CorelDRAW:

1. Using the Freehand drawing tool in Bezier mode, quickly click out two *L* leg shapes, for the top and bottom of a spider leg. Arrange these shapes in such a way that you can visualize how they might actually work, with pivot points in the right places.

2. Add real world details to your illustration, such as pneumatic actuators to create something of a blueprint of a working model. Of course, this project isn't going into actual production at a toy factory or anything, so just use your imagination (see Figure 22.19).

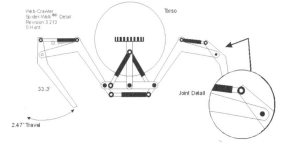

Figure 22.19
Simple shapes destined for CorelDream can also create a blueprint illustration in CorelDRAW.

3. After you complete a set of leg parts, simply duplicate, flip, rotate, and skew the duplicates to create the other sets. This relatively simple task makes creating the blueprint illustration a snap, and with the addition of official-looking arrows and captions, you can make the results look downright convincing (see Figure 22.20).

My problem with the blueprint illustration was that, because I didn't start out with that in mind, my results were a very complex set of pieces in black and white, and did not have that blueprint feel that I was after. To really sell the blueprint, I first imported a border from an actual AutoCAD drawing, which has the official-looking legend box in the bottom corner as well as numbered border elements to aid in navigation (joint detail in G-2, and so forth). These pieces would have been really

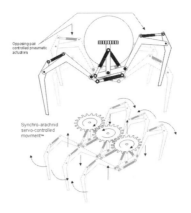

Figure 22.20
Even a totally fictitious project takes on a realistic look with captions and arrows.

easy to generate again in CorelDRAW, but because I already had the file, I just imported it. But, that still didn't give me the blueprint look that I was after, so I returned to the drafting table. Here's how to convert the black-and-white images into a blueprint graphic:

1. Draw a box over everything, open the Lens dialog box (Alt+F3), and apply the Invert Lens effect. This reverses the theme to white lines on black, but still doesn't finish the job (see Figure 22.21).

Figure 22.21
The Invert Lens effect reverses the traditional artwork look to white text on a black page.

2. Export (Ctrl+E) the image as an RGB bitmap. Launch Photo-Paint and choose File|Open to open the file that you exported from CorelDRAW. Choose Image|Adjust|Level Equalization to open the Level Equalization dialog box. Change the Channel option to Blue Channel and then drag the bottom-left slider of the four sliders (just above the words Output Range Compression). Dragging the bottom-left slider to the right changes your black-and-white image into a

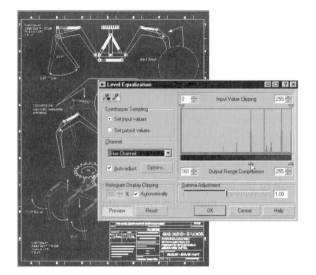

Figure 22.22

Use the Level Equalization dialog box in Photo-Paint to change a black-and-white image to blue and white.

blue-and-white graphic, perfect for the blueprint illusion. Click on OK to exit the dialog box (see Figure 22.22).

3. After you recolor the blueprint graphic, use the File|Save As command to save a copy to disk. To use the image in CorelDream, save it as a BMP file.

Before diving into CorelDream totally, I needed my leg pieces. To keep things simple I combined the legs into two curves; the top and bottom pair. Then I selected one each of the leg elements (top and bottom), gave each no fill and just a black-hairline outline, and exported each as a separate EPS file (or you can use the Adobe Illustrator [AI] format). EPS and AI are vector formats that CorelDream can use to create the leg shapes later on.

Exit CorelDRAW and Photo-Paint to give CorelDream all the RAM that it needs. Then, follow these steps:

1. To create the blueprint in CorelDream, construct the basic box by using the cube primitive. Shrink it vertically into a sheet of paper. This technique will allow for the application of a decal on one side of a box object, but if it's flattened it will appear to be a piece of paper.

2. From the Shaders browser, choose Shader|New, title the shader Blueprint, and click on OK. This creates a new default shader sphere (in red). Double-click on it to open the Shader Editor. Change the View to Flat Preview and choose Type|Texture Map. Locate and click on the bitmap that you created for the top of the box and then click on Open. Now you have the sticker inside of CorelDream (see Figure 22.23). The new image should appear in the Shaders browser.

Figure 22.23
The blueprint bitmap from
CorelDRAW becomes a Shader in
CorelDream.

3. Under the Objects tab in the hierarchy window, locate the object that
   you want to stick this image to. Right-click on the object name and
   choose Properties. In the Object Properties dialog box, click on the
   Shading tab to reveal its options. Under Mapping Mode, click on the
   Box Mapping button; then click on the side of the box you want the
   sticker to appear on. Click on OK when finished.

4. Now, when you drag the sticker image from the Shaders browser
   onto your cube, it will color the selected side. If nothing seems to
   happen, change the options under the View menu to Default
   Quality|Better Preview and Object Quality|Better Preview. You can
   use this technique to stick any image to objects in CorelDream.

5. To create the leg parts in CorelDream, grab the Free Form Modeler
   icon and drag it into the Perspective window. Name the object
   Legtop and click on OK. Choose File|Import to import the vector leg
   piece file that you just created in CorelDRAW. CorelDream may
   warn you that the image is complex, but just click on Proceed to
   continue. This imports the wireframe and extrudes it, but at very
   strange proportions (see Figure 22.24).

6. To bring the extrusion back into the desired proportions, use the selection tool to click on the pink line (sweep path) on the right wall. Grab
   the right point of the sweep path and drag it left, while holding down
   the Shift key, until the legs have the dimensions that you desire.

7. Repeat this process with the other leg curve.

8. Using the blueprint as a guide, add other elements within
   CorelDream to finish off a single leg set (see Figure 22.25). These
   additional elements are all simple geometric shapes (boxes and
   cylinders) that are easy to create within CorelDream. The pneumatic
   struts are just a silver cylinder inside of a larger black duplicate.
   Adding little details like these shapes is easy, enabling you to create
   a convincing, real-looking mechanical machine in virtual space.

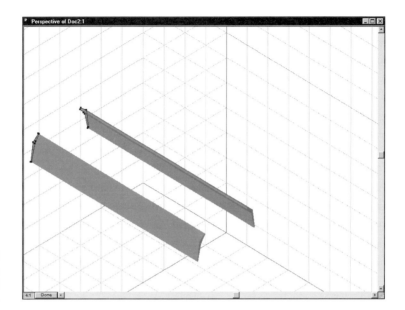

Figure 22.24

The leg shapes created in CorelDRAW gain depth and substance in CorelDream.

Figure 22.25

The CorelDRAW leg pieces, with additional details created within CorelDream, come together to create a realistic robotic-leg assembly.

After I had a complete leg, I selected all the objects and grouped them (Ctrl+G). Then it was a snap to duplicate the group and arrange the duplicates to create the other leg sets (see Figure 22.26).

The front set was reduced in size and rotated. Simple circle shapes became the body segments and eyes of the spider (see Figure 22.27).

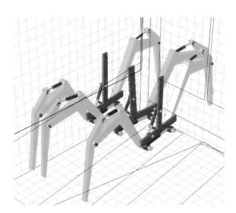

Figure 22.26

Taking advantage of the computerized design medium, the single leg set is duplicated to create the other sets.

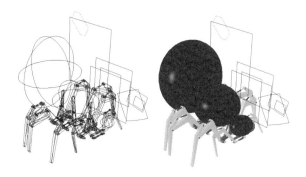

Figure 22.27
Simple geometric shapes drawn in CorelDream create the bulk of the spider robot.

With the basic elements in place, it is now just a matter of arranging everything in the CorelDream 3D set to get the right camera angle and lighting. For my first attempts, I had spidey on a table, but then I decided to stick him in a web. To create the web, I started again in CorelDRAW and created a bitmap to stick on the table-top, in the same way that I created the blueprint (see Figure 22.28).

Figure 22.28
A full-color image, created in CorelDRAW, creates the background in the 3D scene.

The difference is that I also created a black-and-white version of the web graphic to use as a *bump map* in CorelDream, to give the artwork some 3D attributes in CorelDream (see Figure 22.29). A bump map is a graphic

Figure 22.29
A black-and-white version, in the same layout and size as the color background image, is used as a bump map in CorelDream to add a 3D texture.

that gives a flat surface a 3D texture, according to its coloring scheme. The 3D application reads the colors of the bump-map bitmap, and creates a tall or short bump according to the corresponding pixels in the bump-map bitmap. Black is neutral, white calls for the tallest bump, and grayscale everything in between. To create a bump map, use the following steps:

1. Create a new shader element, just as you did for the blueprint, by importing the colorized graphic as the texture map.

2. In the Shader Editor dialog box, use the arrow button to reveal the Bump tab. Again, under Type|Texture Map, select Pre-created Image, only this time use the grayscale image of the web for the bump map. In CorelDream, black is flat and white is the tallest setting for a bump map. So, the black areas won't change the colored web background, but the gray-to-white web area in the bump map gives some subtle depth to the colorized web image on top (see Figure 22.30).

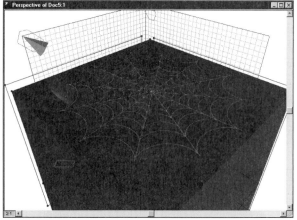
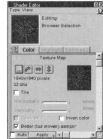

Figure 22.30

Using the matching bump map under the color image in CorelDream creates a web that rises off of the flat object to which the corresponding Shader is applied.

WORKING BACKWARD, AGAIN

I've seen several magnificent pieces of artwork created in CorelDRAW and wondered, "Hmm, how did they work out all the geometry for that virtual landscape?" A totally fictitious landscape has no reference material, yet all the laws of illustration apply.

The answer lies in another working-backward technique. A scene is blocked out in CorelDream and then rendered as a bitmap. This bitmap can then be altered even further, say with a Fish Eye lens, to create a very surreal landscape. The image is then imported into CorelDRAW where it serves as a reference image to redraw the shapes. It seems like a long way around, but it isn't as crazy as it sounds. Things like mirrored reflections, chrome effects, and so on can all be easily worked out in CorelDream; then the image can be duplicated in CorelDRAW to regain all of the resolution flexibility and other benefits of that program. A CorelDRAW file is crisp at any size, can be enlarged or reduced without changing the file size, and is usually markedly smaller in file size than a bitmap image or even a native CorelDream file. Just log this as miscellaneous information, and someday you may use it to solve a unique illustration problem.

With everything in place, it's time to render the final version, which can be seen in the color section in the middle of this book. For the high-resolution graphic needed for the printed version, it took over six hours to compute!

CorelDream is a great program, but I don't like to work in it without first preparing some artwork in CorelDRAW. Creating artwork such as the marbled patterns for the box or a product label adds much more visual interest than the 3D objects can generate on their own. I also find that generating the parent shapes in CorelDRAW and then bringing them to life in CorelDream is a huge time saver compared to working in CorelDream only. When you plan a project in advance and lay out all the pieces ahead of time using whatever program you need, you'll have a much smoother and more productive workday. The triple threat of CorelDRAW, CorelDream, and Corel Photo-Paint serves to increase your design potential threefold. You paid for the privilege, so don't hesitate to unleash the power in the box.

Beyond f/x

These days, 3D applications continue to emerge as the avant-garde design field of choice. Everything from movies to magazines, graphic artists are taking advantage of this technology to render incredible images that would simply be impossible or too expensive to create in any other way. This makes the look of 3D very popular, and even traditional artists are being called upon to create these kinds of images.

Although CorelDream is no longer bundled in the CorelDRAW 9 design suite, many graphic artists are adding RayDream or other 3D-modeling programs to their software toolbox. If you are upgrading from CorelDRAW 8 to 9, you own CorelDream already. If you don't, and are serious about keeping up with the pace of computer graphics, you should consider purchasing RayDream or a similar software package.

If you use the technology when it makes sense in your projects, you may find a new source of revenue, but if you try to use it where it isn't appropriate you may venture into the digital equivalent of opening Pandora's box.

Here are some ideas to spark your imagination. Create full-color stickers in CorelDRAW and apply them to CorelDream objects to transform flat artwork into something totally unique. Imagine your client's logo altered to look like a fuel additive and then wrapped around an oil can for a get-up-and-go ad campaign. Or extrude a logo and create an animation of it spinning around in space in CorelDream. The technology has plenty of applications (all the buttons on my original Web site started as wireframes in CorelDRAW and were then made into pools of metallic fluid in CorelDream). Remember that 3D media is literally and figuratively without boundaries.

Conclusion

In this final chapter we solved some 3D design problems in both CorelDRAW and CorelDream. We saw how to use CorelDRAW to create objects and images for use within CorelDream. We created full-color stickers to apply to CorelDream objects, which gave us unlimited coloring options within that program. Then we saw how to use simple shapes generated in CorelDRAW as the starting point in CorelDream to make some very unique 3D items. Finally, we combined both techniques to flesh out a 3D scene in CorelDream, using artwork generated in CorelDRAW. With these tricks, you can build and color anything within the virtual design landscape of CorelDream. Get in there and get crazy.

And as they say in Hollywood, "That's a wrap!" I hope you have found this book to be a worthwhile purchase and an entertaining read. I have tried to squeeze as much as I could get away with into this monster. Anyway, I had a great time putting this book together and discovered many great techniques along the way.

Why are you still reading? Fire up CorelDRAW and get busy!

INDEX

Y

Z

Colophon

From start to finish, The Coriolis Group designed *CorelDRAW 9 f/x and design* with the creative professional in mind.

The cover was produced on a Power Macintosh using QuarkXPress 3.3 for layout compositing. Text imported from Microsoft Word was restyled using the Futura and Trajan font families from the Adobe font library. It was printed using four-color and spot UV coating.

Select images from the color studio were combined with new figures to form the color montage art strip, unique for each Creative Professionals book. Adobe Photoshop 5 was used in conjunction with filters from Alien Skin Eye Candy 3.0 to create the individual special effects.

The color studio was assembled using Adobe Pagemaker 6.5 on a G3 Macintosh system. Images in TIFF format were color corrected and sized in Adobe Photoshop 5. It was printed using four-color process.

The interior layout was built in Adobe Pagemaker 6.5 on a Power Macintosh. Adobe fonts used include Stone Informal for body, Avenir Black for heads, and Copperplate 31ab for chapter titles. Adobe Photoshop 4 was used to process grayscale images. Text originated in Microsoft Word.

Imagesetting and manufacturing were completed by Courier, Stoughton, Ma.

WHAT'S ON THE CD-ROM

The *CorelDRAW 9 f/x and design* companion CD-ROM contains elements specifically selected to enhance the usefulness of this book, including:

- All of the tutorial files in native CorelDRAW format, to load and learn
- Sample animation files
- Button and interface design examples
- Sample Web pages and Web sites
- Clip-art images from Time Tunnel
- Graphics goodies such as Ulead WebRazor Pro, Ulead FX Razor 2.01, and Ulead's GIF-X-Plug-ins
- Auto f/x utilities such as Universal Animator, Photo/Graphic Edges 4.0, Typo/Graphic Edges 3.0, Photo/Graphic patterns, and The Ultimate Texture Collection 1.0.

System Requirements

Software:

- CorelDRAW 9
- Your operating system must be Windows 95, 98, NT4 or higher.
- Media Player to play the sample movie (AVI) files.
- A Web browser is needed to view the sample Web pages available both on-line and on this book's CD-ROM.

Hardware:

- An Intel (or equivalent) Pentium 100MHz processor is the minimum platform required; an Intel (or equivalent) Pentium 200 MHz (or faster) processor is recommended.
- 32MB of RAM is the minimum requirement.
- A Microsoft (or compatible) wheel mouse is recommended, but not necessary.